Corporate Amnesia

To my family

Corporate Amnesia

Keeping know-how in the company

Arnold Kransdorff

OXFORD   BOSTON   JOHANNESBURG   MELBOURNE   NEW DELHI   SINGAPORE

Butterworth-Heinemann
Linacre House, Jordan Hill, Oxford OX2 8DP
225 Wildwood Avenue, Woburn, MA 01801-2041
A division of Reed Educational and Professional Publishing Ltd

ℛ A member of the Reed Elsevier plc group

First published 1998

© Arnold Kransdorff 1998

HD
58.82
.K7
1998

British Library Cataloguing in Publication Data
Kransdorff, Arnold
    Corporate amnesia: keeping know-how in the company
    1. Management   2.   Corporations – History
    I. Title
    658.4

ISBN 0 7506 3949 0

Printed and bound in Great Britain by Biddles Ltd, Guildford & King's Lynn

FOR EVERY TITLE THAT WE PUBLISH, BUTTERWORTH-HEINEMANN
WILL PAY FOR BTCV TO PLANT AND CARE FOR A TREE.

Contents

ACKNOWLEDGEMENTS

'Failure is but delayed success!'

Like any work dependent on observation, my roster of 'thank you's' is long. While the people I talked to directly in putting together this book number in the hundreds, the inventory actually goes back to my teens to a family acquaintance whose legacy to me was an oft-repeated *'Failure is but delayed success'*, a commentary that no doubt reflected her perception of my own catalogue of life's disasters at the time. It was an adage to which I always retreated when things were not going well but it only assumed its true significance when I took an interest in the whole concept of Organizational Memory, its amnesiac potential and its relationship with Experiential Learning. Thank you Kay Brown, alongside all those others who unknowingly corroborated in this book's underlying theme, including industry's rolling army of managers who, by their decisions, keep on confirming amnesia and discontinuity's endemic consequences for their employers.

It is interesting that, in researching and writing this book, almost everyone I consulted passed on exactly the same advice. *If you can possibly avoid it, don't use the words corporate history. Find another euphemism. The whole genre has been devalued. It'll go down like a lead balloon.*

They were absolutely right, of course. I had been using the genus for at least a decade and mention of the words always fogged the eyes of many of the unwitting interrogators into my interest in the subject. Hence *Organizational Memory (OM)*, which seems to have taken the sting out of what most people mistakenly perceive to be a topic akin to the classroom learning of the dates of British kings and queens, a subject which has always been so badly taught in British classrooms. Even then, OM is still not a comfortable topic to discuss for many people, in spite of the fact that all (without exception) acknowledge its importance in its other guise – experience. For the reasons discussed in this book, the recall of one's own business experiences – and even acceptance of the principle of experiential learning – is still an unwelcome and/or difficult labour for many companies, professional organizations, government departments and academic institutions, even business schools, which made the research for this book particularly arduous. In fact, the reaction by some individuals was so aggressively defensive that I often wondered if it was ever going to be possible to illustrate the concept convincingly beyond my own work in the field.

Of course, the evidence was invariably buried in places where I had not looked or where, ordinarily, I had no access, so my next set of acknowledgements goes to a small band of supportive academics who regularly sent me relevant information down the years. I am particularly grateful to South Bank University's Dr Bruce Lloyd, who never tired of putting a postage stamp on obscure and interesting journals and articles, and the network of academics worldwide with whom the Internet has provided such convenient access.

With industrial champions of the concept so thin on the ground, I am indebted to the late Sir Alistair Pilkington, of float glass repute, whose long-standing efforts to kick-start academic involvement in experiential learning through the Business History Unit at the London School of Economics reflected a conviction that has yet to be realized. I remember him being somewhat surprised at my interest – not in the subject *per se* but that the conception had generated so little attention in the UK down the years among his fellow industrialists, academics and legislators of whichever political colour. His help was uniquely supportive, as was the encouragement of individuals like patriarch businessman Sir Peter Parker, whose Harvard background in the 1950s – when the US's interest in business history was burgeoning under the pen of people like Professor Alfred Chandler, Richard Tedlow and Tom McCraw – first fired his interest in the genre as a valid teaching tool. Elsewhere, the Bank of England's Sir George Blunden was an unexpected ally. Many of the others to whom I am grateful are quoted in the text, including around 200 companies in the UK, the US, Germany, Japan and elsewhere that have made attempts – often vainglorious – at capturing their OM. At this level, the subject's discussion is, interestingly enough, always more embracing among the non-Anglo-Saxon respondents whose grasp of the distinction between explicit knowledge (the 'what' of know-how) and so-called tacit knowledge (the 'how' of know-how) is invariably more cognisant. Among those with the more resistant disposition, notably those in the UK , Knowledge Management invariably excludes the latter.

It is just as interesting to note that what little work that is being done to mitigate the effects of employee discontinuity is almost exclusively directed at exiting individuals (through outplacement, retraining, etc.). The irony is that the very organizations that actively advocate the flexible labour market are doing so little to mitigate the downside effects on *themselves*. If it is a perception thing, I hope OM will do for corporate and business history what redefined Human Resources (HR) did for Personnel in the 1980s.

The text's other unspoken helpers have also played a key role. With a book of this nature, I thought it was necessary to gain the perspective of as many people representing as many different interests as possible. At the management consultant level, where the concept of experiential learning *should* be a recognizable and common currency, Price Waterhouse's Andrew Coleman was especially helpful, as was Omnia Consultant's Dr Cyril Levicki. For the accountant's viewpoint, I found Stephen Godfrey's outlook immensely valuable. Notable, too, was BP's Sas Aslan. He has been with his employer longer than most, so his observation that job rotations' effects on companies are not too dissimilar to short enterprise tenure was invaluable corroboration. I am also grateful to Brian Berman at the World Bank who helped me develop the Oral Debriefing applications for management development and induction.

One of the domains to which I'm privy is the small band of academic and non-academic chroniclers who have specialized in documenting long-term OM – the so-called corporate historians. As the primary recording resource of the subject companies, their experiences were especially pertinent to how this unique corporate asset is being assembled – and how their work might be made more creditable and useful. While confirming that the conventional way in which they are asked to produce them is typically less than amenable – many admitted they came out of the experience frustrated, disillusioned and browbeaten – almost all were happy to relate their experiences at producing this detailed, creative and, because of the sensitivities involved, extremely difficult history product whose employment is most often – and sometimes unfairly – relegated to low-key public relations.

As a project manager who deals with knowledge issues on a day-to-day basis, I am also familiar with the 'consumer' end of the know-how chain – the people who, ultimately, determine the efficacy of OM. Their feedback, candidly given, has been a benchmark for this book's underlying theme.

The *Financial Times'* Michael Cassell, a corporate historian who has demonstrated that serious biography need not be unreadable or lack an application, saved me months of research with voluminous texts emanating from newspapers and other sources. Thanks, too, to members of my family with relevant business experience, especially my brother Basil, who gave me long hours.

Finally, I must thank my literary agent Ros Edwards, of Edwards Fuglewicz, who expertly filtered the list of potential publishers and secured the attention of Butterworth-Heinemann's Publishing Director Kathryn Grant. Although it was always possible to use my company's own publishing resources to print this book, the decision to use a non-Pencorp agency was deliberate. If, as this work proposes, independent publishing is one of a number of ways of helping to demonstrate the integrity and application of an OM product that is almost always dependent on client patronage, then an independent publisher should help to do the same for this book.

Arnold Kransdorff
Beagle House
80 Hill Top
London NW11 6EE
Tel: (44) 181-458 9343
Fax: (44) 181-455 7828

E-mail: ak_pencorp@msn.com
Internet website: www.pencorp.co.uk

February 1998

New brooms sweep clean!

Consider the following state of affairs at a medium-sized company in any Western-style country in Europe, North and South America, Australia, New Zealand, even in developing countries like South Africa, where the local policy of Affirmative Action is mimicking the effects of the flexible labour market in the workplace of its First World rivals.

The Chief Executive resigns at short notice after two years in the job. He's the fourth incumbent in 14 years and there's no obvious successor. Among his 10-strong board of directors, only two individuals have been in office more than six years.

At senior management level, about 15 per cent of individuals are in the first year of their employment, with another 10 per cent having been in situ for two years. A long-serving executive with a wide knowledge of the company's property portfolio is about to retire. In the key planning department, where there was a headcount of six in 1996, there have been four departures and six arrivals inside 18 months. There's talk of the factory manager being lured away after just two years; this post has had four incumbents in ten years.

In the next tier of organizational command – the middle managers – a re-engineering exercise two years ago disposed of 15 per cent of individuals while another 10 per cent have been rotated to new jobs, mostly to new locations. Non-rationalization departures are running at the rate of 20 per cent a year. Only half of their replacements have come up through the ranks, the balance having to be recruited externally. The most visible effect of the high staff turnover is in sales, where customer retention is now very low.

At white collar level lower down, where rationalization has cut numbers by 30 per cent since 1995, the company is moving into a hiring phase because of an anticipated increase in demand for a new product. A succession of HR managers and consequent departmental disruption is slowing this down. Administration has had to rehire half a dozen people previously made redundant when the company could not achieve promised 24-hour turnrounds.

Similarly at blue collar level, where staff roles have been halved over a three-year period, the average turnover of remaining staff is running at 22 per cent a year. Recruitment needs to be stepped up but appropriate skills are difficult to find, with school leavers having little or no conception of the realities of commercial life. Outsourcing machinery maintenance has cut costs but increased down-time has cut inventory's ability to respond to demand.

A Group Employee Audit shows that only 17 per cent of employees have been with the company more than six years, with many younger workers staying just three years. Part-time workers, which number about 8 per cent of the workforce, stay on average just 11 months. At any one time over the last three years, slightly less than 30 per cent of all group employees were in the acclimatization period of their tenure. The induction period of new employees is estimated to be five months for manual workers, up to 12 months for more senior staff and up to 18 months for top executives. The key people in the company who can personally remember what it was like before 1992 are thinly spread. The Property Manager, the chairman's secretary and a cleaner have the longest tenure – they were appointed in 1978, 1979 and 1981 respectively, around the time Mrs Thatcher and Mr Reagan came to office.

While this particular account is fictional, the scenario is actually not far from reality right across the industrial spectrum, where the flexible labour market is turning over huge numbers of people every year. However beneficial this policy is perceived to be for companies, what is also happening is an altogether new phenomenon that is *Corporate Amnesia*. The constant dissipation of staff means that institutions – from bankers to manufacturing companies, traders and service organizations – are losing their organizational knowledge at a rate that is greater than their capacity to retain it. In fact, most organizations now end up having to re-invent themselves continually.

Simply, every time someone resigns, leaves to join another company, retires, is 'rationalized', rotated or dismissed, the organization's hard-won and expensively acquired knowledge literally walks out of the front door. Relearning is a time-consuming and expensive process – especially if replacements are duplicating work and not learning effectively from tried-and-tested experiences. Flexibility may well give organizations the ability to duck and dive at will but the cumulative effects of discontinuity are grossly undermining its benefits.

The following chapters explain the effects that this new work model is having on industry and how to manage that disappearing resource called Organizational Memory so that institutions – government, private sector, small or large, academic, professional, whatever – can learn more effectively from their experiences.

Without the benefit of hindsight ....

This is a book about corporate amnesia, which occurs when companies and other business concerns lose their 'Organizational Memory' (OM), the institutional-specific knowledge accrued from experience that is more prosaically – and dismissively – called corporate history. The root-stock of any organization, OM's existence is perhaps the most important constituent of any institution's durability. When it disappears – through inherent short and selective memory recall, natural wastage when employees leave to join other organizations, the retirement of key individuals and/or redundancy, even through staff rotation – the organization's ability to learn and develop naturally is interrupted, often with expensive consequences. Alongside today's workplace environment of short employee tenure – the result of the flexible labour market – its management is one of the most overlooked and undervalued of the corporate competencies, a neglect that has guaranteed a deceptively high built-in degree of inefficiency to Western industry.

My interest in the subject of Organizational Memory, which is sometimes called institutional memory, goes back to a period in the 1970s and 1980s when I worked for the *Financial Times* in London. It spanned a decade of commercial activity in the UK that overlapped the economic difficulties which ended the Labour Party's hold on power in 1979 and the first six years of Mrs Thatcher's 12-year incumbency, the first four of which trailblazed the heady days of the 'enterprise revolution' that swept the country.

It was a time that I characterize as the point when Britain belatedly changed itself from a cash economy into an investment economy. Unplanned and unheralded, it happened towards the end of the 1970s when the majority of workers stopped being paid weekly in cash and bank accounts became the norm for the majority of citizens. The effect of these seemingly unimportant and related developments was that individuals unconsciously changed their budgeting habits from a seven-day cycle to a 30-day cycle, a remuneration preference that had been commonplace for at least 40 years in the US and was introduced in neighbouring France by President de Gaulle immediately after the Second World War. Rather than having to budget for seven days at a time, the extra cash at the beginning of each month meant that Britons had to think in ways that encompassed interest rates and financial planning. At a stroke, money that was traditionally kept in the back pocket – commentators often referred to it as cash that was stashed in the proverbial mattress – also issued straight into the mainstream economy through bank accounts and other forms of investment. It felt like a seminal moment in the nation's commercial history at the time.

My role on the *Financial Times* was as a company commentator and specialist writer for the newspaper's Management Page, which gave me the opportunity of meeting on an annual basis literally hundreds of middle- to senior-ranking business executives across the industrial spectrum. In terms of my job, the industrial transformation over this time couldn't have been more dramatic, with the period up to around 1980 marked by companies being mainly defensive in character. Thereafter, once Mrs Thatcher's government started demonstrating through legislation that the industrial initiative was being shifted to the boardroom, companies literally mutated before my eyes. If they weren't innovating and investing, they were expanding through either organic growth or acquisition. If it wasn't a family concern that was coming to the stock market, it was former government-run organizations that were actively promoting share ownership to everyone for the first time. Privatizations were thick on the ground, Big Bang was the common currency and jobs that were lost in the thick of rationalizations were re-created in a rash of new, exciting enterprises.

The bubble would burst a little later – and do the usual thing of inflating once again, five years on – but for the moment Britain was experiencing a new Industrial Revolution. Among the areas in which I took a special interest were personnel, management education, management consultancy and management itself, including emerging issues such as profit-sharing schemes and the introduction of more non-executive directors into the boardroom. I also covered the early examples of companies addressing the issue of radical jobs change that would herald the onslaught of downsizing and the industry-wide white collar shake-out, outsourcing and working from home. Privately, I was always fascinated by the characteristics of successful business executives, in particular why some untrained managers – among them in family-run businesses or in countries without sophisticated management training resources – did so well and the success of the extended family network as a successful business model in many minority communities, as in the Asian, Chinese and Jewish examples in many Western economies. I also had an interest in the nature of authority, why many management buyouts were more successful outside their parent groupings and, probably above all, why so many companies seemed to misapply their past successes, repeat prior mistakes and re-invent the wheel. This last puzzle had become evident in even the span of my own short career.

Perhaps because of this interest, I started to notice something unusual. In my conversations with all these fast-running business executives, it was conspicuous that the most successful all had a keen historical perspective of their industries, business in general and their own companies in particular. For a journalist, memoir – and the quality of recall – is one of the important elements of their stock-in-trade, so this was not a particularly difficult quality to spot and appraise. They were easily able to refer to precedent and incremental developments within a longer historical timeframe. Yes, there was selectivity in their recollection and the expected public relations gloss that I always had to filter out but on the customary cross-check, the information invariably had an authority that extended beyond the expected publicity briefings that most managers would receive ahead of any meeting with the press.

In contrast, the less successful managers, defined as those whose companies either ranked in the second division of their sector or who did not seem to last very long in their jobs, were notably non-reflective about their activities to the extent that they were distinctly dismissive – and even hostile – about looking back. A fairly typical response from this group of people – the majority, it seemed – would be that reflection was no more than nostalgia or sentiment, that they had no time, that they considered it more important to look forward, that past models didn't apply because circumstances and tools changed or that they wanted to *change* their culture, not perpetuate it. Often, they would insist that many decisions were taken in defiance of precedent, conveniently ignoring the associated reality that one had to know what the precedents were in order to take a contrary course.

The other observation was an almost obsessive disposition to avoid admitting to – and discussing – mistakes. When it was unavoidable, the blame was invariably placed elsewhere – except by the more successful managers.

The interim conclusion I came to at the time was that some managers probably had better public relations advisers. But as the anecdotal evidence built up and reinforced my surveillance, why, I kept asking myself, would an awareness of how one's predecessors did things – and the events they had experienced – make the difference? Especially in an environment where – as my defined set of unsuccessful managers kept reminding me – circumstances seemed to change so often?

The answer didn't come immediately but it eventually struck me that business decisions were no different from decisions taken in other areas of life – better made with the benefit of hindsight. Further research at the time revealed an unexpected observation – that British workers at all levels acquire little historical awareness of business from the wider educational system or the workplace. While there was a reasonable level of exposure in our schools and universities to the 220-year-old Industrial Revolution and economic history dealing with macro-fiscal issues, there was a noticeable absence of corporate and business history that would familiarize the emerging generation of workers, consumers and potential investors with how – at the practical level – their parents and grandparents earned their livings .... the type of information, for example, that traced the development of companies in particular and business in general. It was puzzling because there was plenty of political history, social history and military history in the curriculum to demonstrate the *bona fides* of the genre as an educational tool and as a means to reinforcing a culture. Even musicians and artists studied their respective histories. But for the people who had to go out and earn their living in the business world – i.e. practically everyone – virtually nothing in the way of corporate or business history.

Apart from illustrative references – called case studies but usually no more than summarized snapshot examples used to explain the workings of some functional management disciplines – the subjects were even neglected at business schools, where management educators were teaching the nation's future business executives how to manage *without* the perspectives of their predecessors or an awareness of their corporate past. It was equivalent to Britain's Sandhurst, the armed forces academy that trains the nation's future military leaders, not referring to the First and Second World Wars, the Korean War, the Falklands or the Gulf Wars in their classrooms.

Alongside this, and against the background of the accelerating demise of the job-for-life work model, very few British companies were passing down their own experiences from one generation to the next. It seemed not uncoincidental that apprenticeships – the side-by-side training process whereby a youth acquired proficiency by inheriting both the skills and the experiences of an elder mentor – had also been abandoned.

By way of contrast, the level of activity in corporate and business history in countries like the US, Germany and Japan was significantly higher, although the evidence there, too, was of an under-exploited resource.

For the UK at least, my conclusion was that, without any corporate or business history to connect the generations, there was very little continuity at both the wider industrial and individual organizational levels. In effect, each new generation of workers was obliged virtually to re-invent the wheel for themselves when they first entered the workforce and whenever they joined new companies. Yes, the lateral movement of employees across the workforce provided a constant source of new ideas for employers, but without access to their own hindsight, this also meant that corporate requirements were increasingly being driven in isolation to their own experiences and circumstances. It also meant the constant dilution of each organization's individual culture.

At about the time my interest in organizational memory was gestating, the importance of – and relationship between – hindsight and continuity then reinforced themselves in two different ways. I was listening to a radio programme on heavyweight boxers in which one of the 1930s champions was explaining how he had beaten his opponent. One of his throwaway lines in the archive crackle was that he had spent time examining the newsreel footage of his opponent's previous fight and, from that, was able to derive a strategy to beat his adversary.

It struck me that the film clip he had seen all those years ago was, to all intents and purposes, the technological equivalent of Organizational Memory and that the individual was using experience – this time someone else's experience that wasn't distorted by time or ego – as a learning tool.

My imagination then took flight. Was not the boxer (I can't for the life of me remember who it was now) the forerunner of hundreds of thousands of other sportsmen and women who, since then, have accelerated their performances to an extent greater than in any previous period in history? Yes, training techniques have improved, as have athletes' diets, medical procedures and that prime incentive, money, but – I asked myself – could their employment of 'memory' in this way also be a factor in the dramatic improvement in performances over almost the entire range of sports? The fact that film and video usage in sports reporting has been around for about the same amount of time – and that most top sportsmen and women routinely use the medium to examine their own and each other's performances – seemed not uncoincidental.

If this *was* the case, why, then, could not industry apply the same principle to equally good effect? For a stark illustration of the downside potential of discontinuity, my attention was then drawn to the unwinding repercussions of one of the world's best examples of bad succession planning. The infamous General Idi Amin's decision 23 years ago to cleanse Uganda ethnically of its Asians also removed the country's corps of businessmen and the collective equivalent of its business 'memory'. The outcome was that the 'businessmen' who replaced them could not rely on the example of how their predecessors did things. The hapless general had, in effect, stripped the replacement managers of their ability to use the departed Asians' experience. The result has been an emerging generation of entrepreneurs having to re-invent the wheel entirely from first principles, a rate of managerial evolution that has inhibited national prosperity ever since and a stark illustration of the downside of ignoring one of the fundamental elements of all progress: continuity.

Fortunately for countries and organizations elsewhere, not all job-change occurs at the same time, so there is some element of overlapping continuity. But the low levels of enterprise tenure now evident across industry are progressively ensuring that companies are becoming what the *Financial Times* has described as the corporate equivalent of Alzheimers[1]. While the analogy may well misappropriate the medical complaint, the underlying suggestion is such that, having reduced and changed their workforce in the name of change, organizations recall very little of their own corporate memories and experiences, with the result that few have any facility to benefit from their own hindsight.

There is another aspect to the widespread non-employment of corporate and business history in the educational system or the workplace. It provides few role models to act as motivators. Without the necessary exemplars, is this a possible explanation why, for example, the vast majority of British school leavers have always been more interested in public service jobs than industry? Or why business executives continually complain of widespread employee ignorance about business and the role of companies? Or, even, why corporate enterprise has never firmly established itself in the national character? Given that the whole ethic of enterprise is such an uncommon currency, is it a reason why investment in the stock market is not as instinctive as it is in other developed economies?

Continuing the possible consequences at the corporate level, is the widespread disregard for corporate and business history why British industry always seems so surprised and unprepared when the trade cycle regularly turns down – and then up again? And why, in spite of Mrs Thatcher's efforts to change the country's business culture, the UK remains near the bottom of the league table of industrialized nations in new enterprise creation?

Part of the explanation is – I believe – that we are not familiar enough with the dynamics of the marketplace. Also that, at a business level, we do not learn well from our experiences – of both the short and long-term variety. Not that we can't, but that we don't have the inclination or the opportunity to do so because there is virtually no tradition of passing down our own business experiences – our Organizational Memory – from one generation to the next either in our schools, universities or in the workplace.

Simply, because we inherit very little, we – the nation – are constantly having to cold-start our commercial lives.

An aside is that, without the established discipline of one's own corporate and business history to inherit, whatever vacuum there is is filled by others' corporate and business history. I am not suggesting that others' examples are not relevant or appropriate, only that their exemplar then becomes the dominant role model. Even in its minimalist way, the superimposition of another's experiences by default is a less effective learning tool and motivator than using one's own as the principal building block of progress. Is it not more effective, for example, for Britons, Australians and South Africans to learn from and be motivated by their own role models than those of the US or Germany?

This is a business book about Organizational Memory or experiences, what others loosely call corporate history and, when it is put into a broader comparative context, business history. As a business historian and management journalist, I offer as my credentials for doing it half a lifetime's striving to be a perceptive re-assembler of corporate experiences, a passion for business and a belief that both success and failure – the primary components of all experience – are equal partners in the learning process of change.

My role with Pencorp has given me a unique perspective of a whole range of companies and industries. Whereas most people's interests are focused on the relatively short term, mine has necessarily extended over a much longer period, where the business of business takes on a completely different hue. Even though things like technology have changed many working practices, the issues, for example, with which early twentieth century businessmen like Henry Ford were wrestling suddenly look remarkably familiar to those on the agenda of 1990s managers, as do the outcomes. If outcomes are, ultimately, the only way of truly assessing efficacy, then the wider picture can in no way flatter the comparative ability of British industry to benefit from its own hindsight. Truly, often, it seems that many companies are successful *despite* themselves. As the oldest industrialized economy in the world, it is not unreasonable to argue that it should have some experiential advantage. From the official statistics, this does not appear to be the case.

In the world prosperity league, for example, the OECD's 1996 ranking of gross domestic product per head showed the UK's position to be twenty-first in 1996, down from eighteenth the previous year. In the same year the Lausanne-based International Institute for Management Development (IMD) put Britain nineteenth, down from fifteenth, in the world economic rankings. In the same year, Oxford Economic Forecasting (OEF), the leading economic research group, found that Britain's investment record – the key to industrial success – was among the worst of industrialized nations, with spending on research and development 'well below that of many other countries'. Excluding housing, total investments, for example, were a third lower than Japan while manufacturing investment per worker was almost half that in France and the US.

When it comes to share ownership, another key indicator of national investment attitudes, figures[2] in 1996 reported that while just 8 million people had been enticed into buying privatization shares since the wave of popular sell-offs began in 1984 with the flotation of British Telecom, the number of private shareholders had been declining. Only 200,000 privatization investors had invested in other shares, leaving many to brand the whole programme to promote private share ownership as a flop. Since then, the only increase has come from the free handout of shares from the latest crop of building society and insurance mutuals that have converted into public limited companies.

Scottish Enterprise, the official development body, found[3] that the birth rate for medium-size companies between 1978 and 1990 per 1 million of population was 77 in Scotland, 86 in the West Midlands and 116 in the south of England. In Massachusetts, in the US, the comparable figure was 333.

On Britain's managerial abilities, the views of many captains of industry and business academics have been similarly unflattering. As recently as 1997, Allen Yurko, the US chief executive of Siebe, one of the UK's top 50 companies by market capitalization, was complaining that the UK was one of the most difficult places in the world to turn on the growth switch. His observation was that industrial managers in Britain lacked skills at expanding their businesses. *'The UK is an excellent place for manufacturing but on the whole UK managers are downsizers. They are restructurers and wonderful at it. This is necessary but at some point you need to grow.'*

For Exeter University's Professor John Adair, managerial abilities were just as unpraiseworthy. In March 1996 he told the Institute of Personnel Development's annual training conference that he could not name a single company in the UK developing the quality of leadership needed for the country's future success. *'Any leaders Britain does have are a result of accident, not design. We tend to wait until we're on the beaches at Dunkirk before looking for our Winston Churchills,'* he said. A research study's findings, which were announced at the same conference, found huge swathes of British industry still unconvinced of the need for training, with these attitudes inbred at management level and where almost a third of line managers were *'not interested in people management'*.

Although this book has its origins in the UK, it also carries a message for other industrialized countries, and especially for those that qualify as emerging in the new economies of China, Eastern Europe, South America and Africa. My argument is that, like any area of life, a lack of objective reflectiveness about one's own performance slows down the capacity to change progressively. Workplace discontinuity and the associated problem of migratory knowledge, which inhibits the ability to be objectively reflective, is a problem that the West's main competitors in the Far East do not have – at least in the generous measures evident in the UK, the US and, increasingly, elsewhere in Western Europe. Whereas the Anglo-Saxon economies argue that flexible labour markets help organizations better to respond to consumer demand, the Pacific Basin countries believe that they inhibit both productivity and profitability over the long term. Although these policies are coming under strain in their recent recession, I suggest that Japan's business history, rooted in a more stable workforce and with a greater consequent ability – and, it seems, desire – to be more objectively reflective, carries its own explicit lesson about industrial success that we ignore at our peril.

That said, if, for the West, workplace discontinuity is the preferred strategy option for dealing with changing consumer demand, then we at least have to find ways of mitigating its effects. How, then, does one sustain the internal knowledge chain in a flexible labour market?

Rather than an academic treatise, I have chosen a prescriptive format that I might have used were I still to be writing for the *Financial Times* in the hope that it will be more reader-friendly to both managers and academics, both groups of which – I submit – are missing an opportunity. I have structured it in a way that shows practical solutions to the range of tenure- and experience-related problems that workplace discontinuity has imposed on industry, among them the brain-drain from departing employees, the prolonged induction of new appointees and the disposition not to learn the lessons of hindsight, the combined effects of which are unaccountably expensive. They are the very meat of change management.

Because of the widespread scepticism of corporate and business history's applications, I have deliberately structured the narrative with as much supporting evidence as necessary. Also, knowing how busy managers are, I have tried to keep it short. Business executives have enough on their plates without another long and tedious book to contend with.

The techniques I relate, which explain how companies can retain and use their experiences, are not sophisticated management tools that academics and management consultants might ordinarily blind with jargon, complex number-crunching and expensive software solutions. Nor are they a cure-all for all the problems arising out of short enterprise tenure or even a substitute for the emerging management discipline called Knowledge Management. Largely unutilized by industry, they are relatively simple, commonsense techniques that can be classified under the wider Learning Organization's precepts. To make them most effective, they just require imagination in their conception and a professionalism in their execution. Their cost is typically a fraction of the price-tag of labour and the on-going expense of rehiring, prolonged induction, not learning from prior successes, repeating mistakes and re-inventing the wheel.

Only one of them is brand new – an alternative to the traditional post-implementation review that I call the Learning Audit, which is designed to help managers benefit more effectively from their on-going experiences. It is still in its development phase but I have included it because it directly addresses a key learning issue and the application of organizational memory – and academic endorsements of its methodology and conceptual principles have been very encouraging.

Because of their attendant role, I include academia's attitude to corporate history and wider-based business history, in particular how they have applied the genre as a learning tool, particularly in the UK. Except for a few domestic champions, their enthusiasm for what is potentially one of the most effective ways of teaching the business of business is generally dismissive. On examination, a common response is shortage of suitable indigenous material, which is undoubtedly true, but my own view is that there are deeper, more political explanations, not least academia's cultural estrangement from industry in the UK. Among other reasons, the genre is viewed as a budgetary threat by the more macro-orientated economic historians within whose departments such a discipline might most comfortably reside while industry – the real participants in business history's rich recall and without whose active cooperation any interpretation is only half the story – have never felt as comfortable as their political, military, literary, artistic or musical counterparts to being exposed to the rigours of historical review. The result is a mutually agreeable stand-off – and a potentially valuable discipline neglected by under-employment.

I have also taken a close look at the humble corporate history, which is undoubtedly one of the most devalued of management tools. Alongside the more voluminous company archive, which is a subject I have intentionally not covered (its effective management is a book in its own right and, of which, there are many), it is the heart of all Organizational Memory, without which history's recall is confined exclusively to the vagaries of living memory and contemporary newspaper cuttings. Of all the formats, it is – because it is so portable – the most dispensable repositories of OM. While other forms of history achieve high readership levels, corporate history, which is arguably just as interesting, colourful and useful, has the distinction of being widely unread, largely because of the way it is produced. There is another reason. Because of the frequent unavoidability of client patronage in their production and public relations being the subject company's typical motivation for their production, the genre is widely condemned to sweeping derision and general obscurity – *however well they are done*. To professionalize them – and give them real corporate employment – I relate how companies can overcome the commonplace perception that the published accounts of their corporate life lack credibility and are merely boardroom indulgences. The principle of client sponsorship already exists in academia, architecture and the arts (the BBC, etc.), where *their* results are not automatically maligned and where benefit accrues. Why not in corporate literature as inherently erudite – and just as important – as corporate and business history?

In my own mind there is no doubt that the absence of good corporate and business history over the years has contributed to the continuing polarization of the industry debate between labour and capital and also ill-served the development of business and companies themselves.

Alongside applications that address specific problems like day-to-day induction and the slow integration of acquisitions and mergers, my critique also examines how companies in other countries use them. For most of this century Japanese and German companies, for example, have been printing their corporate histories in English and other European languages and distributing them to their target markets abroad. In contrast, less than a handful of English-speaking companies in countries as export-reliant in non-English-speaking markets as the US and UK have used the same marketing technique to break into *their* non-English-speaking markets.

It may *seem* to some that any preoccupation with how we did things yesterday will distract from how we do things today and tomorrow. But in an environment where intense competition is transforming the marketplace at a rampant pace and individuals will be changing their employer many, many times in their working lifetime, corporate productivity is always going to be inhibited by a workforce unenlightened by precedent, particularly one's own precedent.

At its most simple, the theory – practised, it seems, more readily in most other aspects of life, perhaps the most effective of all being the major religions, which all unashamedly use their 'experience' to secure their continuity – states that if you inherit nothing, you have to start from scratch, sometimes from first principles. As such, the continuous learning curve is inevitably steeper and longer than it might otherwise be. In another way, better hindsight gives you better foresight. It is one of those ideas whose simplicity understates its significance and overlooks its importance – and for which I'll gladly stand accused.

Its rationale can be simply illustrated by veteran British politician Tony Benn's comments in the House of Commons in 1974, when he was Secretary of State for Industry and the Minister responsible for Posts and Telecommunications. He said: *'In developing our industrial strategy for the period ahead, we have the benefit of much experience. Almost everything has been tried at least once.'* The point here is that our experience – whether or not it was successful in its accomplishment – is a knowledge resource. If it can't be recalled accurately and in context, it might as well never have happened, which might help to explain why the nation seems to have so little experiential advantage. Simply, its disregard diminishes the options we might successfully choose to shape today's decisions for tomorrow's world.

In this respect, the observations[4] of Martin Jacques, a co-founder of the apolitical think tank Demos and one of the UK's prominent commentators, have a resonance. One of Britain's problems, he wrote in 1993, is that history has become disembodied from the present.

> *'Japan has a very powerful sense of its history, but this is the handmaiden of the present and is combined with an intense interest in the future. The culture is forward looking and strategic. The United States, though possessed of a short memory, is also driven by a sense of its own history, the frontier for example, but nobody could possible describe American culture as nostalgic or historically escapist. One of the most embarrassing attempts I have witnessed was at last year's Expo in Seville. The British pavilion was a magnificent piece of architecture but the concept of Britain projected inside was restricted to a series of presentations by large companies with no sense of culture, life, society or even, ironically, history.'*

In explaining how organizations can manage this dissipating resource, this is a book that goes to the heart of the debate between those who think we can learn from the past and those who think that old lessons are misleading or irrelevant because times change. It will also try to illustrate that there is much less danger in dwelling on the past than remaining in ignorance of it.

For just one example is the lesson that history teaches about how often dominant companies complacently ignore the effects of mature markets and new technologies. In the 1980s a smug Remington yielded dominance of the typewriter market to the electronic age – and IBM. Almost immediately IBM made the same expensive mistake by reacting inappropriately to a technology that threatened its own core business. On the surface it simply misjudged one of its product's life cycles but in reality, it mishandled the emergence of personal computers, under-rating vastly the impact that they would have on its larger mini and mainframe businesses. A memory of how Remington reacted to similar conditions might have encouraged IBM to give its originally independent PC unit a longer life – and avoided the US's biggest annual corporate loss of $4.9 billion in 1992.

The fact that IBM is among a string of companies that have not attempted to record their OM because their executives will not allow access to their records makes the episode seem not unsurprising. That the precedent was also not new could, moreover, have been gleaned from an awareness of business history going back to the last century. Over four decades to 1880, the New England ice cutting industry, for example, built a formidable delivery business across large swathes of America[5]. When mechanical ice-making machines from France allowed the product to be manufactured near its markets, the local companies refused to embrace the new technology. Over the next 30 years machine-made ice steadily took over, even though the cutters ploughed more resources than ever into process improvements.

This book's title – *Corporate Amnesia: Keeping know-how in the company* – is a graphic allusion to the organizational memory loss that a flexible labour market imposes on individual companies but it could equally have been entitled *History as a Management Tool, How to Sustain the Internal Knowledge Chain in a Flexible Labour Market* or, more literally, *Experiential Learning*. I hope the medical analogy, which is less awkward than its traditional description of 'organizational forgetting', is accurate enough to spark the attention of decision makers to a problem that is invisibly sapping the existent life out of our companies. Also, disavow those who derogate the wider genre and give the tried and tested past a more useful future within the wider precepts of the Learning Organization.

I am not suggesting that companies displace their traditional learning processes, although there is plenty of evidence that these, too, are not fully employed in industry and are often less than efficacious. Whether in the UK or elsewhere, my proposition is that academics and industry start treating what they otherwise call their business and corporate history as Organizational Memory to be valued just like another corporate asset.

OM is knowledge accrued from experience. We are all participating in a knowledge revolution where its management is becoming just as important – some are saying even more important – than the traditional factors of production like labour, capital and land. Given that the flexible labour market is now also a fact of life, is it not time that industry started associating discontinuity with lost experience that is a valuable knowledge resource in need of management?

Treated seriously, and with application, OM's employment is a powerful change tool with a range of applications that addresses many of the problems that Western industry has imposed on itself in recent years. In financial terms it can provide experience very cheaply, it can help smooth the inevitable discontinuity that all change imposes, reverse the conventional model of having to be wise after the event and give the experiential advantage older economies and companies *should* have over the emerging young bloods. In short, it can abbreviate everyone's learning curves and make us, the people who have to make work work, far more professional at the way we earn our daily bread.

References

1. Editorial comment, Management Page, *Financial Times*, 29 July 1996.
2. Committee for Private Ownership, study, 1996.
3. Scottish Enterprise research, 1993.
4. 'Time for Britain's Lost Soul to Shake off the Shroud of History', *Sunday Times*, 16 May 1993.
5. J. Utterbach, *Mastering the Dynamics of Innovation*, Harvard Business School Press, Cambridge, MA, 1994.

CHAPTER ONE

The ABC of data, information, knowledge and organizational memory

If corporate amnesia or organizational forgetting entails the loss of Organizational Memory what exactly *is* OM and some of the other associated jargon, all of which can be categorized under the wider and equally esoteric lexicon called the Learning Organization? Given their imprecise appreciation, their explanation is fundamental to any discourse on the subject.

As a generic term, the word 'memory' itself has a variety of definitions. Most commonly it is described as knowledge retention, the difference between learning and relearning, what is *not* forgotten, the reconstruction of experienced events or the total of recollections. Within this context, organizational memory – sometimes called corporate memory – is viewed variously as the aggregation of individual experiences or as the capability of the organization itself. Most people give it a technological and/or quantitative orientation, equating it with the information documented in the records of company archives or on corporate databases[1]. In truth its nature is more metaphysical and qualitative – and goes largely *unrecorded* in all the organizational paperwork that is generated by managers and other employees down the years.

With the exception of the process of management itself, OM is only peripherally related to actual professional or vocational skills such as the particular faculty related to being an accountant, a machinist or a nurse or the latest technical advance in telecommunications and pharmacology. It is more akin to the ways in which individuals – of whatever discipline – apply their jobs in the establishments for which they work. This comprises the awareness of wider organization-specific experiences and knowledge, including the information that is related to understanding and accommodating an employer's individual corporate culture, management, communications and decision-making style, and the detail of job-related events.

To be more specific, OM is the difference between information that is explicit, often called skilled knowledge, and knowledge that is tacit and cognitive, sometimes known as 'state of play' knowledge or 'coping skills'. The former is the type of technical information that is codified in the abundant manuals, textbooks and training courses available while the latter, much of which is implicit and ambiguous, is acquired only by experience that is personal and context-specific. Its cognitive dimension, which is essentially subjective and arrived at more perceptively than the other types of knowledge, would include contemplative insights, intuition and hunches based on thoughtful reflection. It is difficult to articulate formally.

This type of knowledge encompasses what is known as episodic knowledge, which relates to the detail of actual events and incidents that occur in the course of using skills. It also includes more intangible factors such as shared values, belief systems and corporate culture.

Corporate culture, which is one of the most difficult types of knowledge to define accurately, is perhaps the most inexplicit feature of the corporate soul. Because of this, it is also the factor that inhibits managers most in their understanding of how OM shapes their response to any given circumstances. With no common definition available, two of my preferred descriptions are the learned product of group experience and the sum total of shared beliefs and knowledge. As much of the sum total of our knowledge has been learned as culture from older generations, both indicate the extra dimensions that organizational memory covers.

OM is knowledge accrued from experience. It is the non-technical 'how' of doing things, which Edward de Bono, the champion of lateral thinking, calls 'operacy' or the skill of action. Embedded in the personally held skills of individuals, it is the essence of being practical, ownership of which enables, for example, a good theoretician to also become a good practitioner. In terms of management, it would be described as corporate enterprise, the craft of entrepreneurship or the technique of being a good business executive. Its awareness provides the type of expertise that is simultaneously an organization's adhesive and lubricant that both keeps it together and allows it to operate smoothly and efficiently. Without it, organizations – even if they employ the most qualified people in their field – run like a gearbox without oil. It is assuredly the single most important element of any organization's success or failure. In his *Post Capitalist Society*, Peter Drucker goes some way to identifying it through the word *techne* (Greek for 'skill'), the understanding of which, he contends, cannot be explained in words, whether spoken or written. It can only be *'demonstrated'*, he says, through apprenticeship and experience although some commentators suggest that it is possible to communicate it through metaphor and analogy.

Because companies find OM difficult to characterize and document in conventional ways, much of it typically exists only in the minds of individuals – a reason why, perhaps, so many managers disregard its importance and find it so difficult to manage?

Managers also hold on to the misconception that OM is constant across the organization. Thus, they believe, so long as there is someone around who remembers *'the old days'*, there is sufficient memory for continuity to exist. The trouble with this assumption is that every employee's OM is distinct. Thus, a chairman's OM is very different from a machinist's OM. In only selective cases would one functionary's OM be relevant to another.

In its migrated form, it is often labelled the 'brain drain' where national frontiers are involved, 'poaching' in the commercial sphere or 'secondment' in the public sector.

For practical purposes, OM can be broken down into three distinct time frames. Realistically, short-term OM lasts up to about five years, medium-term OM occupies a time frame up to about ten years, with anything longer qualifying as long-term OM. As a general rule, short- and medium-term OM's applications are more relevant to operational issues because of their contemporary and contiguous nature while long-term OM's employment is more conformant with strategy and culture.

To fully understand its nature, one has to appreciate the difference between data, information and knowledge, a distinction that is often blurred in the minds of managers. In many cases, they are frequently used to describe each other. Although interrelated to the extent that they have no useful existence without each other, data and information are not the same; nor are data and information synonymous with knowledge. By way of illustration, take a typical announcement of a company's annual performance, which is usually published alongside the previous year's achievement. The figure published for either year is data – a fact depicted as a figure or a statistic. The relationship between the company's two sets of annual figures is information, i.e. data in context. In essence, information is essentially rooted in data relevant to a historical timeframe. In contrast, knowledge – around which Organizational Memory is constructed – is interpretive and predictive in nature. Its deductive character allows its owner to understand the implications of data and information – and act accordingly.

It is in this act that the acquisition of knowledge, which can only come about through learning, becomes the basis of all planning. By its very nature, this is prophetic, which also makes OM a key component for what is otherwise called scenario planning and anticipatory competence development.

For more than two decades now, the whole subject of knowledge as a management resource has been the focus of socio-economic and management theorists, who have been emphasizing the importance of so-called knowledgement management. Perhaps the best-known advocate is Peter Drucker, who is said to have coined the phrase the *'knowledge society'*. Assessing knowledge's importance as a management resource, he elevates its nature above the traditional factors of production of labour, capital and land, an appraisal reinforced by the likes of fellow gurus Alvin Toffler and James Quinn.

Their common endorsement of the genre's emerging pre-eminence would suggest that industry might be taking a little more notice. Unfortunately, its application, at least in its broad sense, is still mostly confined to the rigour of academics, some management consultants and a few computer whizkids. The whole concept of the Learning Organization is a mantra whose popularity is matched only by the confusion that besets almost everyone over how to put it into practice. Even gurus like David Garvin, professor of business administration at Harvard Business School, admit[2] that the topic in large part remains murky, confused and difficult to penetrate, part of the blame for which he places on academics whose discussions on the subject have often been *'reverential and utopian, filled with near mystical terminology'*. As a result many who court its gift pay only lip service to its application.

The need for continuous organizational learning to accompany the need for continuous organizational change is its most frequent justification. In their examinations, the theorists have identified various types and stages of learning. These different kinds of learning have variously been described by G. Bateson as *'Learning 1'* and *'Learning 2'*, by Chris Argyris and D.A. Schon as *'single loop learning'* and *'double loop learning'* and by Peter Senge, perhaps the most zealous proselytiser of the Learning Organization, as *'generative'* learning and *'adaptive'* learning.

The first – the collection of know-how in order to solve specific problems based on existing circumstances – deals with the conscious and obvious levels of organizational learning when, for example, a business deals with a downturn in customers by changing its image through marketing. The second – which usually arises when the first attempt to solve the problem is unsuccessful – establishes new paradigms to build on the existing model. It typically employs a deeper level of scrutiny and action. Using the same example of the business with falling demand, managers might, for example, then examine product quality or services – and change accordingly.

More recently, L. Swieringa and A. Wierdsma have identified a third learning loop when fundamental organizational beliefs begin to be addressed. In the example of declining levels of activity, the organization might then question the very business it is in.

Because of its intrinsic importance to any good decision, the 'conceptualization' of knowledge, and its acquisition – i.e. learning – in particular, has created a whole new field of study and applications into what is commonly called information systems. Systems researchers and practitioners have even tried to store the knowledge of experts such as engineers and physicians into software systems that imitate 'human reasoning'. These information systems – sometimes called Management Information Systems or Executive Information Systems – are collectively known as Expert Systems. Modern computer and networking technologies have allowed relatively sophisticated processing of data from one form to another, its storage and retrieval and the assembly of background data, which can then be turned into information for decision making.

Among these, one of the most refined attempts at using data and information as a learning tool is one that has been developed by the Strategic Planning Institute, a non-profit membership organization housed in the Massachusetts Institute of Technology in Cambridge, Massachusetts. This was developed into the theory of planning strategy called 'Profit Impact of Market Strategies' (PIMS).

PIMS's origins go back to the 1960s when, in an exploratory investigation organized by the Marketing Science Institute, a research institute affiliated with the Harvard Business School, the General Electric Company's internal efforts to analyse its own strategic experience produced a so-called Profit-Optimizing Model called PROM, which was used to test the reasonableness of plans submitted by the general managers of operating units. At the time some of GE's managers wondered if the strategy–performance relationships incorporated into the model were valid only in the company's existing kinds of business. This led to the idea of 'spinning off' the activity and inviting other companies to join. An initial thirty-six other companies joined the programme and contributed information and financial support, rising to fifty-seven companies and 620 business units by the end of 1972. Today, the database comprises more than 3,000 separate business units owned by around 450 companies. The database, described by management guru Tom Peters as *'the most extensive strategic information database in the world'*, was set up in 1975 by Sidney Schoeffler, the man who directed the original GE model. It provides factual evidence about the linkages between strategy and business performance and claims to contain more than 20,000 years of business experience.

Schoeffler's claim is not that PIMS can foretell the exact results of every business in any given short period; rather, that most outcomes are predictable within certain limits. It is possible, he says, to estimate the approximate results of most businesses over three to five years on the basis of observable characteristics of the market and of the strategies employed by the business itself and its competitors. While PIMS demonstrates how IT has provided an efficient example of how data and information is being used, effective knowledge-based systems are still elusive. Unfortunately, the critical reasoning process, which allows conclusions to be reached based on facts and information, is still not well understood or, in software terms, yet achievable.

To compensate, many companies employ a parallel range of tactics to try to improve their knowledge base through 'sharing' systems. Among these are Benchmarking, a concept first developed by the Xerox Corporation that formalizes the ongoing investigation and learning experience to ensure that best industry practices are uncovered, analysed and implemented. This can be done internally, which enables the comparison of performance across different business units within the same organization or externally, which is typically done through collaborative arrangements between non-competing organizations that have common or comparable processes. Thus, a group of companies will get together to share experiences and collectively build up a databank of best-practice applications, a discipline that also provides a face-to-face forum for understanding and sharing details of best practice. Benchmarking's other leading-edge practitioners include AT&T and Digital Equipment Corporation.

A hard example of how it has been used is at PowerGen in the UK, where the lessons learned[3] from best practice at seventeen US power stations has helped Britain's second biggest power generator to claim it is the world's lowest-cost producer of electricity for the class and age of coal-fired power stations it operates.

Executive coaching is another form of knowledge acquisition. Typically, an executive coach is an experienced business person from outside the organization who works alongside a manager – much like a personal coach works with sportsmen and women. When the 'coach' is an internal individual, the procedure is called mentoring.

One example of this is the 'sempai-kohai' arrangement employed by many Japanese companies, which encourages bonding between new and older employees. A senior worker becomes responsible for guiding a younger person by passing down his OM, ensuring continuity between the generations. The bonding – done mostly in bars after work – is as strong on the shopfloor as at management level. This is often complemented by Quality Circles, a management stratagem introduced by many Japanese companies in the 1970s to nurture creativity and job satisfaction, one of the characteristics of which is diligent documenting of all processes so that newcomers can learn what has gone before.

Other forms of knowledge acquisition include the employment of outsiders as consultants and trainers and the hiring of specialists as employees. What they have in common is that they are all so-called 'distance' teachers in the sense that they are – at least initially – removed from the subject organization's unique circumstances and operational culture. From the company's viewpoint, the theory is that their external and independent influences provide the organization the opportunity to adopt others', presumably better, practices. In practice, their input always has to be adapted to the organization's own way of working.

The other – more direct – form of knowledge acquisition is through Action Learning, a system that embraces the proposition that we learn best about work at work and through work. Implemented in various ways, it is an approach that throws individuals into the deep end of a project. The direct practical involvement throws up the knowledge gaps, which can then be filled from existing knowledge sources. Latterly, companies have begun to adapt the approach to get managers to tackle problems through team work; California-based electronics giant Hewlett-Packard, for example, encourages all its operations to develop personnel by putting them on task forces. In business schools, Action Learning is when students bring 'case studies' into the classroom from their sponsoring employers in an attempt to bring together the distinct worlds of theory and practice.

While these approaches are all perfectly valid forms of knowledge acquisition, there is another form of learning – arguably the most effective form of all – that organizations across the industrial spectrum have all but overlooked. These are the opportunities afforded by learning *directly* from their own experiences through techniques that necessarily involve the need to be constructively reflective. It is only from this point that organizations through their employees can create the new knowledge that is essential for efficient progress.

It is a process otherwise referred to as experiential learning – learning from experience – a proposition that starts from the premise that nearly all learning is evolutionary. Thus, a baby learns to walk by first taking one step. Having negotiated that successfully, the child takes another – and so on. On this basis, the most efficient process of knowledge acquisition – and progress – occurs incrementally, from the building of one experience on top of another. Disconnect them – the corporate amnesia that results from a low level of employee tenure would be one way of doing so, staff rotation would be another – and the momentum slows or, in some cases, reverses. Its doctrine is perfectly explained by Harvard scholar Alan Kantrow[4]:

> '*Like it or not, the past infects the world we live in, the decisions we make, the very choices we see to lie before us. If we ignore its influence, we do not escape its power. All we do is remain to some extent its prisoners without ever really knowing that that is what we are. If, however, we acknowledge it, learn to recognize its workings, come to greet it on familiar terms, we can put it to excellent use.*'

It is in the realm of experiential learning – and the disposition towards organizational forgetting – around which most of this book is written.

There are generally four approaches to experiential learning, all of which have little rigorous employment in industry, at least in the West. By this I mean that industry does not generally structure any of the approaches in anything like the formalized way training from external sources is understood and applied.

First, there is the intuitive approach which is, effectively, unconscious learning. It is a process that is completely unstructured, random and depends on the natural process of osmosis. It is the type of experiential learning that is probably the most prevalent of all the learning disciplines. In the majority of cases, this type of learning is often unrecognized as such. Its employment is almost always self-initiated. This approach would include the instance of the child learning to walk but it would also cover the lessons, for example, that Marks & Spencer chairman Sir Richard Greenbury has learned from sport, particularly football, a game in which the 60-year-old has had a keen interest for many years. *'In football everyone has to do their job. If someone lets you down, then the whole team suffers. It is a great leveller. You learn to accept defeat because there is always someone better than you,'* he says.

In Brazil, another example would be lessons that Semco's Ricardo Semler, head of the diversified engineering and consulting group, learned[5] as an 18-year-old in his rock and roll band. *'If the drummer doesn't feel like coming to rehearsals you know something's wrong. You can hassle him as much as you want but the problem remains.'* The way he has applied this to his business life is to focus on how to get people to want to come to work on a grey Monday morning. *'That is really the only parameter we care about, which is 100 per cent a motivation issue.'* Some of the methods used at Semco have been picked up by manufacturing companies in the US, schools in Finland, an Australian hospital and the Amsterdam police force, which illustrates the external form of experiental learning – learning from others' experiences.

Then there is the incidental approach to learning from experience, where the process of erudition occurs through chance circumstances that are out of the ordinary. Like intuitive learning, incidental learning is unstructured, informal and usually involves pondering over incidents like mishaps or frustrations in odd moments. In this case the outcome – the learning – usually, but not always, takes the form of rationalization or justification. Once again, this type of learning is often unrecognized as such and is almost always self-initiated.

While this would also cover the case of the child learning to walk – but this time from the repeated unsuccessful experiences of falling down – a business example would be the lesson learned by Gerald Ratner, one-time head of the world's largest jewellery chain, whose remark that one of his product lines was 'crap' led to his eventual dismissal and the group's demise as an independent business. Sir

Richard Greenbury learned from a similar incident concerning a remark he made about the acquisition he made for Marks & Spencer of Brooks Brothers, the US men's fashion retailer. 'We all do things we regret,' he recalled later. 'I wish I had never said we paid too much for Brooks Brothers. In 20 years people will still be rabbiting on about it.'

In contrast, there is the retrospective approach to experiential learning, which involves deliberate reflection of incidents with the clear intention of reaching conclusions. Like the intuitive and incidental approach, this type of learning is usually initiated by mishaps and mistakes but it also includes routine events and accomplishments. Because it involves a conscious intention to learn, the quality of erudition is often more superior to the intuitive and incidental approaches.

The use of case studies, internal audits, post-project reviews and/or oral post-mortems are illustrations of this approach to experiential learning. Like intuitive and incidental learning, good retrospective learning is entirely dependent on accurate memory recall and overcoming what the academics have identified as the *'defensive reasoning process'*. This type of experiential learning is also relatively rare in industry – and extremely difficult to do well. Often, they take the form of prosecutional inquiries into disaster-like incidents, the nature of which is designed to detect fault or apportion blame, a recent example of which was the one National Westminster Bank set up after its investment banking arm incurred a £77 million loss by mispricing derivatives, an incident that sparked the resignation of the subsidiary's chief executive and the departure of six other senior managers.

Lastly, there is the prospective approach, which is the most structured form of experiential learning and, arguably, the most effective in terms of preventing repeated mistakes and re-invented wheels, and building constructively on successes. This kind of learning includes all the elements of retrospective learning along with the more proactive intention of planning to learn *before* an experience takes place. It is even more difficult to achieve than retrospective learning, mainly because of the need to overcome the disposition towards short and selective memory recall and subjective analysis. In Chapter Five I explain a completely new methodology that has been expressly designed to overcome these main drawbacks to retrospective and prospective learning.

Whichever approach is being used – from the informal intuitive and incidental approaches to the more structured retrospective and prospective approaches – the essential component for effective experiential learning is a corporate environment in which the collection and application of knowledge is perceived to be more important than fault-finding, apportioning blame or tip-toeing around managerial egos.

Thereafter, it necessarily includes diligent and accurate observation of experiences (which usually necessitates their accurate recording because of the not uncommon short and selective memory recall of the learners), their profound and honest reflection and the empirical implementation of the consequent lessons. In short, it requires companies – and the people who run them – to be objectively reflective. It is in the less than rigorous implementation of these components, which includes the disposition towards organizational 'forgetting', that makes Western businesses so poor at learning from experience and – because of this – slower than they might otherwise be at creating the new knowledge essential for progress. Headway in the UK, for example, which – as this book will show – is particularly non-reflective in its learning processes, is largely accomplished defensively rather than proactively.

Underlying all this is the classroom attitude to 'history' as a generic subject. From the educational viewpoint, particularly in the UK, history is most commonly perceived to be a subject whose instruction encompasses the study of dates and events, whether of British kings and queens, wars or plagues. Rarely is it taught as an applied science, where its inventory of tried and tested experiences is a knowledge source that is part of a natural process of progress and change. Its nature is more commonly seen as immutable rather than evolutionary.

When it comes to experiential learning in industry, there are generally three directions from which input arises. The first is from external disciplines such as the military and politics, which are perhaps the most documented of all subjects, certainly when it comes to recording their history. Then there are the lessons that emanate from within industry, even from within the same sector. Finally, there are the lessons that a business can learn from its own experiences, the substance of which derives from an organization's own OM. Perhaps because it is the most personal, it is this kind of learning to which businesses are most resistant.

It is instructive to note the differing regional attitudes towards information, knowledge, decision-making and the creation of new knowledge. Managers in Western economies generally focus on explicit information to make their decisions. The emphasis of the Japanese, on the other hand, is on tacit knowledge. This deeply rooted difference is explained more fully by Professors Ikujiro Nonaka and Horotaka Tekeuchi in their 1995 book on *'The Knowledge-Creating Company'*. Academics who have also worked in industry in both the US and Japan, observe that Western management is deeply ingrained with the view that the organization is a machine for information processing. While this provides a valuable analytic edge to information gathering, it is a view of knowledge that is necessarily explicit – and viewed synonymously with a computer code, a chemical formula or a set of general rules.

Japanese companies, on the other hand, recognize that knowledge expressed in words and numbers represents only a small part of the exercise in new knowledge creation and decision making. They view knowledge as being primarily tacit, a characteristic which is also deeply rooted in an individual's action and experience, as well as in the ideals, values or emotions embraced. In its application, corporate culture is axiomatic.

The difference, they explain, goes to the heart of the traditional philosophies of Western rationalism and Eastern empiricism, the former based on the theory that knowledge comes about through deductive reasoning and the latter that it is derived inductively through actual experience.

While Western managers use mainly explicit knowledge to make their decisions, the Japanese manager's approach to creating new knowledge – focused as it is on tacit knowledge – is to convert tacit knowledge into explicit knowledge and then back into tacit. In this, sharing of experiences – and being constructively reflective – is key, as is the learned ability to communicate tacit knowledge through figurative language and symbolism. Whereas the premise of Western managers is that knowledge can be taught through formal education and training, the Japanese belief that the most powerful learning comes from direct experience, including trial and error, is rooted in their Zen Buddism heritage.

In the West the systems approach is expressed in almost all formal management education and staff training, which generally consists of technically oriented, mostly explicit, knowledge. The so-called tacit knowledge that comes from actual experience, reflective thinking and experiential learning is studiously avoided. The only concession to this approach is perhaps the management training that occurs 'on the job' and/or between jobs, when the theoretical instruction given has a practical context.

Evidence of the West's inattention to reflective thinking is highlighted in Peter Senge's conclusion in his writings that *'trial and error learning is a delusion, since the most critical decisions made in an organization have systemwide consequences stretching over years and decades, a time frame that makes learning from direct experience an impossibility'*. If anything, his conclusion is an admission that experiences do have a consequential effect, however long the length of time it takes to manifest itself. More importantly, if his perception is in any way also an accurate reflection of management views generally, it is clear reinforcement of the West's short-term view of business as the lessons of history do *not* have to be confined to a timeframe that is long removed from the actual event.

Another characteristic of Western managers is that, if there *is* any attempt to learn from experience in any formal way, the effort is typically directed towards learning from *successes*. Very few Western organizations tend to focus purposely on their failures until they become too big to ignore, preferring not to admit to any form of managerial infallibility and hoping that if they are disregarded, they'll not be repeated. As a result, failure has the disposition to become a recurrent syndrome rather than one that is actively avoided, as this book will show.

This is invariably associated with a spirited argument that it is impossible to be objective about 'facts', a reaction that reflects the cynicism towards the pursuit of knowledge that is more prevalent in the West. There is a further element that compounds the differing regional philosophies – the conflicting attitudes towards employees, who are the main repositories of OM and the ultimate decision makers in any organization.

In the West, where the heavy emphasis on flexible labour markets has encouraged very short individual enterprise tenure, the organization's core information and knowledge – their organizational memory – is usually held by individuals who guard its ownership proprietorially and jealously as a bargaining weapon in job and salary negotiation. When they move on, they take the organization's OM with them, leaving their successor to relearn their new employer's organization-specific information and knowledge. For the Western manager, the conventional wisdom is that an incoming appointee's experience and expertise, although acquired elsewhere, will generally compensate for those of the departed individual. The reality is that every organization's OM is different and only partially transferable. As such, the organization is constantly cold-starting itself and also exposing itself to the constant risk of repeating its mistakes, re-inventing the wheel and not building properly on its past successes, consequences that go a long way to offsetting – and in some cases overturning – many of the advantages attributed to the flexible labour market.

In contrast, continuity is a policy that is deliberately and formally encouraged in many Pacific basin countries, as is information and knowledge sharing between employees, procedures that are enhanced by a greater level of socializing and mentoring among Japanese workers.

While the likes of Senge may have introduced the concept to the modern generation, its origins, in fact, go back to work done in the 1920s and 1930s on learning organisms and learning systems, also by Western academics. This was followed up in disparate fields by the pioneering work done by von Bartalanffy in biology, Bounding in economics and Parsons and Shils in sociology. The concepts they developed – how organizations use external inputs and feedback loops to implement change – led to a systems approach to learning in many disciplines, notably in the political sphere in the 1960s by Easton, McClelland Deutsch and others. It is only now that the business world is realizing that these insights can equally be applied to industry, a reflection, perhaps, of the systemic gulf that has traditionally existed between industry and academia and industry and other life disciplines.

But, of all the languages in the domain, the Learning Organization is still a conceptual catch-all phrase that has little meaning to the majority of business organizations, who will generally suppose that if they employ any form of staff training they are, *ipso facto*, a Learning Organization. Alongside a myriad different definitions, the one to which I am most drawn is an organization which has consciously elected systematically to manage with purpose the knowledge it holds and creates to enable employees continually to discover why and how to create and change their reality to corporate advantage.

In this book I am not attempting to contradict or restate the traditional approach to the Learning Organization, which is well documented in a number of excellent books by the likes of Peters and Senge and an army of other management academics and management gurus. Nor have I dwelt on the complexity of the decision-making process itself, which is the product of creating new knowledge. This is a book about an aspect of the whole subject that academics and business organizations generally have missed or treat only peripherally – how to benefit *specifically* and *directly* from one's own hindsight. It is an approach to learning that some Western managers give only ornamental house room to once or twice every hundred years in their corporate histories, which are considered to be no more than fairly inexpensive publicity exercises sitting somewhere between prestige advertising and patronage of the arts.

Although, strictly, it is individuals, rather than corporate bodies, who create knowledge, organizations can't create new knowledge without old knowledge, at least not *efficiently*. By definition, they have to be aware of what the old knowledge is – somewhat difficult if time has blunted the corporate memory or the flexible labour market sees off a large proportion of the workforce every year. Also, knowing how the old was created is the most proficient guide on which to base the procedure for creating the new.

In pure business terms, the logic can be clearly seen in management's role, which is all about making decisions for the future. To address this unpredictable scenario, a decision-maker has to understand the range of likely possibilities that lie ahead. Taking account of one's previous experiences allows estimates to be made in the light of past experience, a discipline that necessarily reduces the uncertainty over decision making.

In truth, one's own organizational memory is an invaluable inventory of the experiences that have already been tried and tested. It is intellectual property alongside other strategic assets like customer trust and brand images. While OM may have happened yesterday, it has assuredly shaped today's performance and will, along with present-day experiences, condition tomorrow's – *however* fast is the rate of change in the process. If one disconnects it by not being constructively reflective, the inevitable consequence is that change will be less smooth and more expensive than it might otherwise be.

In essence, companies can implement essential change more efficiently by *using* the past rather than trying to avoid its significance and its consequences. As such, one has to manage one's OM. Why, why not, how, and how not to are the subjects of the following chapters. In particular, they explain how OM – the tacit element of which most managers (West and East) acknowledge is extremely difficult to communicate – *can* be articulated. And how yesterday's experiences, whether they occurred one day ago or fifty years ago, can be applied to how today's decisions are designed for tomorrow.

References

1. J. Yates, 'For the Record: Embodiment of Organizational Memory, 1859-1920, *Business and Economic History,* Second Series, Vol. 19, 1990.

2. 'Building a Learning Organization', *Harvard Business Review*, July-August 1993.

3. Management Page, *Financial Times*, 2 July 1997.

4. A.M. Kantrow, *The Constraints of Corporate Tradition*, Harper & Row, New York, 1984.

5. Management Page, *Financial Times*, 15 May 1997.

CHAPTER TWO

A job-for-life no more!

Of all the factors that contribute to corporate amnesia, the single biggest is the modern policy that has given rise to the flexible labour market. It was not so long ago that individuals had one, perhaps two, employers in their working lifetimes. Alongside job rotation within organizations, which can often take place every two years, job-hopping to new employers is now responsible for the second greatest measure of peacetime jobs disruption this century after the 1930s depression.

The flexible labour market is the name given to the managerial stratagem that gives companies and other organizations the adaptability to change their workforce, almost at will. Usually identified with bankruptcy, downsizing, radical jobs-change in the workplace and the consequence of acquisitions, mergers and restructurings, its nature is also associated with job creation and expansion.

In the West, the work model in its present form has been around for more than two decades now, occupying two recessions and, now, two recoveries. Its accelerating course first emerged in the mid- to late-1970s, which was perhaps the zenith of corporate corpulence in the West, at least as it applied to employment numbers within organizations. It was a period that is identified with the emergence of serious competitive threats from the Far East and parts of the Third World.

A collective and growing sense of urgency at the time led to an upheaval in the industrial landscape, with companies suddenly becoming more proactive in their management strategies. In particular, it created a variety of new management techniques, among them the discipline of Change Management, a somewhat amorphous management practice that has overlapped with equally indistinct practices such as Business Process Re-engineering, Continuous Process Improvement, Total Quality Management, Just-in-Time, multi-skilling, de-layering and outsourcing, to name a few.

Underpinning them all has been the flexible labour market which different Western countries have implemented in varying degrees, the argument being that a mobile workforce allows better control of overheads (especially in times of recession), the ability to be more flexible on jobs that change their nature and that new blood allows the importation of new ideas. While intended to improve efficiency, it has also been a cost-cutting and staff-reduction exercise. In many cases it has been an opportunity to displace the higher-paid, older generation of employees and get rid of dead wood in that now familiar management remedy called downsizing.

As a word, 'downsizing' first entered the management lexicon in the early 1970s when it was coined by the car industry in reference to the shrinking of cars. It was given its anthropomorphic connotation in about 1982 as a euphemism for cutting worker roles. At the time, it was typically viewed as a one-time fix but the direction of the new work model has not reverted, incurring widespread insecurity among the workforce. The ease with which the word has entered modern management vocabulary is illustrated by the 1997 imagery used by the chief executive of a troubled pharmaceuticals company: 'We must reduce the amount of DNA in this company.'

The new demography has also been supported by widespread improvements in technology and the social and political changes that have accompanied a succession of governments of different political colours, among them pensions transferability and the accelerating trend towards early retirement following the large influx into middle management of post-Second World War baby boomers. In the UK, government pay policies in the 1970s actually encouraged job-hopping; it was the only way individuals could legitimately increase their pay. More recently, there has been a sizeable trend towards temporary jobs and short-contract work.

Overall, the past two decades have been characterized by a constant succession of layoffs and subsequent hirings. While permanent layoffs have always been a feature of recessions, they now also occur in large numbers during the recovery phases, even at companies that are doing well.

There have been other significant changes in the nature of the workplace. In a reversal of the 1980s, when job losses were mostly the preserve of unskilled workers, it is now those with higher educations whose jobs are more vulnerable. In the US, for example, better-paid, white-collar workers, many at large corporations at the peak of their careers, today account for more of the share of jobs lost[1]. Also, whereas twenty-five years ago the vast majority of people that were laid off found jobs that paid as well as their old ones, only about 35 per cent of laid-off full time workers today end up in equally remunerative or better full-time jobs. Compounding this has been stagnant wages and an increasing unequal distribution of wealth. Adjusted for inflation, the median wage in 1994 in the US was nearly 3 per cent below what it was in 1979. With the average household income during this period climbing just 10 per cent, 97 per cent of gain went to the richest 20 per cent, workplace characteristics that are also evident in Europe.

An indication of the scale of job movements can be seen in the US, where – according to a 1995 analysis of Labor Department figures by the *New York Times* – more than 43 million jobs were erased since 1979, among them the likes of 50,000 jobs at Sears Roebuck, 12,3000 at AT&T, 18,800 at Delta Airlines and 16,800 at Kodak. Over the same period there was a net increase of 27 million jobs. In the UK, where job creation has not been as great or as fast, Britain's top twelve companies – from BT to Racal Electronics and Pilkington – cut their workforces by an average 44 per cent[2] in the five-year period to 1995, a rate of attrition that was mirrored elsewhere in industry. At BT, for example, the worker role was cut by 88,500, by 71,500 at British Aerospace and by 58,000 at Grand Metropolitan. At WH Smith, where workers[3] in their twenties have a turnover rate four times higher than that of older workers, staff reduction in 1995 alone was 30 per cent, the £24 million direct cost of which was equal to more than a quarter of the previous year's pre-tax profits.

Across Europe, the high rate of jobs change was no less evident. In one year alone – in 1993 – at the height of the latest economic slump, about 17 per cent of all workers changed[4] their jobs. By 1994, across all OECD countries, one in five jobs[5] were being newly-created or destroyed each year, with about 80 per cent of job turnover not related to the economic cycle.

It has always been more difficult for the displaced staff to find other jobs during periods of recession but, even with the economy now in recovery, the rate of job-change continues to increase. At the bookstore chain Waterstones, which is currently embarking on an ambitious programme to open fifty new shops, annual staff turnover[6] is running at between 70 per cent and 80 per cent in the company's key central London branches. According to a study[7] of future jobs patterns in the UK financial services sector, 125,000 jobs will go by the end of the decade to be replaced by 113,000 new jobs. In many City of London companies, employees stay on average just four years.

There is no shortage of examples where the same corporate post – from the chairman's to key shop floor appointments – has had a succession of different appointees over a relatively short period. In the mid-1990s, for example, WEW, the former Amber Day chain of discount stores, had three chairmen in less than two years; in the same period the company also lost both its chief executive and managing director.

This phenomenon is evident right across industry, even in the newly commercialized areas of sport. Football clubs like Manchester City, for example, have had twelve managers in ten years. Over a similar period its neighbour, Manchester United, had one manager. Illuminatingly, the former did not win any major trophies during its period of manager discontinuity while the latter, where first success came only in year four, collected a cabinet full, including two 'doubles' of the Cup and the League. By way of confirmation, in a unique study[8] of managerial job change in the English football league over a 21-year period to 1993, when there were 820 separate spells of football managership, the Institute of Economic Affairs concluded that discontinuity had an adverse effect on performance.

In introducing the jobs equivalent of musical chairs, the new work model has simultaneously imposed on industry a largely itinerant workforce. Take the individual case in the UK of David Hankinson's career. After graduating from Cambridge, the now 57-year-old chairman of Nottingham Group Holdings has had ten previous full-time employers, among them Arthur Andersen, Midland Bank, George Wimpey, Guthrie Corporation, Wilkinson Sword, Chloride, Rover, Ranks Hovis McDougall, Lucas and, latterly, Fisons before it was taken over by Rhone-Poulenc Rorer.

Over his working life so far, the *average* time he has spent with any one employer is around three years after taking into account any short periods of unemployment between jobs. However astonishing his individual rate of jobs change may *seem* at first sight, his mobility is not that extraordinary.

Although the rate of job-change varies from country to country, an indication of the wider measure of discontinuity can clearly be seen in the employment statistics. Alongside the day-to-day job movements among on-going businesses across the industrial spectrum, the *average* number of different employers that an American worker had in 1991 – the most recent year when statistics of this kind were gathered – was around six based on a forty-year working lifetime. Seven years later, after the most dramatic period of downsizing ever seen right across the industrial spectrum, the figure is certainly much higher.

The 1991 statistics come from the OECD[9] which puts the US at the top of the discontinuity league, closely followed by Australia and the Netherlands. Not far behind was the UK and Canada, succeeded by the likes of Switzerland, Finland, Norway, Spain, France, Germany and Japan, all of whose rates of discontinuity have continued to increase.

The detailed figures make instructive reading. Seven years ago, the length of time that an individual US employee stayed with the same paymaster was just six years and seven months. In the UK, the figure was seven years and nine months, with Germany and Japan between ten years and eleven years. How much these figures have deteriorated since then can be seen in the latest computation from the Employment Policy Institute, Europe's leading independent think-tank on employment, which puts[10] the number of different employers that new entrants to the labour market will have over their working lifetime at eleven. On this basis, employers can expect the average length of enterprise tenure from the next generation of workers to total just over three and a half years from now on.

These figures, which apply across the jobs spectrum, are put into further perspective by other research[11] that found that, in 1991, fewer than 40 per cent of all workers in the US had been with the same employer for more than five years. The equivalent proportions were 45 per cent in the UK, 57 per cent in France, almost 60 per cent in Germany and 62 per cent in Japan. A similar study[12] in 1995, which found that just 16 per cent of senior managers in the UK had been with their current employer more than six years, suggests how much the tenure rate has fallen since then.

The base shift change in employer attitudes to employee tenure is illustrated by a 1997 report[13] which confirmed that two thirds of companies no longer had a contractual or tacit understanding with their employees that promised a secure job in exchange for loyal and dedicated service. A further 27 per cent said that such an agreement never existed, leaving just 6 per cent where the paternalistic relationship remains more or less intact.

Worker attitudes to employers have been correspondingly affected. In just one of the many opinion surveys[14] at the time, employees' morale was *'in free fall'*. Disclosing the largest decline since the beginning of the decade in worker feelings of insecurity with their current employer – just 43 per cent of workers said they felt secure in 1996, down from 76 per cent in 1990 – the researchers announced that the traditional career had become just a memory.

Just how ingrained the flexible labour market is can be seen by the attitude of the London Stock Exchange, which has also become addicted to companies cutting jobs to enhance earnings. When Sir Richard Greenbury, Marks & Spencer's chairman, announced a plan in November 1996 to create 2,000 jobs – *'sure we could make more money by slashing costs, but I'm not interested in the short term'* – the company's shares, acknowledged to be one of the most resilient of all British stocks, suffered the largest fall in the FT-SE index that day. The fact that the company's 12 per cent profits rise, announced at the same time, was on target did not help.

As an instrument of social change, the collective insecurity that has emanated from the flexible labour market arguably helped to unseat the governments in Britain and France in 1997. Truly, it has seeded a redefinition of employment that has little to do with continuity or corporate loyalty.

Up to now, it has generally been assumed that the new work model has always been an employer's charter, where the organization accrued the main advantages. It is becoming apparent that this is not now the case. Almost unnoticed, the dramatic shift in the nature of employment towards short enterprise tenure has become one of the single biggest damaging influences on productivity and competitiveness in companies today.

Alongside the popular management perception that change necessarily means that old practices are largely redundant and that new tricks are best accomplished by new, usually younger, blood is the conventional wisdom that an incoming appointee's experience and expertise, although acquired elsewhere, will generally compensate for those of the departed individual. The reality is hardly comforting. Whenever an individual leaves an organization – for whatever reason and whether in a period of recession or recovery – the organization's hard-won and expensively acquired experiences literally walks out of the door. If, say, 10 per cent of managers leave every year, then 50 per cent of a company's managerial knowledge potential will have dissipated within five years – a classic case of throwing out the baby of experience with the organizational bathwater. This equivalent of 'forgetting' or 'unlearning' is not uniform because the departing knowledge and experience varies from job to job. Thanks to the complex nature of organizations, a chairman's OM, for example, is very different from a production manager or a machinist's OM.

The 'information' that disappears – usually at three months notice for senior personnel, one month's notice for more junior staff and sometimes just a week for others – is of two distinct types. There is the explicit expertise that is related to actual professional or vocational skills which organizations can – and when required, do – re-acquire when they rehire individuals of similar or better qualifications. The other type of experience that walks out along with the departing individual, arguably the more important kind that can be more properly be defined as the organization's 'intellectual property', is the institution's own organizational memory, which is the accumulation of experiences and knowledge that is organization-specific – and which cannot be rehired. It is also largely job-specific, making a nurse's OM, for example, very different from a hospital administrator's OM in the same organization. This includes the individual's understanding and accommodation of their employer's individual corporate culture, management, communications and decision-making style, contacts and relationships between employees or teams of employees, the detail of job-related events and the knowledge of tried and tested usage as it applies to the organization's own market circumstances and special environment – i.e. all the routines and processes (formal or otherwise) that make an organization tick. Because companies find it so difficult to characterize and document in conventional ways, it is the type of knowledge that typically exists only in the minds of individuals. New appointees are expected to assimilate it informally by way of osmosis from remaining employees who, because of the flexible employment market, have themselves been with their current employer only for a short period.

 An example that illustrates this loss of organizational memory is in the UK aerospace industry, where companies are experiencing serious problems in redesign and improvements of aero-engines[15].

An analysis of 'shared knowledge' within companies in the sector has discovered that because the workforce no longer has the continuity it once had, there is no one around to explain why particular engines were designed in a particular way.

Loss of design memory[16] has also been in evidence at IBM's personal computer division and Ford, both of which have been among America's top job cutters. IBM has suffered because it got rid of staff who worked on previous generations of PCs while the loss of design memory has affected Ford's latest version of the Taurus car. The original model was a hit because it met the needs of big-car buyers better than most rivals, but the latest version, which has been largely re-engineered from scratch, has failed to capture buyers' imaginations. In its design Ford, it seems, has forgotten what its customers wanted. Elsewhere, one US insurance group, which had slimmed its claims department, found[17] it was settling big claims too swiftly and too generously. Belatedly, it discovered it had sacked several long-term employees who had created an informal – but highly effective – way to screen claims. It subsequently reinstated them.

The downside of jobs discontinuity doesn't stop there. Having had its experiences and expertise dispersed elsewhere, the organization then has to re-invest in new appointees. In this, there is first the direct cost of re-employment, which includes the expense of advertising and/or agencies/ headhunters and the management time involved in replying to letters and interviewing. With the UK bill for recruitment of permanent staff put at about £2.5 billion a year[18], the Institute for Management Studies has calculated that the 1997 cost of replacing, for example, a sales assistant at WH Smith was £2,500 while other estimates of more senior personnel put the cost at around three quarters of annual salary. For graduates[19], it has been estimated that the selection cost in 1994 was around £25,000, rising to more than £100,000 over a three-year period when salary, training and overheads were included.

Second, there are the indirect costs associated with the new appointee's ability to settle into their new environment. With anecdotal evidence suggesting that it can take up to 12 months – and sometimes longer – for new appointees to settle into their new jobs and become fully productive, just seven employer moves means that at least 15 per cent of workers' lives are now routinely less than fully productive. For new entrants to the economy, the forecast of eleven different moves within their working lifetime means that up to 27 per cent of business lives will be worked at a pace that is less than premium.

In many companies today, a large proportion of their workforce is permanently in the induction phase of their employment. It is not uncommon to find that one third of an organization's workforce is, at any time, in the first year of their employ. This was the case for most of the first half of the 1990s in one of the UK's leading healthcare companies. Out of a section strength of nineteen in just one of its key management departments, departures were running at the rate of eight – usually to other outposts of the company – every sixteen months.

A low level of enterprise tenure has other unavoidable consequences. Individuals do not have any direct memory recall of any organization-specific events outside their short tenure. On the basis of an average six-year period of employee tenure, companies are employing an increasing number of workers – including managers – whose experience in their organizations does not extend before 1992. Taking the example of the regular trade cycle, which comes round about every eight years, there are few people in place who can directly recall how their employer responded to events related to the last trade upturn or downturn.

Real-life examples are not hard to find. Take the important UK banking and financial services sector, which experienced one of the highest level of employee shakeouts in the most recent recession. At the beginning of the 1989/1990 housing market collapse, the Halifax Building Society, for example, did not have in place any branch managers who could remember first-hand how the organization handled the previous housing market downturn. According to a newly appointed senior manager of my acquaintance, the organization finds itself in a similar position now that the housing market is recovering; there are once again few around who can remember accurately how the organization responded to the last upturn, with the result that the organization's learning curve is steeper and longer than it might otherwise have been. The problem is evident throughout the financial services sector – and beyond.

One unintended consequence of the BBC's reorganization in the 1990s was that it no longer had a middle management capable of getting programmes out if engineers went on strike. British Gas's re-engineering torched its reputation for service. In the US, Delta Air Lines, which shrank its workforce by about a sixth in the mid-1990s, 'forgot'[16] that service was what gave it its edge – and lost the loyalty of many customers. Nynex, a regional telephone group, found itself in similar straits after a restructuring similarly destroyed thousands of jobs; in April 1996, it was forced to pay customers a rebate.

Given that all companies are uniquely different in their management style and market, the reality is that corporate requirements are increasingly being driven in isolation to their own experiences and environment. With the phenomenon applicable across the jobs spectrum, the effects are most acute at middle-ranking and senior levels, where individuals are often expected to start making important strategic and operational decisions within months of their appointment. In most cases, this means that judgements during this period are based almost exclusively on their previous employers' experiences, cultural environment and market circumstances. Without organization-specific continuity, companies have scant ability to learn from their own, special experiences. As already indicated, the consequence of this is that they run the risk of misapplying their prior successes, of repeating past mistakes and re-inventing the wheel.

The evidence for this can be seen in the mountain of academic literature on the subject of strategic and operational change. In a 1988 study of competitive precedents, for example, a team of academics from Warwick University confirmed that many companies reproduce their blunders on a regular basis[20]. Looking specifically at development projects, a high-profile team of US scholars and industrialists also established that projects in the same company tend to suffer from the same mistakes[21], while consultants working for the leading US management consultancy McKinsey & Co. concluded that many companies continually re-invent solutions[22]. These are all findings that I take a closer look at in Chapter Four in connection with another characteristic of experiential learning – the predisposition towards a short and selective memory recall and the defensive reasoning process, and their impact on one of industry's most potentially powerful (and under-utilized) of management tools – the post-implementation review, the post-project review and/or the post-mortem.

The effects of discontinuity have several other insidious consequences. Even though circumstances change, companies generally owe their success to the building of one experience on another. Without access or reference to the practised example, a veteran business is automatically denied the experiential advantage it should have over a brand-new or much younger company. This would help to explain the vulnerability today of many veteran companies to smaller and much newer rivals and why so many newly-formed companies can emerge so quickly. In fact, the continuous assimilation of outside experiences to the exclusion of one's own, also carries with it the prospect of an organization quickly losing its hard-won, competitive advantage, the very thing that made it special in the first place.

Short job tenure also disrupts long-standing cultural and belief systems, which risk breaking down and makes it more difficult for individuals to feel part of a wider company team. When it is associated with divestments and core cuts, it puts additional burdens on retained staff, often leading to a collapse in morale and making it difficult to innovate and respond to a subsequent trade cycle upturn.

Evidence for this was found by a Cambridge University academic's research[23] into the flexible labour market which identified what he called a *'survivor syndrome'* among those left after redundancies. The manifestation of this was decreased levels of motivation, morale, confidence and loyalty and increased levels of stress, anger and bitterness. Tony Eccles, a visiting professor of strategic management at Cranfield School of Management, has quoted[24] similar US surveys reporting a collapse in morale in 70 per cent of delayered companies; interestingly, 30 per cent found that their costs actually went up after delayering and 22 per cent found that they had fired the wrong people.

An example of how difficult it becomes to innovate and grow is at ICI, where corporate downsizing resulted in a cut in head office staff from 1,200 in 1976 to just 240 in 1996, a rationalization that cut the top executive team to just four executive directors. In an interview with a management magazine[25], a senior manager admitted the smaller head office function has made it extremely difficult to 'seed' new markets by placing a promising individual in a key HQ department for a couple of years before sending them out into the field with a rounded experience of the company. The company also found it difficult to roll out a figure of the expected seniority when a major customer came calling.

The inability to innovate is further confirmed in research studies[26] undertaken in both the UK and the US by Peter Herriot, director of research at Sundridge Park Management Centre, and his research assistant Carole Pemberton. They point out the consequences of lost experience. *'Organizations are now in no position to innovate. When you can't innovate you can't compete. Slow death is the inevitable prognosis for many companies. Delayering and downsizing has produced a conformist, homogenized workforce used to keeping their heads down and too frightened to take risks.'*

The effects of discontinuity can be seen elsewhere in a variety of institutions across the world. In Israel, for example, the effectiveness of the country's defence forces, which has saved the fledgling country on numerous occasions over its fifty-year existence, has been questioned by reports[27] to the government which suggested that the early retirement of thousands of senior officers and the subsequent dislocation of the traditional promotional path had compromised the ability to respond effectively to external threats.

In the new South Africa, the government's own auditors have admitted that the recent restructuring in the Civil Service has irretrievably damaged the nation's financial management capacity. The government's original target was to cut 300,000 jobs in three years. Up to 1995 – the end of the first year of downsizing, when only a small percentage of the workforce had been dispersed – the calculation was that R1 billion had been wasted.

The restructuring has involved replacing existing job-holders with black appointees as part of the policy of Affirmative Action Appointments to encourage black economic empowerment. The government has admitted that its best brains have literally walked out of the door, leaving their inexperienced stand-ins to re-invent what had already been learned at great expense. Much the same is happening in the police force and elsewhere in industry, where a whole swathe of companies are undergoing huge rationalization, some of them for privatization.

The results of discontinuity are particularly acute in South Africa, where a fifty-year-old management culture has been replaced virtually overnight. While the political imperative argued that the clean break would enable a fresh start to create new paradigms and new solutions, the reality is very different. Even though some of the new appointees have modern technical proficiency, the economy now has few 'coping skills' among the new captains of industry that would otherwise derive from experience. This has imposed a widespread dearth of confidence in managers' own abilities and a correspondingly inert decision-making process.

As all the examples show, the aggregated effects of the flexible labour market on productivity and competitiveness are unaccountably costly.

It is an approach to business that fosters change through employee change. What this corporate equivalent of 'musical chairs' ensures is that organizations recall very little of their own corporate memories and experiences, with the result that few have any facility to benefit from their own hindsight. What is actually happening is that, if they *do* have the capacity to respond, they are more commonly reacting to the experiences and environments of other organizations.

Curiously, it is a viewpoint that the West is only now beginning to appreciate, although there is little evidence that the voices of concern are being listened to. In the UK, for example, the attitude towards downsizing, is being questioned by organizations as diverse as the Institute for Personnel and Development (IPD), the main professional body for human resources professionals, and the Employers Forum on Age (EFA), a small group of companies concerned about industry's preoccupation with making redundant the more experienced members of the workforce. The IPD's studies[28] on the subject found that *'too many organizations are unable to differentiate "fat" from "muscle"'* and generated workforces *'unable and unwilling to make the most of new opportunities as they arise'* while the EFA found that the new youth-cult operated by many employers had led to spiralling recruitment costs and – according to its Ruth Jarrratt, its development director – *'lost continuity'*.

It was at the EFA's launch[29] in 1996 that its chairman, Howard Davies, a deputy Governor of the Bank of England at the time, made one of the first public references to *'organizational memory (OM) loss'* in the context of the flexible labour market. A year earlier he had also referred to *'corporate anorexia'*, a related term coined by two London Business School academics[30] in a book that sharply criticized the Anglo-American managerial habit of reaching for personnel cuts as a first resort.

These perspectives have now gained the support of the European Commission. In 1996, the EC's report[31] on the competitiveness of European industry underwent an important change in its traditional attitude to the flexible labour market. An early version of the report highlighted the benefits of making hiring and firing easier and warned that a lack of labour flexibility could stifle companies' ability to respond to consumer demand. This was substantially watered down after accusations that its approach was too *'Anglo-Saxon'*. The new version's recommendations, which endorsed the Pacific Basin approach to employment, emphasized that a stable workforce can improve company competitiveness in the long run.

Other critics of the flexible labour market even include Morgan Stanley's chief economist Stephen Roach, downsizing's principal proponent in the 1970s and 1980s, who is warning that workplace shrinkage has now gone too far. He admitted in 1996: *'Tactics of open-ended downsizing and real-wage compression are ultimate recipes for industrial extinction.'*

Over in the US, a recent survey[32] by the American Management Association found that fewer than half of those companies that had downsized since 1990 went on to report higher operating profits in the years following the move; even fewer saw improved productivity. Elsewhere, Monitor, the Cambridge, Massachusetts, consultancy extension of Professor Michael Porter, found[33] that 90 per cent of companies that outperformed their industries over a ten-year period had *'stable'* structures, with no more than one reorganization and no change (or an orderly change) in chief executive.

The idea that downsizing's corporate benefits have not materialized is also belatedly being mentioned more and more in academic literature, management journals and national newspapers, among them the *Financial Times*, which has quoted a critic's description of the policy as *'dumbsizing'*[34]. In a specific reference to its amnesic effects, *Management Today*'s assessment[35] is that the result of delayering and downsizing was more often *'a forgetting, not a learning, organization as companies flattened their stock of experiences along with the hierarchy and found they had outsourced the ability to make the wheel, let alone invent it'.*

My critical review of the whole concept of the flexible labour market is not intended to advance the notion that jobs-change, including downsizing, is *all* bad. There are always going to be examples where recruiting decisions are not necessarily good ones, where individuals have, indeed, outlived their usefulness and need to be moved on and where it makes sense to withdraw from non-core activities. Also, it *does* allow better control of overheads in the short term, the ability to be more flexible on jobs that change their nature and introduces new ideas. My point is that the flexible labour market also hides a raft of very serious downside consequences, the significance of which is often disregarded by managers whose own short tenure frequently overrides the wider corporate focus. This has ensured that the organizations for which they work, and then leave, never have in place management processes truly to address the problem of discontinuity and migratory knowledge.

Whatever the arguments for and against the flexible labour market, the West – for its own best reasons – has chosen the alternative of the less stable workforce to run its enterprises. How, then, can businesses retain the advantages of the flexible labour market without suffering the existent – and sizeable – consequences of discontinuity?

While some attention has been given to the new work model's effect on individuals (retraining, etc.), the fact is that, in their preoccupation with managing change itself, companies have largely overlooked the wider consequences that the flexible labour market is having on themselves. In doing so, they have also neglected to build in management systems to mitigate them. Among the neglected areas, for example, are the interrelated aspect of staff/management development and succession planning, which is often limited to vintage induction techniques designed for employees who were hitherto and ostensibly recruited for life.

With 'life' now averaging less than the typical trade cycle, the answer lies in retaining and more effectively applying a company's OM as the lubricant for change. Enabling new appointees to inherit company-specific knowledge will allow transition to evolve at a momentum that will always be much faster than them having to start from scratch.

This can be done through the skilful employment of knowledge preservation techniques to capture relevant OM in forms that can be easily understood and used by successive generations of appointees. There are a number of methods and mediums that I explain in this book, the first two of which, outlined in the next chapter, are ideal for capturing short- and medium-term knowledge up to about twelve years and which are particularly suitable for staff/management development and induction in particular. In deference to Sir Winston Churchill, who authored the terminology, I call them the Jaw-Jaw[36] applications, which uses oral debriefing techniques.

Expertly structured, they are a practical and inexpensive way of retaining custody of OM within an organization. They are also a means of providing the all-important element of job continuity that modern job-mobility has destroyed, a change tool that allows new employees to learn from the experiences of their predecessors at *first hand* and an effective way quickly to empower the next generation of workers.

References

1. US Labor Department statistics 1994.

2. Hemmington Scott, quoted in the *Director* magazine, April 1996.

3. Getting the Right Balance in Recruitment, Employers Forum on Age, 1997.

4. 6th report on Employment in Europe, European Commission. 1994.

5. 1994 OECD Annual Report on Employment.

6. 'A New Chapter', *Financial Times*, 6 August 1997.

7. Report by Focus, Central London Training and Enterprise Council. August 1997.

8. Institute of Economic Affairs study, published October 1997.

9. 1993 OECD annual report on employment.

10. Employment Policy Institute, London. 1997.

11. *Management Practices and Unemployment*, Centre for Economic Performance, LSE. 1995.

12. *Research into Management Discontinuity*, Pencorp, London. 1995.

13. Implementing the New Employment Compact, *HR Executive Review*, The Conference Board. 1997.

14. *Transition and Transformation in the 1990s*, ISR International Survey Research, London. 1996.

15. Feedback to me by supervisor into research study by Bristol Business School's Judith Jordan and Penelope Jones, 'Assessing Your Company's Knowledge Management Style', *International Journal of Strategic Management*, Vol. 30. No 3, June 1997.

16. 'Fire and Forget', *The Economist*, 20 April 1996.

17. Ibid.

18. Job File, *The Sunday Times*, 27 July 1997.

19. *Delivering the promise*, report by Yellowbrick, Glasgow. 1994.

20. 1988 research study 'Strategies and Past Actions: Management Awareness of Competitive Precedents,' by Dr Robert Rosenfeld, University of Warwick's School of Industrial and Business Studies.

21. 1992 research study at Harvard University, the Massachusetts Institute of Technology, Purdue and Stanford universities into 20 development projects. Regaining the lead in manufacturing by H. Kent Bowen, Kim Clark, Charles Holloway, Dorothy Leonard-Barton and Steven Wheelwright, *Harvard Business Review* reprint nos 94501-2.

22. Research into 'design amnesia' by Lance Ealey, Leif Soderberg, published Spring 1990 issue of *McKinsey Quarterly*.

23. Brendan Burchell, 'The Unequal Distribution of Job Insecurity', *International Review of Applied Economics*, 1997.

24. The Incredible Shrinking Company, *Director* magazine, April 1996.

25. Ibid.

26. Peter Herriot and Carole Pemberton, *Competitive Advantage through Diversity*, Sage, London. 1993.

27. *The Jerusalem Report*, 26 August 1993 and 5 September 1996.

28. 1996 report Issues in *People Management* No. 15, Institute of Personnel and Development.

29. *Financial Times* report, 14 May 1996.

30. G. Hamel and C.K. Prahalad, 'Competing for the Future'. 1994.

31. 1996 EC report on Competitiveness of European Industry, reported in *Financial Times*, 9 October 1996.

32. 1996 survey, American Management Association, quoted in *The Economist*, 20 April 1996.

33. Unpublished survey, Monitor, Cambridge, Massachusetts, quoted in *The Economist*, 20 April 1996.

34. Mastering Management, *Financial Times*, 31 May 1996.

35. The Knowledge Within, *Management Today*, August 1997.

36. From "To jaw-jaw is always better than to war-war." Sir Winston Churchill's speech at the White House, 26 June 1954.

CHAPTER THREE

How to sustain the internal knowledge chain in a flexible labour market

As the previous chapter showed, a whole raft of things happen when organizations are exposed to the high rate of employee turnover that is characteristic of the flexible labour market. Among them, its hard-won and expensively-acquired experiences keep walking out of the front door while a succession of new appointees ensures that a large proportion of the workforce is always in the induction phase of their employment.

It is a sobering thought that at the current rate of jobs-change, few companies in the Western world have many employees in place who can personally remember what happened in their organizations just five or six years ago. With little or no organizational memory at hand, there is little or no organization-specific hindsight on which to base the decisions for the future.

I have also outlined the consequences this is having on companies. However difficult it is to quantify the cost of repeated mistakes or re-invented wheels, it *is* possible to put a figure on some of the other downside effects of the flexible labour market. For one, there is the known direct costs of re-employment, which various bodies have calculated in a range of £2,500[1] for a sales assistant to three quarters of annual salary for a senior employee. Then there is the cost of getting new appointees up to speed; on the basis that this can take up to a year, then – using the six-year tenure figure suggested by the OECD[2], which has been long overtaken by events – up to 16 per cent of each individual's productivity can be stripped out of the benefit that an organization might derive from each worker's employment.

Other ways of putting a value on OM is to view its existence as an inventory of tried and tested experiences, the cost of which is represented, at top level, by the value of 'key man' insurance policies that many companies take out against death in office of their important decision makers or the organization's actual cash investment in its employees.

The value[3] that Gianni Versace's company put on the designer fashion tycoon's lost experience after he was murdered by a gunman in Los Angeles in 1997 was $20 million, while the claim

that was put into Lloyds of London for insurance broker and
football personality Matthew Harding, who was accidentally
killed in a helicopter crash in 1996, was £16 million. Using the
other measure of OM worth – the investment in actual salaries
paid out – the average payments made by a UK company to its
employees over a six-year period can range from around
£100,000 for a relatively junior worker to upwards of £800,000,
and much, much more, for senior officers. When their OM –
acquired entirely at the organization's own expense – can wholly
disappear, virtually overnight, this must represent an extremely
poor investment in intellectual capital. What price its retention?
Aggregated – from hiring and firing costs to lost momentum and
dissipated knowledge – the flexible labour market is dispensing a
high built-in degree of inefficiency to Western industry that is very
damaging to wider competitiveness.

Curiously, migratory knowledge and the effects of discontinuity do not feature very high in the priorities of most companies in their management of the core corporate competencies. For the former, they do very little to retain and/or pass down their experiences to successive generations of employees. For the latter, the techniques of succession planning – and induction in particular – are still rooted in the days when individuals were hired for life.

Even when one discounts the effects of high jobs turnover, most organizations have notoriously poor memories. Here, the problem is inaccurate memory recall and the inevitable dispute over the precision of events and their sequence. While the personal memory may be long in parts, it is also highly selective and the quality of recall fades with time, even after a relatively short period. Individuals typically cannot remember what they did, the circumstances in which decisions were made, the rationale for the decisions, who said what to whom and what was meant by what was said.

Lord Armstrong, the former Cabinet Secretary in Mrs Thatcher's administration, knows the problem well. He discovered just how fallible the human memory is when he was conducting the inquiry into the Westland affair in the 1980s. People, he recalled, could not remember the timing of important telephone calls just a few weeks after the event. John Dean (of Watergate fame) claimed fairly total recall but an analysis[4] of the Oval Office tapes found that he remembered neither conversations nor even gists of conversations. Instead, his recall covered an ideal set of possible conversations that encoded his perceived truth of the situation and his fantasies about his own role. For organizations, short job tenure merely exacerbates this incapacity.

In businesses, the supporting documentation that is normally generated at the time is usually of little help. Most of it is usually of a formal nature and contains little of the 'tacit' knowledge that is essential in any good decision-making process. In almost all cases, this documentation is stored away in dusty rooms or on sophisticated computer systems – and rarely referred to. In hard copy, most companies dispose of their archives when the piles get too high. In fact, relatively few companies have working archives.

When it comes to succession planning, most organizations find themselves more concerned with the logistics of hiring (and firing) than ensuring that the inevitable discontinuity is minimized. Take what happens when employees retire or leave to join other organizations. If the individuals are replaced, their successors are either hired from outside the organization, in which case the appointees have to be inducted both into their new organization and their new jobs, or promoted internally, either upwardly or laterally, in which case the individuals still have to be inducted into their new jobs. In the case of internal appointments, the knock-on effect of individuals stepping into other people's shoes creates a domino effect, with consequent disruption all along the chain. At the end of the line, someone is usually hired from the outside.

To help smooth the succession process, organizations sometimes overlap employees, usually the more senior individuals where it is possible and deemed affordable; in most cases, the handover is usually cursory and less than generous in the amount of 'tacit' knowledge and organizational memory that is transferred. Whatever information is transferred is subject to the exiting individual's selective memory recall, deliberate screening and the incoming individual's ability to retain such information. More common, however, incoming appointees never meet their predecessor. Otherwise, conventional induction generally concentrates on familiarizing new entrants with the corporate – rather than the functional – nature of their job. A typical familiarization programme comprises the provision of a short historical pamphlet and associated company literature providing information on, among other things, terms of employment such as holiday entitlement and sickness benefits. Sometimes, new entrants are addressed by a long-serving employee, given a tour of the company and/or are shown a corporate video.

Even though most professionally managed companies run induction courses, most new placements will readily admit that the components that most inhibit their early passage to full productivity relate not to the operational side of their job but to understanding and accommodating their new employer's individual corporate culture, management and communications style, and the detail of recent events. Because of the difficulties of imparting such information in written form, companies generally leave individuals to assimilate these 'intangibles' as best they can, usually by osmosis, often judging the new entrant's ability to acclimatize to their new environment above their actual functional abilities. The process is so unstructured that individuals often only assimilate this type of knowledge by chance and in a piecemeal way.

If OM loss and discontinuity are the inevitable effects of the flexible labour market, how, then, can an organization minimize the effects on productivity and competitiveness? The answer lies in a knowledge-preservation tool that, constructed professionally and with purpose, can simultaneously capture OM and provide a powerful means of management development and induction. The genre, which can be classified under the wider Learning Organization's precepts, is otherwise known as oral history. Professionally undertaken, it is a powerful and cost-effective way of preserving short- and medium-term OM in a form that is easily communicable with following appointees.

While the use of oral debriefing is relatively widespread at a sociological level and in areas like book research, its application in industry proper is rare in most European economies. In a project called *City Lives*, the National Life Story Collection attached to the British Library National Sound Archive is interviewing about 100 top men and women from financial institutions who have lived through the changes since the Second World War. Aside from that, only a handful of British companies have undertaken projects to record the memories and experiences of their employees, among them London Transport, which has made a special effort with their West Indian workforce, the brewers Bass, the telecommunications company Cable & Wireless and, until the project was aborted in 1991 as a cost-saving exercise, Ford UK. The uses to which they have put the information have generally been minimal, usually for museum exhibits or public relations.

This compares with the US experience where oral history has been a more recognized discipline in industry ever since Allen Nivens, a professor of history at Colombia University and a noted biographer, organized the interview in the early 1950s of more than 400 people for a history of the Ford Motor Company. Nivens had already introduced oral history as a tool for serious scholarship through the Oral History Collection of Columbia University, which he founded in the late 1940s to preserve the reminiscences of former slaves and so-called 'unlettered rural folk'. Since then other universities, including Harvard, Princeton and the University of California, Berkeley, have also developed extensive collections of oral history.

Nivens' work is often associated with another American exponent of oral history, the social commentator and writer Studs Terkel, a 1985 Pulitzer Prize winner for his book *The Good War*. Born in Chicago in 1912, Terkel studied law at the University of Chicago before becoming a journalist, broadcaster and social writer. His books are best known for his technique of interviewing a whole cross-section of American society: taxi-drivers and teachers, the poor and the rich, young and old. In his books he pieces together a jigsaw of social opinion and attitudes which gives the reader an overview of a nation undergoing rapid social change.

Among the many US companies that support programmes of oral history are ARCO, Beckman Instruments, Bristol-Myers, Eli Lilly, Kaiser Aluminum and Chemical, Monsanto, Procter & Gamble, Rohm and Haas, Standard Oil Company, Kraft General Foods and the computer company Digital Equipment Corporation.

In the UK, companies most commonly know the tool in its unsophisticated form otherwise called the exit interview, which is usually employed as a formulaic, twenty questions means of trying to uncover reasons why employees leave. Because of their prescriptive nature, many are as limiting in the quality of knowledge capture as simple, written questionnaires. They are usually conducted by a member of the human resources department when individuals resign and are generally loathed by the people who are assigned to undertake them. They are considered largely ineffective, usually because of their unprofessional construction, the fact they are carried out internally, often by juniors who are also sometimes acquainted with the departing interviewees, and that exiting individuals see them as being intrusive and prying because of their purpose. Inasmuch as they are carried out so ineffectually, the organizations that use them don't usually consider the tool as having any other application.

Professionally reconstructed, however, oral debriefing can be transformed into a practical Knowledge Management tool for at least two clear corporate functions – in management/staff development and, in a slightly different form, for induction purposes. Done well, it is the most effective – and cost-effective – of all the media available as a means to retain custody of an organization's important experiences and knowledge before they are either forgotten or walk out of the door.

One of the first things to do is to create a simple 'Knowledge Map' that identifies an organizations's key individuals whose functions and experiences are considered important for the smooth running of the business. In identifying them, the broad rule of thumb is: *'Would we be in trouble if these people fell under a bus?'* While the list clearly depends on institutional size and the rate of employee movement, numbers would also be influenced by the organization's complexity of functional operations and the perceived importance of operatives in less senior positions. Typically, a Knowledge Map might identify around 10 per cent of an organization's employee base.

To facilitate knowledge capture, debriefing programmes can be applied either at regular intervals *during* an individual's tenure or immediately after key projects, and when an employee retires or leaves to join another company, usually in the last month of the exiting individual's tenure. The former will give a time-undistorted record that can be referred to at any later stage while the latter will also provide incoming appointees with a powerful induction tool.

Carried out at regular intervals during an individual's job tenure, oral debriefings can be used to ensure that corporate knowledge and experiences are not forgotten down the years, and that companies do not lose the benefits of hindsight. Importantly, it also allows the collection of the most recent experiences which, often, are also the most relevant but, because of the perceived lack of perspective over time, are rarely documented.

In most cases, it is quite easy to identify the individuals for which such debriefings would be beneficial. They are usually the organization's key operatives, including non-executives such as plant managers and department heads – anyone who, if they were no longer around, would create an operational crisis. Almost every well-established organization can, for example, recall occasions when key individuals have died suddenly in office leaving a void that takes many months and sometimes years to fill.

Gianni Versace and Matthew Harding are high profile examples who have already been referred to. The list is endless .... Mark Wyatt, owner and managing director of Cheshire-based software group General Systems, who died at age 38 in 1997 from injuries received in a car accident .... 56-year-old Bernard Doyle, operations director of diversified engineering group Glynwed International, who died suddenly in 1996 from lung cancer.... Roberto Goizueta, chairman and chief executive of Coca-Cola, who died in office in 1997, also from lung cancer.

The type of debriefings that would provide added value, for example, might be related to individual projects such as product launches, product recalls, relocations, an acquisition, a disposal, the installation of a new machine or computer system, even how a rationalization is carried out.

What price to a corporate strategist the *accurate* recall of the philosophy and mechanisms behind a planned change five years earlier? Or of a time-undistorted analysis of a prior marketing strategy, a company restructuring or investment technique, or how managers tackled declining exports when the local currency was last highly valued? Consider, too, the benefits to a new chief executive of having access to the conceptions of key executives when they planned their way out of the last recession? Or of the lessons of the tested past of a director to his colleagues on a subsidiary board?

At another level, a production director's experiences of a factory extension may also be of considerable value to a corporate planner, a design engineer or a financial controller – and not only in the current generation. Elsewhere, it can provide a useful diagnostic tool for studying organizational cultures and can assist in a wider understanding and interpretation of events. For example, the processes of managing change will frequently go unrecorded; as such, oral recollections can provide much which more formal written material does not.

And what about in the computer industry, where computer programmers, the lifeblood of all software products, have one of the highest rates of jobs-change? One of the essentials of updating software programs is continuity, which requires an evolutionary knowledge of a product. What price a running and detailed explanation of the rationale behind software architecture for successive generations of programmers?

For whatever application, an important consideration in this type of knowledge capture is to secure the on-going cooperation of employees. For this, a positive attitude to learning – on the part of both the wider organization and individual employees – is key. Knowledge Management, and especially the concept of knowledge sharing (which is still largely an alien concept in most Western companies), can then be presented to employees in the same way as external training – as a means to boost individual and corporate performance. Importantly, knowledge sharing needs to be disassociated with the general appreciation of the exit interview's traditional purpose – to ferret out problems.

It is instructive how some companies have used the methodology. At Kraft in the US, for example, the company's oral history archive has been used to fashion a new marketing approach to an old product. Towards the end of the 1980s one of the company's brands, Cracker Barrel cheese, was experiencing a slowdown in growth. Linda Crowder, the brand's manager, used the oral tapes to delve into the brand's origins in 1953 in order to shape a new marketing strategy. By reading the transcripts of interviews, she was able to gain the insights of retiree Med Connelly, national sales manager of cheese products from 1959 to 1962, the period when the brand's sales began to take off. *'He gave us a perspective we just couldn't get anywhere else,'* she says. *'Our research gave us a sense of what the theory was when Cracker Barrel was first introduced, and what we told consumers about the brand in the beginning.'*

At DEC, its oral history archive combines with a 'living' museum – called the 'Collection' – of the company's 33-year-old history to help build on past achievements. To date, its oral history programme has recorded the memories and experiences of more than 300 individuals. In addition to key officers, the company 'debriefs' selected employees who are both retiring and leaving to join other companies. Transcripts are filed on diskette and hard copy, and indexed by topic and individual. Apart from providing valuable anecdotal information for later use, the programme can extract from departing employees their understanding of situations in the past and how they responded to them. Although staff may have left, the company has thus ensured that it still derives benefit from the years they were employed.

DEC's founder and president, Ken Olsen, believes the project enables people in and outside the company to *'study and learn from what we've done in the past, and understand where the company has come from and where it is going'.* Present-day engineers, manufacturing, services and sales people, for example, are put in touch with what it was like doing their jobs twenty and thirty years ago. *'That many of the company's upper management were engaged in designing, building, selling and fixing the systems of the 1950s, 1960s and 1970s provides insight into their goals and perspective,'* he says.

In fact Olsen goes as far to suggest that the internal creative process of the company, which is at the leading edge of computer technology, owes much to its sense of history – *'of one achievement building on another. Examples of this are evident throughout the history of the company, from the PDP-1, the world's first 'personal' interactive computer, building on the values developed in the Whirlwind Project, to the design of new generation VAX systems using design simulations that run on earlier VAX generations.'*

> *Oral debriefing is also a key management tool at Los Alamos, birthplace of the atomic bomb. In the wake of the US Government's decision to stop testing nuclear weapons, officials are concerned that the skills it has developed will atrophy. In the event that it has to resume testing one day – and perhaps actually use the weapon again – it is undertaking a massive programme called the Knowledge Preservation Project to ensure that the expensively acquired expertise it has accumulated over the years is not lost forever as archives progressively degenerate and scientists retire. As part of the programme, retired weaponeers are being brought back to the laboratory for videotaped interviews intended to salvage information about nuclear bombs that can never be gleaned from blueprints and archived documentation. So far, the Los Alamos researchers have recorded about 2,000 videotapes.*
>
> *Behind the need to guarantee that they retain the expertise to build atomic bombs is to ensure that they do not have to re-invent the wheel. 'We don't want to press the erase button on our memory and go back to where we were fifty years ago,' says John D. Immele, director of nuclear weapons technology at Los Alamos.*

A similar approach[5] was used by a major aircraft manufacturer which was faced with the shutdown of an established production line. Unsure whether or not the line would ever restart, it decided to capture as much of the 'learning' embedded in the individual production workers as possible by videotaping workers at their stations prior to the shutdown.

The genre's other application – as an induction tool – involves the oral debriefing of exiting individuals as a way of transferring knowledge and experience across to incoming appointees. Companies generally perceive that departing employees are not of much use any more. In fact, exiting individuals are teeming repositories of all the experiences acquired over their period of tenure. Passing on their experiences in a way that illustrates how a company does its business provides a powerful change tool to familiarize a successor quickly, efficiently and cost-effectively into both their new job and their new company.

The problem with conventional induction processes is that they do not convey these intangibles. Leaving new employees to pick them up in their own time is a risky policy, especially if organizations require them to start making important decisions before they fully understand the way the organization does business.

Carefully constructed, oral debriefings can relate these intangibles at first hand. Recorded during the outgoing individual's notice period, the transcript can be made available to the new entrant immediately on appointment, providing a timely and permanent record to which the new appointee can refer at any time.

One example of its use is by the UK merchant bank N. M. Rothschild, whose decision to use the oral debriefing[6] as a knowledge-preservation and induction tool came when its Director of Corporate Affairs, John Antcliffe, decided to leave the company before a successor could be appointed. The merchant bank was conscious of the need for job continuity and the fact that a key employee was leaving with a wealth of experience that – if not captured in some way – would be lost forever. The debriefing was conducted two weeks before Mr Antcliffe's departure, after which Mr Antcliffe said: *'It fleshed out areas I would not have thought of mentioning to my successor, even had I the opportunity. As a succession planning tool, it has considerable value for the new entrant and the company. It is an extremely effective way to quickly familiarize one's successor with all the subtle aspects of both a new job and their new employer.'* Rodney Lonsdale, Rothschild's Personnel Director who commissioned the project, said: *'The project went far beyond any of our expectations. Unless a new employee reads the culture here right, then they're going to find it extremely difficult, if not impossible, to be productive. The technique is a very insightful and efficient way of reflecting the reality of the job and the company, and a well-balanced way of crystallizing all the issues that someone coming into this organization cold needs to know. When the new appointment is made, it will give the new entrant a very good understanding of how this business ticks.'*

The assignment, which took an afternoon to record, was undertaken by a skilled knowledge manager with an expert knowledge of management issues, human resources and corporate culture. Pre-project research included discussions with Rothschild to define the project's objectives and provide the interviewer with specific guidance on areas of importance to be covered in the debriefing. The resultant transcript was edited and indexed to ensure clarity, continuity and readability.

Pharmaceuticals giant Glaxo Wellcome is another company to have used the technique[7] for its succession planning. Its decision to use it arose when management realized that a key, twenty-man planning department, which is dependent on a detailed understanding of the clinical and commercial aspects of all group compounds and their markets, had eight departures and fifteen arrivals in eighteen months. In addition to the routine settling-in period, each new entrant had to acquire the knowledge that exiting individuals took with them – a time-consuming and expensive operation. This 'know-how' – which existed only in the minds of individuals – was typically held informally and, theoretically, passed over to newer appointees orally at joining and at appropriate junctures thereafter. Because of time pressures and the fact that it was normally so difficult to characterize and document in conventional ways, little was actually being conveyed.

Glen Slade, who commissioned the project, said the company was conscious of the need to manage these transitions more effectively. The problem, he recalled, was compounded by the fact that the managers worked independently from each other, so there was little shared knowledge of the detailed issues each was addressing from day to day.

A pilot project was first set up to discover whether or not an agency from outside the knowledge-intensive pharmaceuticals industry would be able to capture the necessary information to provide a worthwhile handover dossier. The pilot took advantage of some of the internal role changes within the department so that backup routes, by direct reference to the individuals concerned, were available.

> *'The results were considered very successful, concluding that the handover reports would not only be useful when people left, but were worth the expense even for internal moves'*, said Slade. *'This finding is now departmental policy and the service continues to be used as the department undergoes another reorganization. The method proved very easy to integrate into the department since we were quickly able to minimize the management overhead associated with each debriefing (the time to brief the interviewer and collate the background documentation) to less than half an hour. Furthermore, use of this technique has been demonstrated to be fully applicable to middle managers, as opposed to senior executives who may be the more common target for such debriefings. We even used the tool successfully on a junior member of staff who left the company shortly after her departure was integrated into ours.'*

In transcript format, debriefings ran to about one fifth the length of an average novel.

The idea of using oral debriefings as an induction tool is relatively new, although its application for experiential learning has – and is being – used in various formats, usually in first-person written form. Management consultant Arthur Andersen, for example, encourages its clients to use personal web pages on their intranets as a way of capturing and retaining information within the company that might be useful to colleagues in other parts of the company. They suggest, for example, that staff write their own white papers on specific topics detailing how a project was handled.

Semiconductor manufacturer Intel is another example of an organization that uses personal web pages to distribute experiential information. Typically, a manager writes and places his progress report on his personal web pages. Staff are able to view the report directly from the manager's web pages.

Honda in the US uses an associated technique, also in first-person written form. It uses a diary format to help cure the *'design amnesia'* which its consultants, McKinsey, found was costing many companies 30 per cent of their design time in redoing work that had already been done elsewhere in the organization[8]. To help engineers review their collective memory, the company imposes a simple historical discipline by encouraging individuals to keep notebooks in which they are expected to record their work progress, highlighting their own creative ideas. These notebooks serve several crucial purposes. As personal documentation of previous work experience, they ensure that previous ideas and solutions are not lost, providing an effective way to maintain design memory with the organization. In addition, they serve as a recognized form of copyright protection for ideas the individual might have come up with so that credit for any particular breakthrough can be given to its originator.

As the examples illustrate, the Arthur Andersen, Intel and Honda models all rely on the writing skills of individuals and their ability to be accurately observant. The problem with this approach is that managers are notoriously bad communicators, especially on paper. Apart from a selective memory recall they are, after the event, also rarely neutral or objective in their assessments. The quantity and quality of 'tacit' knowledge that they record is also typically minimal. While better than nothing, the learning potential of these approaches is limited.

On the other hand, structured oral debriefings, if they're professionally carried out by a skilled knowledge researcher, are almost always more efficient at capturing a wider range of relevant knowledge. Managers are almost always better speakers than they are writers and their spoken word is a more efficient way of conveying the abstract and complex nature of elements like the nuances of corporate culture, management style and the often obscure issues surrounding decision making within groups.

The debriefing option also has the advantage of first-person presentation, avoiding the hazards of third-party interpretation that is necessary in the other forms of delivery. The trick is in the interviewing. In essence, the better the input – i.e. the questioning – the better the output.

Given that each individual and every job is different, there is no carbon copy formula in the way debriefings are constructed. Their effective utility necessitates them being professionally researched alongside the employment of expert oral research techniques. This best requires the skills of an adept knowledge manager with a keen understanding of management issues, human resources and corporate culture.

However keen companies might want to associate themselves directly with the knowledge capture process, it is often more productive to cede responsibility for this to a specialized professional who is disassociated with the organization's human resource department or library. The reason for this is similar to the reason why individuals often use external counsellors to discuss their problems; a familial link between interviewer and interviewee generally inhibits the quality of knowledge disclosure – and, thus, retrieval. As with management consultants, an external service provider also helps to give the project the authority, autonomy and credibility that is not always attainable by in-house operatives. Equally pertinent is the need to ensure accuracy in knowledge capture. It must be accepted that oral recall is just as partial as any other knowledge source, which reinforces the need for it to be undertaken professionally. While the majority of organizations would deem themselves best qualified to do the job (*we are the people who know ourselves best,*' is perhaps the most common attitude), most, in fact, do not have the appropriate skills – or the necessary distance to be objective. The evidence for this lies in the restrictive corporate applications to which conventional 'exit interviews' and other oral history programmes are put.

Depending on the application, more specialised debriefings can be constructed in a variety of ways to capture a range of different kinds of knowledge. Generally, however, the objective is to capture the type of experiential knowledge that is not codified in manuals and other accessible corporate documentation, much of which is implicit, ambiguous and extremely difficult to relate without skilled prompting. Debriefings, for example, might include how individuals do their job within their organizations and the special internal and external relationships necessary for prime performance. In many cases, this type of knowledge can best be divulged by using anecdotes, figurative language and metaphor which, when they are related as experience rather than information, are extremely powerful 'windows' into the craft of management and organizational culture.

As indicated, much depends on the skill of the debriefer, who needs to have a deep understanding of the nature of tacit knowledge that is rooted in actions and experiences through elemental characteristics like ideals, values and emotions. It is through this comprehension that the interviewee can be encouraged to disclose the OM that companies otherwise find so difficult to identify and communicate. Unlike the typical manager's written word, their spoken word is a much richer resource to yield the illusive tacit knowledge that comes from actual experience, reflective thinking and experiential learning.

Importantly, the debriefing should be context-driven and clearly focused on both an application – whether for management development or induction – and a circumscribed theme or themes. The reason for this is that, for the subject, recollections are usually most fertile when there is a definite task, goal or motive in the questioning. Recollection for its own sake often yields only generalized observations.

Typically, a great amount of research goes into pre-project planning, which will involve discussions with the employee's colleagues ahead of the construction of a detailed interview plan that becomes the outline for the debriefing. This should always generate a range of supplementary questions at the time of the interview. Often, it is in the supplementaries that much of the individual's body of tacit knowledge emerges. The approach is allied to the interviewing techniques used by good detectives, researchers or journalists, only with an astute management and business focus.

In most cases, the preferred medium is the tape recorder, which some practitioners call the 'historical tongue', from which management tapes can also be put together. Some organizations prefer to use video or film, which is much more expensive but also very graphic and which requires a slightly different approach because interviewees are sometime more intimidated with motion pictures. Sometimes, edited clips can be used for other applications, such as public relations or advertising.

Debriefings are best conducted in two- to three-hour sessions at a time, which is normally the optimum period before individuals – debriefer and interviewee – start to lose their concentration in any one session. Depending on the employee, their length of service and the nature of their job, debriefings can run to many tens of thousands of words. A good debriefing will provide an almost verbatim transcript, edited only lightly to ensure clarity, continuity and readability, along with an index to allow quick reference. In addition to hard copy, the edited transcript should also be made available on computer disk.

The categories of employee for whom these oral debriefings are normally applied are relatively senior people who change jobs within an organization, depart for other companies or retire, although there is plenty of evidence that lower-ranking individuals hold equally important OM and take just as long to be inducted. Certainly, many Japanese companies consider supervisors and middle managers as important keepers of OM and actively encourage knowledge-sharing across the organization.

Unlike the attitude of incumbent employees, who could – or be encouraged to – see regular oral debriefing as being in their interests, some exiting individuals would not be as motivated to cooperate. In these circumstances, the most effective approach is often to explain to employees that the organization would like to learn from their experiences. Once the methodology has been given a more constructive purpose, there is usually little resistance from incumbents. With the exception of employees who are dismissed, most departing individuals are generally more than happy to contribute, often viewing a request to 'download' their experiences as an appreciative valedictory gesture on the part of their employer and an opportunity to validate their own contribution. Given the perceived importance that some organizations might give to OM, it is not inconceivable that some businesses might, eventually, include knowledge sharing in this way as a provision of their employment contracts with staff.

There are three other related aspects of knowledge capture that are relevant. Among the categories of employee who leave to join other companies and who retire, it is important to debrief them *before* they leave. The reason is that the corporate memory is always most acute in advance of the individual's change of environment. Both the quantity and quality of recall is always less reliable when an employee is in other surroundings, and especially in a new work setting, even weeks after departure.

The second relates to the relationship between knowledge capture and the process of learning from experience. Most managers obfuscate between the two and then argue that the lessons of hindsight cannot be assessed in proximity to the actual event – i.e. a length of time has to pass before it is possible to be objective. As a result, documenting the knowledge is invariably continually postponed. The trouble with this attitude is that, without accurate recall, *no* objective review is possible – ever. The employment of 'rolling' oral history projects allows organizations to capture their important OM before time blunts the corporate memory and it walks out of the door. The process of learning, while interrelated, is another process entirely. The other viewpoint – that learning cannot take place in proximity to the actual event – is also questionable.

Lastly is the sensitive issue of whether or not organizations should disclose internal information to an external knowledge consultant, some of the detail of which may be perceived as 'confidential'. If necessary, this can be overcome by the use of standard non-disclosure agreements that are commonplace with management consultancy and other external service providers. Organizations should also take care to secure copyright ownership of the tape recordings from the debriefer and interviewees.

Independent endorsement of oral history's efficacy as an effective knowledge preservation tool comes from no less an organization than the

World Bank in Washington. Through its Group Historical Office, the bank maintains an oral history archive with a well-defined set of corporate objectives that go beyond its value to future economic historians. One of its functions is to enable the bank to bequeath its institutional culture to new employees. Jochen Kraske, head of the Group Historical Office, admits that even though most companies' work processes are largely designed around documentation, much remains unrecorded. Decisions taken, especially those regarding policies, are not always reflected in the files. The voluminous paper record may provide no more than bare facts, and even that record often reflects the desire to gloss over disagreements and serious questions. An additional vital source of information is the views and perceptions of those who participated in the decision-making processes.

'We can learn much about what happened and why by asking those involved when a loan was identified and appraised, a crucial policy decision taken, a particular contract awarded. An effective oral history programme can address the problem of this gap by recording, before time dilutes or erases them, the memories of executive directors, borrowers, managers and staff, who participate in key events and developments in the bank's evolution. Catching and questioning key participants in important decisions before time takes its toll will do much to fill in the record. Not that memories recorded (no matter whose) are always reliable. They, too, need checking and confirmation. With the passage of time, and older staff retire, there has been a loss of institutional memory. It is easy today to be unaware of what happened yesterday on important issues. Staff often learn of the past, if they learn it at all, accidentally or incidentally, in a fragmentized fashion. Without the history, new staff in particular may be missing an important component of institutional culture – of understanding what the bank is and how it got there.'

In the UK, Kraske's views get the support of Robert Rosenfeld, a senior research fellow at the Centre for Corporate Strategy and Change at the School of Industrial and Business Studies, University of Warwick. His support of the genre results from a study[9] he did on the evolving competitiveness of nine British businesses over a period of thirty years. He concluded that aside from the lessons that could be culled from the selective collection of key documents, one of the most fruitful ways of collecting relevant data was by asking senior or retiring employees to provide an oral history of their recollections. *'This can be particularly important when trying to understand some of the forces for inertia and change which characterize every organization. While written accounts may provide a more accurate*

*representation of chronological events, the processes of managing change will
frequently be unrecorded. Oral recollections provide much which more formal
written material does not.'*

With the near universal adoption of new communications technology,
the last twenty-five years have seen a marked decline in the volume of
written material circulating within companies. On this basis alone, it is
arguable that oral history is of increasing importance to make good what is
omitted from the written archive. At one level, it can – in the hands of a
skilled professional – bring management helpful information, perspective
and insight by assisting the understanding and interpretation of events that
might otherwise have been forgotten, and thus benefit companies trying to
cope with the pace of change in the modern economy. At another, it can be
used specifically to help solve a range of industry's tenure- and experience-
related problems, among them the brain-drain from departing employees,
the prolonged induction of new employees and the disposition of many
companies not to learn from their experiences. While its employment cannot
totally overcome job disruption, it *can* improve job continuity, shorten the
new appointee's acclimatization period and – because the transcript is in
the outgoing individual's own words – allow the new placement to benefit
from a predecessor's past experience at *first hand*. Importantly, it can help
the incoming individual understand *quickly and comprehensively* both the
company's unique corporate character and the job's singular demands and
requirements. In this environment of low job tenure, not to retain one's
experiences when an employee moves jobs, leaves or retires is the equivalent
of treating knowledge in the way an auditor eventually deals with plant and
machinery. Write them off.

In the words of Procter & Gamble's former Vice President J. G.
Pleasants, *'no company can afford the luxury of rediscovering its own prior
knowledge'*. Professionally employed, the various debriefing techniques can
provide rolling generations of employees with a company's business
experience very cheaply – and the necessary company-specific continuity
to ensure that the individual corporate engine does not have to be continually
cold started in times of transition. Mr Pleasants's advice is equally relevant
to some other corporate problems, one of which relates specifically to the
disposition of companies to repeat their mistakes, to re-invent the wheel
and not learn properly from their successes.

References

1. Getting the Right Balance on Recruitment, Employers Forum on Age, 1997.
2. 1993 OECD annual report on employment.
3. *Financial Times*, 23 July 1997.
4. U. Neisser, 'John Dean's Memory: a Case Study'. *In Memory Observed: Remembering in Natural Contexts*,

W.H. Freeman. San Francisco, CA 1985.

5. Internet discussion on corporate memory loss on Learning Organization bulletin board (LO13097), Stuart C. Harrow, April 2 1997.

6. Post-project review, Pencorp. 1995.

7. Post-project review, Pencorp. 1997.

8. Research into 'design amnesia' by Lance Ealey, Leif Soderberg, published Spring 1990 issue *McKinsey Quarterly*.

9. 1988 research study 'Strategies and Past Actions: Management Awareness of Competitive Precedents,' by Dr Robert Rosenfeld, University of Warwick's School of Industrial & Business Studies, presentation to British Archives Council. 1988.

CHAPTER FOUR

'You have not had thirty years' experience. You have had one year's experience thirty times'

Even before one takes into account the effects of short job-tenure on organizations, corporate amnesia is already an erstwhile player in the lives of most businesses. There is now a huge body of evidence affirming that loss of organizational memory (OM) is intrinsic to the workplace among permanent workers. Without accurate recall, organizations are unable to learn effectively from their tried and tested experiences, a disposition that is responsible for many businesses repeating their mistakes on a regular basis, routinely re-inventing the wheel and misapplying their successes – with enormous downside consequences for productivity and competitiveness.

The evidence, which asserts that this happens on both the shopfloor and at management level, including the boardroom, and does not discriminate between small and large companies or between the private and public sectors, all points to individuals and organizations being poor experiential learners. The flexible labour market, which accelerates and intensifies migratory knowledge for businesses, just exacerbates the problem. This chapter's title, taken from the pages of one of English novelist J. L. Carr's texts[1], is an apposite image of what happens in the absence of effective experiential learning.

Business is all about making the right decisions. Given that to err is human – and managers are as mortal as anyone else – the reality is as much to do with the frequency of *wrong* decisions. With no organization immune from them, the businesses that misapply their successes, re-invent the wheel and/ or repeat the same mistakes on an on-going basis are invariably less competitive than the businesses that do not.

While the connection between these events may seem obscure, their association is, in fact, axiomatic. Unless they are deliberate, they involve a lapse of memory and a related inability to learn from one's own – and others' – experiences.

When it comes to corporate amnesia, the phenomenon basically occurs at two different levels. There is first the corporate amnesia that takes place at the 'motivated' level, which is normally associated with negative or embarrassing experiences that could have a disadvantageous effect on individuals and/or the organizations for which they work. In some cases this triggers a defensive process that invariably includes a measure of deliberate memory loss and even distortion that covers lying. Allied to this is a variant of recall – so-called 'wishful' remembering – that tailors memory to a desirous conclusion.

The other type of corporate amnesia occurs at the unconscious level, which covers what I describe as unmotivated forgetting. This is plain old-fashioned memory loss that can occur for reasons varying from disinterest in the subject to distraction and untrained recall ability.

Examples of the former occur every day in the courts along with instances such as the 'forgetfulness' of many managers of some German companies when they were questioned in Nuremberg after the Second World War and, more recently, some Swiss banks à propos Second World War frozen bank accounts.

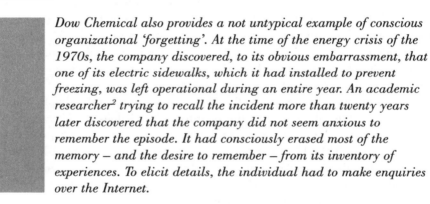

Dow Chemical also provides a not untypical example of conscious organizational 'forgetting'. At the time of the energy crisis of the 1970s, the company discovered, to its obvious embarrassment, that one of its electric sidewalks, which it had installed to prevent freezing, was left operational during an entire year. An academic researcher[2] trying to recall the incident more than twenty years later discovered that the company did not seem anxious to remember the episode. It had consciously erased most of the memory – and the desire to remember – from its inventory of experiences. To elicit details, the individual had to make enquiries over the Internet.

While amnesia of the motivated type might be understandable, even of long-term OM if there is no accurate documentation, it is in the realm of unconscious corporate amnesia that companies also seem predisposed in a big way. This even occurs with short- and medium-term OM, with the amnesia apparent very soon after even very recent events in many cases. Organizations, it seems, forget faster than they can remember.

Evidence that confirms the link between staff discontinuity and corporate amnesia as well as the inability – and in some cases reluctance – of many organizations to learn from their own experiences is buried in the mountain of academic literature on the broader subject of strategic and operational change. For conceptual advocacy, it is a view reinforced by Harvard scholar Alan Kantrow, whose perception[3] is that '*When we go to work, we forget.*' To Kantrow, who has worked for two of the world's most prestigious management journals, the *Harvard Business Review* and *The McKinsey Quarterly*, and for the Cambridge, Massachusetts-based business history consultants, the Winthrop

Group, managers' choices and actions may find a ready place in memory but the reasons and the intended significance of their deeds quickly float away out of reach and beyond recall. In his book, *The Constraints of Corporate Tradition*, he observes that while all organizations have some form of recall, their memory is frequently inaccurate.

> *'The style of a business presentation, the kinds of evidence that tend to sway decisions, the shared sense of what constitutes relevant information about a new market or product, the deep-seated visceral preference for certain lines of business – all these characteristics, and a thousand others like them, are the subtle products of memory. In no two organizations are they exactly the same, nor in any two parts of the same organization. Intuitively we know this. But on the job we usually disregard it. In particular individuals forget both the density and duration of the activity underlying the surface facts. We forget that, like an iceberg, nine tenths of their mass lies hidden, well below the normal waterline of vision. And we forget that the part we can see is not just "there" but is very much something built, something constructed or pieced together over time.'*

He describes the categories used to structure experience as the cumulative product of artifice, selection and manipulation that are built in the same way that a work of art is constructed. *'In practice, however, we forget the artifice that shapes them and treat them as if they were hard nuggets of fact.'* Kantrow's observation is that *'we do not commonly treat a corporation as the cumulative result of an historical process of development, nor do we think of it as an edifice held together by the bricks and mortar of tradition. Yet it is, and we should.'*

These things, he explains, are not idle matters with no real bearing on corporate performance.

> *'A maker of computer peripherals like disk drives or colour monitors comes to grief because its people are so used to viewing the world in a certain way that they cannot see how their market has become a systems market .... A financial institution persists in ignoring the threat posed by the in-house financial operations of capital goods producers like GE or GM .... A capital budgeting scheme designed to move a commodity producer of metals downstream toward manufactured end products fails to skew the pattern of investment .... Domestic manufacturers pump massive infusions of capital into new flexible technologies like robotics but continue to use them in high volume, low-variety environments ..... In all these cases history is making itself felt. Of course, in all these instances there*

are other forces at work. But we are, for the most part, able to recognize them with some ease. It is the unseen, subterranean influence of history – institutional memory – that regularly eludes us. With few exceptions, the great helpings of prose and urgent advice under which managers increasingly finding themselves buried reads as if the past – of an individual, a company, a product, an issue – were thoroughly irrelevant to present concerns or, at best, an ornamental reminder of other days and other times. Like it or not, the past infects the world in which we live, the decisions we make, the very choices we see to lie before us. If we ignore its influence, we do not escape its power. All we do is remain to some extent its prisoners without ever really knowing that is what we are. If, however, we acknowledge it, learn to recognize its workings, come to greet it on familiar terms, we can put it to excellent use.'

The evidence for the prevalence – and effects – of corporate amnesia doesn't stop there. In a study[4] of competitive precedents, a team of academics from Warwick University, which looked at key problems of strategy and change over thirty years in nine private and public sector organizations from four mature sectors of the British economy, found that many companies reproduced their blunders on a regular basis. This was a conclusion[5] also reached by a high-profile team of US scholars and industrialists looking into a range of development projects in five leading US companies and by Peter Herriot, director of research at Kent-based Sundridge Park Management Centre, whose research[6] covered both British and US companies. Elsewhere, the leading US management consultancy McKinsey & Co. has found[7] that many companies continually re-invent solutions.

The Warwick University study found managers having little awareness of past actions or rationales and that some companies were unable to communicate appropriate lessons from one part of the organization to another in sufficient time. They also found that organizations continually re-invent solutions.

One of the objectives of the Warwick research, which covered the activities of companies like Kleinwort Benson, Robert Fleming and Hill Samuel in the merchant banking sector, Jaguar and Peugeot Talbot in the automotive industry, life assurance companies The Prudential and Clerical Medical and publishers Longman and Associated Book Publishers, was to provide a means by which organizations could learn from strategic precedents within their own firms as well as from others. Funded by the Economic and Social Research Council in the mid-1980s, their study, which concluded that most managers have only a partial view of the forces which influence the speed and ability of firms to manage strategic and operational change, revealed three common characteristics

– the inability of organizations to remember and use the lessons learned from previous successes and failures, that senior managers tended rigidly to maintain a set of beliefs regarding appropriate strategies and managerial tactics and that the same managers devoted little time or energy to understanding the variety of internal and external forces which influenced the organization's ability to manage strategic and operational changes. *'A common feature seen in many organizations today is the efforts made to recruit outsiders to help inform the organizations about alternative ways of operating or perceiving the environment,'* they pointed out. *'The value of recruiting such individuals is that the organization consciously tried to learn from their experience in other firms. It is ironic that many of the same organizations have tended to devalue lessons which can be learned from prior events within their own organizations.'*

They cite the example of two of the companies studied – a merchant banker and a life insurer – where senior management frequently lamented the inability of their subordinates to be more entrepreneurial in their activities. Both firms opted for the selective recruitment of outsiders as a tactic to make up for this perceived shortcoming. Yet, the researchers found, within the recent history of both firms, there existed evidence of individuals and groups who had created new operations in-house. When confronted with this evidence, both firms felt that the chaotic and sometimes disorganized nature of these entrepreneurs did not fit with the orderly activities which senior management desired. Similarly, when questioned, the in-house entrepreneurs commented that they felt their efforts were often resented internally and that the culture of their organizations inhibited such activity.

The high-profile project in the US that also found that projects in the same company tended to suffer from the same mistakes was undertaken by the Manufacturing Vision Group, a team of researchers from Harvard University, the Massachusetts Institute of Technology and Purdue and Stanford Universities. They worked closely with top executives from Chaparral Steel, Digital Equipment, Eastman Kodak, Ford Motor and Hewlett-Packard, looking at twenty different development projects, concluding that while the companies succeeded in learning from some of them, they failed dismally in others.

The close relationship between discontinuity, corporate amnesia and repeated mistakes was one of the research observations[6] of Peter Herriot, director of research at Sundridge Park Management Centre, and his research assistant Carole Pemberton. Based on studies in the UK and the US, they concluded that many organizations are going wrong because they have lost their collective memory. Experience, they say, has become devalued. It is now viewed negatively because it is said to hold back the speed of change with the organization. In their book *Competitive Advantage through Diversity*, they note that lack of experienced staff helps to explain the poor performance of at least one unnamed High Street bank. *'By sacking long-serving managers every time they [the bank] made a business mistake, they wiped out the organizational memory and increased the chances of making further mistakes.'*

Warwick's observation that manufacturing companies continually reinvent solutions is also validated by McKinsey & Co., the US-based international management consultant. Staff consultants Lance Ealey and Leif Soderberg, working out of the consultancy's Cleveland, Ohio, office, discovered that in one automotive supplier, for example, more than 40 per cent of the troublesome design issues that plagued a recent new product programme had already been resolved in prior programmes. Because engineers did not review the work previously done by others within the company, they wasted about 30 per cent of their design time solving problems that had been solved before.

Their experience with other large organizations led them to believe that such design amnesia was a much more common drain of cash and creativity than most managers believed.

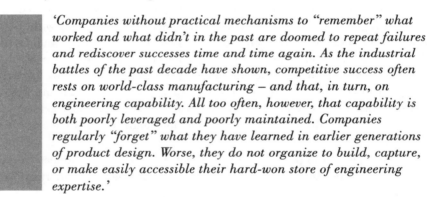

'Companies without practical mechanisms to "remember" what worked and what didn't in the past are doomed to repeat failures and rediscover successes time and time again. As the industrial battles of the past decade have shown, competitive success often rests on world-class manufacturing – and that, in turn, on engineering capability. All too often, however, that capability is both poorly leveraged and poorly maintained. Companies regularly "forget" what they have learned in earlier generations of product design. Worse, they do not organize to build, capture, or make easily accessible their hard-won store of engineering expertise.'

Their finding that companies continually re-invent solutions extends to organizations redoing the same work without realizing it, which is another form of corporate amnesia. Recently at IBM, for example, the company suffered a *'serious constriction in the distribution of competitive information'*[8]. At the peak of confusion there were forty-nine departments in twenty-seven organizations each studying the same competitors. Literally hundreds of people were analysing the data but they seldom knew what others were doing. Neither did they share their conclusions.

For the most part, the evidence I have ventured so far for corporate amnesia's prevalence and its effects has been of an academic nature. To get organizations to admit to its existence within their own businesses, at least publicly, is more difficult, but one hands-on manager to do just that is American Marc Demarest, Chief Knowledge Officer of Portland-based Sequent Computer Systems. His experience[9] of commercial firms, particularly US firms, is that they have notoriously poor memories. The corporate past is *'lost'* almost at the very minute it becomes *'the past'* – *'we cannot remember what we did, the circumstances in which we made decisions, the rationale for those decisions, who said what to whom and what they meant by it,'* he says.

> *'This is exacerbated by our collective tendency to view discontinuity, in the form of mistakes, errors in judgement, or misperceptions as evidence of "bad management" and our resulting predisposition to "revisionist history" and the rewriting of the corporate past to erase all discontinuity and replace it with a smooth "evolutionary view" of decision-making and policy-setting that, while it creates great cognitive dissonance within the rank-and-file, makes us feel better about ourselves when next we speak to the board of directors or shareholders.'*

The problem with this forgetfulness, he confirms, is that we are unable to learn from the past. Forward thinking firms are, paradoxically, simultaneously embracing learning organization precepts like *'fail early and often'* and at the same time erasing the traces of the failures through forgetfulness or revisionist myth making, depriving themselves of one half of the knowledge-creation machine: experience. *'It is truer today than ever that it is easier to know what not to do and how not to do it, based on past failures, than it is to know what to do and how to do it based on either experience or more conceptual knowledge bases.'*

However difficult it is to quantify the cost of corporate amnesia's influence on repeated mistakes or re-invented wheels, consultants working on Total Quality Management (TQM) programmes have estimated[10] that a staggering one third of all effort expended in British businesses is wasted on correcting errors, checking late deliveries, redoing, apologizing and generally making good, mistakes. If the academics, management consultants and hands-on managers are right, many of industry's problems are simply reruns of previous mistakes, either unobserved, unacknowledged or – if noticed – unheeded.

Hard examples of this abound. The finance sector's experience is especially rich, particularly banking, where the record of failures has left a decent trail of evidence that successive generations of bankers continually forget. A graphic example, which illustrates both the magnitude of the phenomenon and its pervasive nature, can be seen in the banking crises of the 1980s and 1990s. It also demonstrates the short-term nature of memory loss and the importance of constant reminders. In the early 1980s the banking community was badly mauled by bad debts in South America. Less than ten years later it was again overwhelmed, this time from loan defaults elsewhere in the Third World. Speaking in 1991 Lord Alexander, chairman of the

National Westminster Bank, admitted there were plenty of historical precedents on Latin American lending which *'should have put the red light up for everyone'*. He added: *'We have got to ensure that the lessons of the recent past are not forgotten by the rising generation of bankers.'*

As he was talking the banks were once again making similar errors of judgement – this time at home – with High Street lenders having to chalk up further provisions collectively totalling almost £4 billion in their 1992 accounts. This prompted one City analyst to comment that *'The biggest worry is that banks do not seem to be capable of learning from their mistakes,'* a warning echoed in 1994 by a banking industry think-tank[6] that analysed the massive write-offs.

> *The repetition of the same mistakes, without any reviewing backup to ensure that lessons are learned, is also a recurrent theme in local and central government, where the consequences are also enormous. Take the management of computer systems, where the rerun of errors has wasted billions of pounds in public funds. The list of squandered resources is seemingly endless: £63 million at Wessex Health Authority, £500 million by the National Health Service on a system to reduce staff costs at a time when the number of administrators increased by 40 per cent and a £2 million budget overrun by the Department of Health and Society Security on its Operational Strategy system, which failed. The same pattern[11] emerged in every case – the hiring of expensive consultants to design a ludicrously complex, over-ambitious, one-off system which failed to allow for the requirements and capacities of its users, an overtight schedule, an almost psychotic reluctance to admit that things had gone wrong and then, finally, when the systems crashed, no one was found to be accountable, and no one was concerned to learn why it went wrong. Tony Collins, the computer specialist who identified the recurring blunders, predicts that the additional £1 billion that the DSS plans to spend on Operational Strategy is doomed to go the same way.*

Elsewhere in the public sector, the changing ethos towards improving productivity is enforcing another form of corporate amnesia. With its increasing emphasis on the inherent importance of competition and rivalry, previously helpful departments are now deliberately withholding know-how that was previously shared [12]. The result for many public service organizations is that they are simply having to 're-invent the wheel' in the work they are undertaking. Examples of this can be seen in the widespread unavailability of business plans of NHS trust hospitals and services and the simultaneous exploration of the same undergraduate markets by London's higher education institutions.

The disposition not to learn from previous experience is not confined to bankers or the public sector. A striking example of how corporate amnesia plays a part in raising costs occurred in 1993 when the BAA, the UK airports company which spends around £250 million a year on construction projects, reported the outcome of a market 'test' to compare building costs in another country. It asked US contractors to tender for an office block identical to a development already underway at Heathrow for British Airways. The tender was for a project at an airport where labour and material costs were similar to those in Britain. Built to US designs and specifications, the American building came out 32 per cent cheaper. One of the reasons, according to the BAA, was that the US architects and engineers spent less time *'re-inventing solution wheels'*.

If, indeed, corporate amnesia and the flexible labour market are two of the reasons why experiential learning goes wrong, what is the answer? How does an organization, in Alan Kantrow's words, *'construct the artifice of experience?'*

In an attempt to understand the problem – and examine the solutions – it is instructive to examine Kantrow's commentary on the subject of the importance of institutional memory and both the UK and US academic teams' mention of the management tool they recommend for experiential learning.

Is there anything that can restore lost awareness, asks Kantrow? '.... *by restoring lost detail, the recovery through institutional memory, through history, of salient facts about the many pieces of things that make up our constructed world. Effective memory helps us see artifice for what it is. Does such clear vision matter – especially, does it matter to managers? Absolutely. Data does not become information until we are able to see the patterns in them, to see which bits and pieces cluster together in some kind of order.'*

While Kantrow mentions *'history'* as the medium, it is the unconnected studies on both sides of the Atlantic that specifically refer to the post-implementation review or post-mortem as the management tool that organizations could use to restore the lost awareness necessary for experiential learning. Both teams also make mention of a widespread corporate reluctance to use the tool, which is potentially one of the most effective methods of performance appraisal and learning from experience. The Warwick researchers pointed out that the more successful firms seemed to be very concerned with conducting post-mortems on key events to learn and communicate lessons. They noted, however, that amnesia was actually self-imposed because of the concern about individuals' feelings and a reluctance to allocate blame. Specifically they found that companies were more concerned to maintain a friendly and cohesive atmosphere than to impose a discipline to help avoid repeating mistakes. They suggested that by attempting to learn from previous strategic changes, managers would be able to better understand the context and processes by which change can be handled. *'It appears that the more successful firms do show some signs of a greater awareness of the past.'*

The high-profile US academics' observation was that for any organization to learn, someone had to step back and ask what a given management team, and the company in support of that team, did right and wrong. Then management had to find a way to implement the needed changes in the next project.

Systematic post-project learning, they confirm, is surprisingly rare. Only a handful of companies have any kind of auditing system. Moreover, audits tend to be done merely to ensure that a project complies with formal procedures rather than to analyse its positive and negative aspects from which the company can learn. As with the Warwick team, they observed that when auditing was done, reviewers were often reluctant to highlight problems for fear of embarrassing people and seeming unfair. As a result, a string of projects in the same company tended to suffer from the same mistakes.

If post-implementation analysis has any purpose at all, it is to learn from experience, yet the traditional methods of identifying and conveying the lessons of the tested past are often ineffective learning tools and – as the academics observed – often deliberately avoided.

Alongside the evident disinclination of many managers towards being objectively reflective, the reasons are complex and varied. Much depends on the underlying attitudes towards learning of managers and their employers. If, for example, a company's belief system embraces the notion of executive infallibility or individuals sense that the purpose is to find scapegoats, the exercise immediately becomes sterile.

It is this fear that encourages a more general management rejection of experience as a learning tool. Typical reactions to its proposed validity are that business life is not based on reflections of the past and that past models don't apply because circumstances change. Often the reaction is unequivocally hostile, with managers insisting that many decisions are taken in defiance of precedent. As already noted it is conveniently overlooked that one has to know what the precedents are in order to take a contrary course.

This smokescreen invariably leads to a selective vision of management education and development – that success is the predominant building block. As a result, industry's role models are generally winners while the losers (and their mistakes) are frequently disregarded, which was one of the observations of both the UK and US research. In an argumentative way, this is like wearing tinted sunglasses – and believing that the view is a faithful interpretation of the world outside.

Behind the rebuff lies human nature in the form of a particularly well-developed managerial ego, an observation graphically described by Thomas C. Barry, former President and Chief Executive Officer of New York-based Rockefeller & Co. and, latterly, President of Marlboro. Commenting[13] on the difficulties of teaching managers how to learn, he describes the apparent amnesia evident in many of his top employees. *'For many years I have been troubled by the inconsistent attitudes of high-achievement professionals who have superb intellects yet appear not to learn from experiences or colleagues,'* he observed. His explanation is that professional service companies in particular attract what he calls *'the stereotypical self-motivated, supercharged MBAs whose past successes build their defences against being incorrect, hence against any need to learn or change. I suspect that the defensive reasoning process is well developed early in the life of a high-achievement person.'*

Barry's observation is reinforced by a substantial body of academic research into organizational learning, much of which confirms the reluctance of companies and their managers to objectively examine their performance, especially mistakes. Defining the defensive reasoning process, Harvard's Professor Chris Argyris, one of the main exponents of the Learning Organization's precepts, explains[14] that whenever a manager's performance comes under scrutiny, the individual begins to feel embarrassed, threatened and, because they are so well paid, guilty.

'Far from being a catalyst for real change, such feelings cause most to react defensively. So, when their learning strategies go wrong, they become defensive, screen out criticism and put the "blame" on anyone and everyone but themselves. In short their inability to learn shuts down precisely at the moment they need it the most.'

Most companies believe that people learn through motivation, says Argyris. As such, they focus outwardly on external organizational factors such as job redesign, compensation programmes, performance reviews and leadership training instead of also looking inwardly towards the individual's own performances.

Elsewhere, the likes of Arie de Geus, a former director of Shell UK (as head of Group Planning in 1981 he championed the concept of scenario planning) says that nobody should be surprised to see aggressive mechanisms surface in individuals who are being asked to bare their souls and to self-criticise in a group of their colleagues and superiors. De Geus, whose work on how people learn from each other as well as from the past has given him a singular approach to organizational learning, says[15]: *'Everybody's stored observation of what exactly happened or what one knew at the moment when a decision was made depends on the position of the observer, then and now. Therefore, one should not be surprised that people find it difficult to communicate about the past.'* He has also worked closely with Peter Senge (of *The Fifth Discipline* fame) at MIT.

His comments masks the other problem inherent in all reflective exercises – the uncertain nature of accurate memory recall and the inevitable dispute over the precision and sequence of events.

Academic studies of how people remember confirm the accuracy problem. Typically, they take[16] the present as a benchmark and then work from a currently held belief about change or stability in their attitudes. Thus, when asked how one felt six months ago, one's memory will necessarily be coloured by what has happened since.

Alongside this is the questionable nature of individual managers' objectivity after the event. Because post-implementation reviews are mostly reflective exercises, it is extremely difficult for managers, who are rarely neutral in their assessments, to be unprejudiced. Imperfect input into any post-implementation review will, inevitably, abet flawed lessons.

While all these apparent difficulties have given the traditional post-implementation review a less than attractive hue as an efficacious learning tool, industry – meanwhile – has been developing other approaches. The best Total Quality Management (TQM) programmes, for example – pioneered by the Japanese in the 1970s – are systematic attempts to build company learning. Elsewhere, institutionalized learning procedures have been undertaken by the likes of Motorola's company university.

Although approaches like TQM – and even familiar procedures like job rotation and networking – show that the principle of experiential learning has not been entirely lost on management, the flexible labour market and the associated problems of migratory memory and corporate amnesia have imposed an entirely new dimension on the problem. Although slow in coming, especially in the West, the growing awareness that human capital cannot now be owned for very long has reinforced the realization that the only way to capitalize on a resource that has the disposition to walk out of the door is to find ways of locking the departing knowledge into the business in some permanent way. The more they can upload knowledge from brains into systems and procedures, the more they can control it, so the argument goes. To achieve this, the main thrust to organizational learning in recent years has been through Information Technology (IT) applications and modern communications technology such as the Internet. Under the banner of the Learning Organization – and specifically Knowledge Management and knowledge sharing – some large companies are spending millions trying to convert individual knowledge into OM via huge databases using custom built or off-the-shelf software systems. In most situations this data is filed and forgotten.

The standard IT approach has been to construct so-called knowledge bases of useful information already floating around the company and outwardly make it available to employees, usually via an intranet, the in-company version of the Internet. Almost all large companies now have their own web site and three quarters either have or are constructing an intranet. Businesses like the US computer company Silicon Graphics, for example, have an internal web site known as Silicon Junction which carries information covering everything from engineering projects to on-line training. Every day, about half the employees are said to call up the site. Elsewhere, some basic Knowledge Management projects like BT's electronic internal telephone directory, Hewlett-Packard's directory of 'expertise' called the *Yellow Pages* and Dow Chemical Company's analysis of the 29,000 patents in its portfolio have been highly successful.

Other attempts have been more sophisticated. US-based Buckman Group, for example, has created a global network that is said to store and continuously replenish the company's collective expertise. IBM has formed so-called Competency Networks – informal networks of professionals with common interests – that create, identify, store and re-use intellectual capital by leveraging the collective brain power of groups of individuals. Elsewhere, Canada's Mutual Group has created a system to bring to life previously redundant knowledge embedded in individual expertise and learning while Monsanto, which has formed a separate Knowledge Management group within its IT organization, has developed a number of related projects in sites across the world. Other companies to embrace Knowledge Management include Xerox Corporation, Hughes Space and Communications Company and – on behalf of its clients – Thomas Miller, which provides facilities management for insurance mutuals.

Among the most advanced practitioners of Knowledge Management are perhaps the management consultancies which, as prime purveyors of knowledge themselves, need the ability to draw on huge reserves of knowledge. Arthur Andersen, Booze Allen & Hamilton, KPMG Peat Marwick, Price Waterhouse and Ernst & Young all have systems up and going.

Arthur Andersen, which first tried a CD-ROM approach to codify and share best practices around the firm – unsuccessfully – now uses a computer network to spread information around its staff about best practices, contacts within the organization and case studies. As well as this information, which is vetted and filtered, it has a second system on which it encourages its staff to post anything that they find useful. The network is known as the Knowledge Xchange. At the end of every consultancy project, information concerning proposals, presentations and contacts is loaded onto the system. Anyone who wants to know something on the subject can download it with the help of proprietary search software known as a Knowledge Map.

Similarly, Booz Allen & Hamilton's Knowledge Management programme, which is called Knowledge on Line, is an electronic database and data map of what the firm knows and who knows it. Developed in 1995, the concept has been introduced to a wide range of clients. Basically what happens is that, at the end of each client engagement, any 'frameworks' or generic lessons that have emerged are fed into the program both by the firm's global innovation teams of senior staff and from operational consultants. Incorporated into a third-generation intranet network, the program – headed by a chief knowledge officer and managed by some twelve to fifteen knowledge managers or super-librarians and supported by some eighty-five researchers – now contains more than 3,000 documents and it is constantly augmented. The decision on the nature of the firm's 'corporate memory' is the responsibility of the knowledge managers, who work closely with partners when launching client engagements, and consultants. The program operates at three different levels – as an educational tool to basic consultancy skills in a workforce where 43 per cent of staff have a year's company experience or less, as a repository of IT knowledge and standardized methodologies for journeymen consultants and as a means of developing leading-edge strategic thinking among the partners at the top.

But how effective are IT applications at capturing OM and providing the wherewithal to learn from one's tried and tested experience? While acknowledging some successes, the general feeling of many leading practitioners in Knowledge Management is of caution, at least as far as predicting the practical and financial benefits of their work in these early days of Knowledge Management's development. At a Knowledge Management conference in London in 1996[17], one of its pioneers, Gordon Petrash, the global director of intellectual asset and capital management at the Dow Chemical Company, admitted that the perceived leadership of companies like Dow did not amount to very much. The leading companies were still feeling their way, he said.

Chuck Lucier, chief knowledge officer of Booz Allen & Hamilton, calculated[18] that just 15 per cent of the programmes he monitored were successes in the sense of producing real business results, while another 35 per cent showed no return for the effort. His estimation was that the meagre proportion of successes may, in fact, be going down. *'There is more to the business of knowledge than a mechanistic systems approach,'* he admitted.

Knowledge Based Development's Mike McMaster, one of the independent consultants in the field, said most Knowledge Management programmes attempted to simplify the nuances away by acting as glorified expert systems, aiming to capture, verify and make available existing knowledge on a systematic basis. A lot of Knowledge Management, he said, seemed to be no more than *'sexy up-to-date databases'*.

The general consensus was that IT applications were unsuitable repositories for some of the most useful knowledge within an organization – in Arthur Andersen's words: *'Knowledge that is highly coded is easily transferable – but often of little strategic value, one of the reasons being that some of the useful knowledge within an organization cannot be codified or even made explicit.'*

Terry Finerty, partner of the firm's knowledge services, warned against putting too much emphasis on the technological approach. IT tended to be more of an enabler than the key, he said. The view of Elizabeth Lank, director of ICL's knowledge programme called Project VIC (an acronym for valuing ICL knowledge) designed to release the value hidden within intangible assets and support the company's transformation into a service-led business, was that while technology helped, *'what knowledge management is absolutely about is the way people work together'*. According to McMaster, what was missing, *'is the generative aspects of intelligence – the life to make knowledge systems work'*. Even McKinsey & Co., whose work[7] in design amnesia found that many companies continually re-invent solutions, admitted: *'Technology can help, of course. There is no question that such things as expert systems, design databases, and design networking can help maintain a vital design memory. But without the appropriate 'humanware' systems to tap this knowledge hardware, nothing much will happen.'*

What they were all referring to is tacit knowledge, that prime constituent of OM that ranges from the practical understanding of how a process works to cultural issues. An important element in any core capability, it was – they found – well nigh impossible to re-create on a database the actual interplay between theory and practice, structure and experiment and human and organizational intent. Indeed, it is arguable that the high rate of failure in the existing Knowledge Management programmes is precisely the result of IT's inability to capture knowledge's most precious quality – the humanware element contained in the tacit portion of OM.

The problems with IT-based systems don't stop there. They – indeed any experiential learning approach – also require a fundamental culture shift toward greater openness. The practitioners made the point that many individuals were often unwilling to share ideas and best thinking on the basis that their status is based on their possession of their knowledge. Simply giving up their knowledge made them less valuable and employable. There was also a resistance to *'not invented here'* ideas, that contributing and documenting knowledge took too much time, a perception that Knowledge Management was yet another passing fad and that most companies were treating Knowledge Management programmes as glorified expert systems without any understanding or the commitment to link it with business issues.

Notwithstanding all this, the new breed of knowledge managers would agree that however expensive it is to manage their knowledge, it is even more expensive not to manage it. With the whole subject still in its infancy, it is clear that most businesses still do not have effective information management, let alone Knowledge Management practices embedded throughout the organization to learn effectively from their experiences. If the IT approach is also flawed, how else do companies attempt to benefit from their own hindsight?

References

1. J. L. Carr, 'I've never been spoken to like this before in all my thirty years' experience,' she wails. 'You have not had thirty years' experience, Mrs Grindle-Jones,' he says witheringly. 'You have had one year's experience thirty times.' Harpole Report p. 128. 1972.

2. Internet enquiry from Economics Department, California State University, to Business History notice board, 28 July 1997.

3. A.M. Kantrow, *The Constraints of Corporate Tradition*, Harper & Row, New York. 1984.

4. 1988 research study 'Strategies and Past Actions: Management Awareness of Competitive Precedents,' by Dr Robert Rosenfeld, University of Warwick's School of Industrial & Business Studies, into key problems of strategy and change over thirty years in private and public sector organizations, among them Kleinwort Benson, Robert Fleming, Hill Samuel, Jaguar, Peugeot Talbot, The Prudential, Clerical Medical, Longman and Associated Book Publishers.

5. 1992 research study at Harvard University, the Massachusetts Institute of Technology, Purdue and Stanford universities. Findings published in *The Perpetual Enterprise Machine*, Oxford University Press. 1994.

6. Peter Herriot and Carole Pemberton, *Competitive Advantage through Diversity*, Sage, London. 1993.

7. Research into 'design amnesia' by Lance Ealey and Leif Soderberg, published Spring 1990 issue McKinsey Quarterly.

8. Mastering Management series. *Financial Times*, 26 January 1996.

9. Understanding Knowledge Management, *Long Range Planning*, Vol. 30, No. 3 June 1997.

10. University of Warwick pamphlet 1994.

11. T. Collins, *Crash: Ten easy ways to avoid a computer disaster*, Simon & Schuster, New York. 1997.

12. C. Talbot and J. Harrow, *Public Services and the Wheel: Re-inventing, Swapping or Buying*, Centre for Public Services Management, South Bank University, London. 1993.

13. *Harvard Business Review*, July/August 1991.

14. *Harvard Business Review*, May/June 1991.

15. Letter to author, 1995.

16. M. Linton, 'Transformations of Memory in Everyday Life', in U. Neisser (ed.), *Memory Observed: Remembering in Natural Contexts*, W. H. Freeman San Francisco, CA 1985.

17. Knowledge Management conference organized by conference group International Centre for Business Information and sponsored by Arthur Andersen.

18. 'The Knowledge Within', *Management Today*, August 1997.

CHAPTER FIVE

Harvesting 20:20 hindsight

In order to adapt, an organization needs to know what to change and how. As such, companies are forever – and rightly – being advised to improve their learning. Hence organizations' emphasis on techniques such as benchmarking and networking, on closer contact with customers and suppliers, and on more effective ways of marrying advancing technology with emerging consumer patterns and behaviour.

As the previous few chapters have shown, the problem with this advice is that organizations mostly look outside themselves for their learning and training. Few companies, for example, use the traditional experiential learning approaches like post-implementation reviews or post-mortems while the IT approaches, although providing a valuable repository of 'experiences' that would otherwise dissipate via the flexible labour market, have been shown not to be able to convey some of the key components of OM necessary for effective experiential learning.

It is instructive how some companies have adapted the traditional 'conscious' approaches[1] to experiential learning, in particular the retrospective approach, that involves deliberate reflection, and the prospective approach, which embraces the plan to learn *before* an experience takes place. Michael Smurfit, chairman of the Jefferson Smurfit Group paper packaging empire, keeps a personal list of his mistakes to remind him not to repeat them. Believing that mistakes go hand-in-hand with risk, the 61-year-old calculates[2] that his blunders so far have cost the group £120 million. In a novel twist to the conventional way the lessons of experience are passed down from one generation to another, Roger Enrico, the chief executive of American soft drinks giant PepsiCo, spent several months in the 18 months *before* he joined the company in 1996 with nine corporate executives at his Cayman Islands home. At these meetings he passed on his own experiences. Part of the programme[3] involved the executives working on specific projects, the lessons of which were then passed on to others.

 *Benetton, the Italian clothes company, intentionally learns from experience through trial and error, notably by experimenting and retaining what has worked at each stage of the company's development. This is based on its refusal to accept established knowledge as the ultimate truth. Instead, its philosophy is based on the evolutionary principle that today's process can be improved.*

The process[4] starts with collecting opinions on a specific issue. These are then used to create a hypothesis about causal relationships. To confirm or disprove the hypothesis, data is then gathered and analysed to make their meaning clear. This is then repeated several times, each time improving the quality of the hypothesis, data, analysis and synthesis until the hypothesis is accepted as meaningful information. Based on this, decisions about the allocation of resources are made and implemented. Then the results are compared with the expectations and the reasons for any deviation are reviewed. The new insights this produces are used to update the existing body of knowledge.

BP in the UK has a completely different approach[5] to experiential learning. The petroleum exploration and refining company has a special post-project appraisal unit to review major investment projects, write up case studies and derive lessons for planners that are then incorporated into revisions of the company's planning guidelines. A five-person unit reports to the board of directors and reviews six projects annually. This type of review is now conducted regularly at the project level.

Yet another approach to experiential learning[6] is taken by the US company Chaparral Steel, a mini mill specialist which is especially known for its 1980s innovations in horizontal casting techniques. Founded more than twenty-five years ago, the company has become one of the largest US steel-makers. Where Chaparral stands out from other companies is in the systematic way it selects projects and then applies learning from one project to another. It requires every project to advance the company's capabilities, and plans combinations of them in a logical flow to ensure that they do so. After each project has been completed, Chaparral analyses it to find out what it achieved or failed to, and why.

In their efforts to improve subsequent decision-making, General Motors and Hewlett-Packard used retrospective historical analysis[7]. GM systematically reconstructed the development of its 'X' and 'J' platform cars in 1981 to search for lessons about success and failure. These new cars, which had experienced severe quality, schedule and cost problems, had been rushed through the development process in the late 1970s to give GM fuel-efficient models at a time when petrol prices were high and volatile and when small foreign cars were successfully invading the US domestic market. Almost eighty managers were involved in the study to reconstruct the development process. The outside consultants which conducted the study uncovered a range of important deficiencies in GM's methods while many participants of the study 'found their attitudes about project management and product quality transformed for the better, and the results are today visible in the high-quality rankings given to several GM models and manufacturing facilities'.

In Hewlett-Packard's case, the company used post-project reviews to internally benchmark its scheduling practices. In 1987 each of its fifty-six R&D centres was charged with doing post-mortems on a number of their recent development projects. Events and processes seen as contributing to project scheduling failures and successes were then shared among all units.

Microsoft, which is among the most successful companies with a good record of learning from both within and without the organization, has an integrated[8] approach to its experiential learning. Part of the process is to deliberately learn from past mistakes, which occurs at regular post-mortems at the end of each project and at which analysis takes place to extract lessons for future projects. Customer feedback is built into the design process through market research, customer support hotlines and usability testing. Input also occurs while the projects are underway in terms of metrics and quantitative measures.

One of the best examples of experiential learning taking place at the prospective level is Boeing's approach[5] when it developed its latest generations of aircraft. Before the company started to evolve its 757 and 767 aircraft, a group of senior employees spent three years on 'Project Homework' comparing the managerial failures and successes of past development processes. They produced hundreds of recommendations. Several members of the team then transferred to the 757 and 767 start-up projects. Guided by this experience, Boeing produced the most problem-free product launches in its history.

To try to share its tacit knowledge management consultants Arthur D. Little complements its employment of expert systems through constant on-the-job coaching and networking on different assignments.

From Benetton's form of trial and error learning to Boeing's prospective learning technique, such systematic self analysis is rare in industry. Yet it is one of the main requirements for any business wanting to be a genuine Learning Organization. To be a learning organization, a company has to be skilled at systematic problem solving, experimenting with new approaches, learning from all experiences, and transferring knowledge quickly and efficiently throughout the organization. Part of this is to be able to learn effectively from one's own experiences, which necessitates being able to review both successes and failures objectively, assess them systematically and communicate the lessons in a form that employees find open and accessible.

The problem with traditional experiential learning – however it's done – is that it is always executed in retrospect. At first sight, this statement might appear to be transparently obvious. To learn from experience, the experience must first happen. Then, to learn from it, it must be reviewed. However, for this to happen, the primary requirement is for full and accurate recall.

The difficulty with the traditional ways of recording experiences – whether the information is transferred to a computer or left on paper – revolves around this one crucial element: accurate and comprehensive recall. If the data/information/knowledge – the main constituents of experience – is incomplete or flawed in any way, any conclusions will, *ipso facto*, also be less than efficacious. In the case of conventional post-implementation reviews (sometimes done as case studies), what happens is that a manager – or if it is done independently, a management consultant or academic – comes in after a project is completed and reviews the evidence, usually through existing documentation and oral discussions with the key decision makers involved. They then go away and produce their reports containing, hopefully, the recommendations for future action in which lie the fruits of experiential learning. Similarly, with IT applications – the computer being the means of storage and conveyance – the data/information/knowledge is still dependent on the quality of recall of individual managers who, as previous chapters have shown, invariably bear the scars of inherent corporate amnesia, the underlying disinclination towards being objectively reflective after the event, particularly about mistakes, and their predilection towards defensive reasoning.

In most computer systems, the recall – i.e. what will eventually go into the computers – is the responsibility of individual managers who provide the data/information/knowledge in their own written hand. Alternatively, their accounts are rewritten by third parties as in the case of Booz-Allen & Hamilton's knowledge managers. The problem with this approach is that most managers are notoriously bad communicators, especially on paper. The other drawback, as knowledge managers have acknowledged, is the common difficulty of communicating one of the most important elements of any core capability – 'tacit' knowledge. In essence, the traditional methods of data collection and review – almost all of which are executed in retrospect, often long after the event – fail to capture the real circumstances in which decisions are made. With flawed or incomplete data, the learning potential of these methodologies is clearly limited.

However difficult learning might be in ordinary situations, the additional complication of the flexible labour market will automatically make decision making a less rigorous process, especially in flattened organizations where self-directed work teams are often used to manage important projects. In these cases, the loss of an individual can be very difficult for the team and the organization, not least because the nature of teams is such that the group typically forms itself in a way to take maximum benefit of the skills and talents of each person, regardless of how they were formally trained. After the loss of a team member, the team normally has to close ranks to try to cover those lost skills, or hire another person. The new person usually has different skills, so the team has to spend time redistributing its roles and tasks, and to 'relearn' their team job. If conventional methods of data/information/knowledge capture are imperfect, how, then, can an organization construct a workable method of experiential learning?

In Chapter Three I explained how, using oral debriefing techniques, it is possible to apply short- and medium-term OM for corporate applications like management development and induction. Using similar techniques, it is also possible to help overcome the specific problems that arise in both the traditional forms of post-implementation review and IT applications. An alternative to the customary post-implementation review, it could quite effectively be used alongside the IT applications. There are two quite different approaches. One involves what is known as the Oral or Learning History approach, which is the recall of an event in oral form by participants. The transcripts can then be used to extract lessons that can be applied elsewhere in the company and on other occasions.

The principle of recording staff's experiences of change programmes to ensure that mistakes are not repeated is one that has been accepted by companies like Ford and BP in the US, where oral debriefing techniques are now being used to impressive effect[10]. The two companies hired researchers from the Massachusetts Institute of Technology (MIT) to produce a Learning History, where interviewees recalled their experiences anonymously and in their own words in a way that reflected their collective learning experience. The transcripts have been used to extract insights that become a best-practice manual that managers and staff read before starting another project of a similar nature and which personnel specialists are using to design training.

Ford, which has debriefed 1,200 employees tracking the progress of teams in the US, Hungary, Ireland and Brazil, has Learning Histories currently underway in its car parts division, at an assembly plant and in product design and development. Vic Leo, a systems dynamics and organizational learning manager at Ford in Detroit, estimates that the assembly plant factory has achieved quality improvements of 25 per cent a year since 1995 compared with less than 10 per cent achieved for two comparable factories. *'The plant was ranked third out of the three when we started. When we stopped our learning history it was number one.'* Among its benefits, says Leo, the learning history has helped to expose unexpected problems such as culture clashes and knock-on effects on other systems when a new working practice is spread throughout Ford's 380,000-strong workforce. He dismisses traditional consultancy reports – they can put *'too much of their own spin on a story'* – as formulaic. *'Often*

you read reports about teams which are filed away and forgotten. But the
learning histories captivate the readers. I also feel they give a much rounder
picture.'

At BP, where Learning Histories are calculated to have saved £22.5
million in a three-year trial at one of its refineries, the company
plans to introduce the technique to its overseas subsidiaries through
an efficiency project called Pacesetter. Learning Histories came to
BP when a group of Ohio employees solved a dangerous butane
leakage problem that had gone unnoticed by managers for eight
years. Since then dozens of other efficiency projects and two
Learning Histories have been launched at the refinery, helping staff
to increase productivity – says BP – by 35 per cent in the last two
years. Paul Monus, who launched BP's first Learning History at
Ohio, is now advising other refineries how to introduce the
techniques of oral debriefing.

The other oral debriefing approach is designed to avoid the retrospective
application, which is susceptible to the characteristic partial and selective
memory recall by participants who, after the event, are rarely neutral or
objective. Underlying this methodology is the use of oral debriefing *during* an
'event' or project's lifecycle. Like the Learning History, the oral approach
negates the requirement for managers to 'pen' their own experiences and –
skilfully done – will have a better chance of yielding the usually elusive
'tacit' knowledge element of OM that is crucial to any core competency. And
by doing the job virtually contemporaneously with the event or project, it
sidesteps the inherent problems – including uncertain memory recall – that
occur with knowledge-capture exercises undertaken after the event.

Unlike the conventional retrospective approach, it is first necessary to
pre-select the particular event or project that needs to be post-analysed. This
can be done on the basis of prior performance of *important* and *recurring*
events such as an acquisition, a refinancing, a rationalization, a disposal, a
new product launch, a product recall, a construction project, the analysis of a
competitive strategy, the assessment of a investment technique or corporate
change itself. Anything, in fact, an organization feels may be less than efficiently
handled or where it is thought that lessons can be learned for subsequent
application.

With the help of skilled researcher/debriefers, key decision makers record
their actions on tape at regular intervals *during* the event or project's lifecycle
in the equivalent of an oral diary. At project's end, a suitably edited verbatim
transcript contains unequivocal – and thus indisputable – sequential and
philosophical evidence of how and why individuals made their decisions at
the time. These are then subjected to the scrutiny of independent functional

experts who – alongside the verbatim record and exactly as a manager, academic or management consultant might do – jointly produce a list of recommendations for the company that specifically identifies lessons that can be applied in the future. I call it the Learning Audit. The crucial difference with regular consultancy techniques is that it allows access to *accurate* hindsight as opposed to hindsight that has been tempered by poor memory recall and defensive reasoning.

As with the previous applications of OM, the reason it is done orally is that managers are generally better speakers than they are writers, a factor evident by the formal and incomplete nature of most business archives. Also, their spoken word is a more efficient way of conveying the abstract and complex nature of elements like the nuances of corporate culture, management style and the often obscure issues surrounding decision-making within groups. As such, it is an efficient way of filling the gaps that otherwise exist in the written and remembered record, while the use of an independent and expert researcher imposes the necessary discipline, the requisite non-partisan attachment and the employment of professional oral debriefing techniques.

Professionally structured, the methodology goes to the heart of good decision-making and the principle of the learning organization. Crucially, data needs to be captured immediately in retrospect, the frequency and timing depending on the event, its duration and the personalities involved, with the *full* cooperation of individual decision makers. The important feature is to ensure that a record is made while events are still fresh in the mind and, significantly, *before* the event's conclusion.

A typical recording exercise for a project might consist of separate weekly 20-minute debriefings over the period of the event or project with five main decision makers, who give the researcher/debriefer a blow-by-blow account of what they did over the preceding seven days and why they did it. The objective is to record actual events within a time-contextual framework, the underlying philosophy and mechanisms for actions and inactions, their perceived importance at the time and the tacit 'humanware' elements of OM. It is this element that makes it different from conventional post-project reviews and how data/information/knowledge is captured for IT applications, all of which normally have to rely on post-event recollections that invariably bear the scars of inherent corporate amnesia.

In effect, events can be assessed in real time as opposed to hindsight – and without the emotive fog and factual disputes that come with written accounts by third parties and the confrontational elements of group-based retrospective examinations. Not unlike the principle of the black box flight recorder that is installed in all modern aircraft; if something goes amiss, the 'real-time' data that it stores within itself can be used to find out what went wrong.

Specifically, the methodology ensures that the evidence on which conclusions are made is incontrovertible, a feature that overcomes Arie de Geus's concern about the capricious nature of memory recall. Equally, because the experiences are captured *before* the event or project's conclusion and individuals do not have to confront each other in face-to-face analysis, Professor Chris Argyris's *'defensive reasoning processes'* are side-stepped. At a stroke it improves the qualitative character of the evidential input and the learning potential of the subsequent analysis. In short, it enables managers to learn specifically and directly from their – and each others' – experiences while providing a workable method of arresting the costly cycle of unlearned successes, repeated mistakes and/or re-invented wheels.

Depending on the nature of the event or project and its length, the Learning Audit can also be used to produce interim reports. Thus lessons gleaned from early stages can be applied in later ones. As with oral debriefing's application in staff development and induction, the key to the Learning Audit is in the quality of the debriefing.

Although the technique can be applied in a variety of management situations, one of its primary applications is in project management, which is one of the most fertile reservoirs of learning within an organization. Corroboration of this comes from the Manufacturing Vision Group, the team of academics from Harvard University, the Massachusetts Institute of Technology and Purdue and Stanford Universities who studied[6] twenty development projects in five leading US companies. The academics commented that managers seldom realized that the learning to be gained from a development project was often more important to the company than the new product or process itself. By selecting projects carefully, a company can use them to develop new skills, knowledge and systems. The reason why development projects were such a good source of learning, they said, was that they are a microcosm of the whole organization. Since project teams are usually made up of people from many parts of the company, development projects *'test the strengths and weaknesses of its system, structures and values'*. The academics exemplify this by using contrasting examples from Ford in the late 1980s: the development of the compressor for an air conditioner from which all sorts of organizational lessons were learned and applied on other projects and the almost simultaneous development in a different part of the company of the 1989 Thunderbird, where potential lessons were neither planned for nor learned.

Project management was first made popular in the 1960s on the back of US space and defence programmes. It fell into disrepute in the 1970s with notorious failures such as the Concorde programme and the construction of Sydney Opera House but its star has lately been resurrected by the new interest generated by so-called 'lean manufacturing' techniques, tools like

JIT (Just-in-Time), supply chain partnering, TQM (Total Quality Management) and the worldwide growth in concession contracting exemplified in the UK by the Conservative government's private finance initiative. Construction companies, for example, are today almost totally project orientated, along with car manufacturers and aircraft constructors. In theory, this should bring chronic problems like cost and time overruns under greater scrutiny but – as the academics have observed – few companies employ any rigorous post-project analysis to learn from their experiences.

The Learning Audit has another bonus that would not be available in conventional post-implementation analysis – by default it overrides management's obsessive disinclination to examine their mistakes, which is another prime source of effective learning for organizations. Because it is executed contemporaneously, the event or project's outcome is still unknown, thus preceding any definitive conclusion that might fall below success.

Evidence for the learning potential of mistakes[10] is also widespread. IBM's 360 computer series, for example, one of the most popular ever built, was based on the technology of the failed Stretch computer that preceded it. Elsewhere, to understand why the company's new business initiatives failed so often, Xerox gained valuable insights by studying the product development process of three of its troubled products. The researchers who examined these examples among more than 150 new products concluded that *'the knowledge gained from failures [is] often instrumental in achieving subsequent success. In the simplest terms, failure is the ultimate teacher'*, a sentiment articulated in Professor Morgan McCall's new book[11] on high flyers, in which he says: *'Learning from failures can prove essential for a successful career. The real leaders are those who learn from experience and who remain open to continuous learning'.*

IBM also provides one of the most famous examples of failure's role in experiential learning. Company folklore has it that when IBM's founder, Thomas Watson, Sr, called in a young manager who had just lost $10 million in a risky venture, the man began by saying: 'I guess you want my resignation?' Watson's reply was: 'You can't be serious. We just spent $10 million educating you.'

Underlying an appreciation that the ability to learn from experience is entirely dependent on a faithful organizational memory is a necessary constructive corporate attitude to experiential learning. Bluntly, this also means nurturing a managerial climate where learning is considered more important than individual managerial sensitivities. As the Warwick research team noted[12]: *'Once individuals realize that there is a positive atmosphere to learning – with no punishment for providing the lessons – then an organization starts to remember and incorporate hard-won lessons into present-day activities.'*

In terms of cost-benefit, the rewards can be considerable. Against the corporate expense of firefighting, what price, for example, a construction project that doesn't make the same mistakes a second, third or fourth time? Take any form of imposed corporate change, a prior marketing strategy, a company restructuring or investment technique. What price the accurate recall of the philosophy, mechanisms and lessons of similar exercises five years earlier? Consider, too, the benefits of having access to the strategy and colloquial conceptions of key executives – probably now all departed – when they planned their way out of the last recession? And what about the banks? Not getting it wrong three times in little over ten years would have saved them a pound or two. It is tempting to speculate how lessons better learned earlier in the day might have saved countless millions in long-running and overly costly projects like the Channel Tunnel and the British Library.

Because of its newly conceived nature, the Learning Audit is still in its development phase but I have included it in this book as an alternative to the traditional post-implementation review because of the academic and professional interest in its methodology both in the UK and abroad. Academic journals such as *The Learning Organization*, *Managerial Auditing* and *Internal Auditing* have all carried articles on it while an approach to undertake collaborative research has been made by the Manufacturing Engineering Group at Cambridge University's Engineering Department. President of the Institute of Internal Auditors – UK & Ireland, Professor Gerald Vinten's reaction has also been encouraging: *'Your technique*, he says, *'places business history consultancy right at the centre of organizational effectiveness and strategic need. The technique has real potenential to win through, to save significant expenditure, and to lead to sustainable and long-lasting improvement.'*

To illustrate how it works, I have – in collaboration with Kent-based project management and benchmarking specialists Human Systems – constructed a simulated example from a six-month project to install a new computer system which networks three regional offices, each of which had previously been separate. The project involves modifying software and operating procedures for stock control, sales ledger and accounts. The project as a whole is divided into four distinct phases – system specification followed by system design and build, after which came integration and parallel running and then live operation and maintenance.

The Oral Diary – transcribed from regular tape recorded debriefings with key members of the project team – is conducted by an independent and skilled researcher. Each debriefing, which takes place at weekly intervals, examines five aspects of the project and its environment to include processes, strategies and policies, organization and structure, people and culture. The Analysis part of the Learning Audit is carried out at key points of the project by several project management experts skilled in the relevant competencies.

The following case scenario occurs at the end of Phase Two when prototype systems are being demonstrated. There is a slippage of six weeks and the overall time scale, which was expected to be completed after twenty-seven weeks after launch, was looking to be under threat. At this stage of the project there is also some danger of cost escalation, although this aspect has not yet been fully investigated.

In the course of one of the regular oral debriefings, the project manager says: 'This has been a difficult week for us. The meeting of user representatives last Wednesday was pretty stormy. They still don't think that the new sales system will work the way our customers are used to working, and there is a lot of resistance to the whole design concept. That made me realize we can't recover from the current delays, and we're probably going to over-shoot costs as well. I've got Steve [planning] to try to produce an ETC [estimate to complete] pretty urgently, and I've called a steering group meeting for next Friday.'

In the Analysis part of the Learning Audit, the consultant's observation is: 'This project is creating a lot of waves about how people work, and relatively little time has been spent so far on it winning the hearts and minds of the people who will need to make the system work. Our earlier comments about the superficiality of the risk management process is now being borne out by the evidence of six weeks programme delay and its associated cost (as yet unquantified). Regular ETC represent best practice. On the other hand, how is this estimate likely to be more accurate than the earlier one? No action has been taken to improve the estimating process.'

At around the same time, the manager responsible for sales says in his Oral Diary: '.... I've been under attack from all sides this week. First, the user representatives from all three regions were really bloody-minded at last Wednesday's meeting, and they are calling into question the whole design philosophy of the software. Each region seems to be wanting something different from the others, and they all claim they'll lose customers if we can't meet 100 per cent of their needs. I've got to try to square the circle by matching what they want to something that the new system is designed to be able to do. I've called a design review for next Wednesday, and see what action we can take. On top of that, I've had Steve [cost control] breathing down my neck and insisting that I revamp my estimates for time and for cost by Monday evening. I'll do that, but they won't be worth a lot since our meeting on Wednesday could throw them up in the air again. I'll also have to see how any changes affect Alan [accounts] and Bob [stock control] before I can commit to firm estimates ....'

In the Analysis part of the Learning Audit, the consultant's conclusion is: 'The prevailing culture in the organization is leading to several undesirable practices. The project manager feels under pressure both to involve the steering committee in "firefighting" (even though the seeds of this problem have been germinating for at least three months, as we commented in an earlier note), and to present them with an "estimate to compete". This estimate could be much more soundly based in a week than it can now, but that would seem too much like "delay" to the JFDI practitioners ["Just Flaming Do It"].'

At the heart of all good business is good decision making. In this, there is no substitute for good judgement, which is necessarily dependent on good information derived from the experience *accurately* recalled – of one's own success and failures. Constructed imaginatively and skilfully, the Learning Audit can overcome many of the common drawbacks to the conventional ways of learning from hindsight.

References

1. A. Mumford, 'Four Approaches to Learning from Experience,' *The Learning Organization*, Vol. 1 No. 1. 1994.
2. *The Sunday Telegraph*, 14 September 1997.
3. N. M. Tichy, with E. Cohen, *The Leadership Engine*, HarperBusiness, New York. 1997.
4. Mastering Management series, *Financial Times*, 22 March 1996.
5. 'Building a Learning Organization', *Harvard Business Review* July-August 1993.
6. 1992 research study at Harvard University, the Massachusetts Institute of Technology and Purdue and Stanford Universities. Findings published in *The Perpetual Enterprise Machine*, Oxford University Press, New York. 1994.
7. Leucke, *Scuttle Your Ships before Advancing: and other lessons from history on leadership and change for today's managers*, Oxford University Press, New York. 1994.
8. M. Cusumano and R. Selby, *Microsoft Secrets*, Free Press, New York, 1995/ HarperCollins, London. 1996.
9. *Personnel Today*, July 1997.
10. M. A. Maidique and B.J. Zirger, 'The New Product Learning Cycle', *Research Policy*, Vol. 14, No. 6.
11. M. McCall, *High Flyers: Developing the Next Generation of Leaders*, Harvard Business School Press, Cambridge, MA. 1997.
12. 1988 research study 'Strategies and Past Actions: Management Awareness of Competitive Precedents,' by Dr Robert Rosenfeld, University of Warwick's School of Industrial & Business Studies, into key problems of strategy and change over thirty years in private and public sector organizations, among them Kleinwort Benson, Robert Fleming, Hill Samuel, Jaguar, Peugeot Talbot, The Prudential, Clerical Medical, Longman and Associated Book Publishers.

CHAPTER SIX

Looking over the horizon

In Chapter Three I explained how it is possible to employ short- and medium-term organizational memory for applications such as management development and induction. Chapter Five illustrated how short-term OM can be used in post-implementation reviews to help organizations benefit from their own hindsight.

But what about longer-term OM, the type of experiences that go back a decade and much longer? Up to now my references to OM have mainly referred to 'experience' which, in semantic terms, implies organization-specific occurrences of a 'contemporary' nature. Because they are recognizably co-existent with the present day, they can be seen to have some measure of continuity – and, as I've shown, some bearing on how organizations can deal with today and tomorrow's decisions. In this chapter I take a look at experiences of the longer-term variety, when they become far enough away to be designated as true corporate 'history'.

Does what happened – and how things were done – outside the immediate past have any corporate relevance? And if so, how can it be put to good corporate use?

While I have already rehearsed some of the arguments in prior chapters – and will venture others later – the most compelling evidence lies in several associated areas of business concern, the most important of which are perhaps the enduring nature of corporate culture and the interrelated subject of institutional identity. Corporate culture is primarily the concern of managers with responsibility for broad-based issues like the organizational environment and decision-making processes – i.e. how the corporate psychology, its inner 'spirit' that is characterized by its shared beliefs and attitudes – affects the way business is done while institutional identity has a bearing on all employees and especially new entrants.

In operational terms, corporate culture is among the most potent constituents of any organization's fabric. Yet, of all the corporate 'ethers', it is probably the most obscure to define, difficult to understand and forbidding to change. Of all the traits of the corporate psyche, it is also the most tenacious.

Illustrating this is the Transport and General Workers' Union, which is one of Britain's most progressive trades representative bodies. The Financial Times review of the union's own history

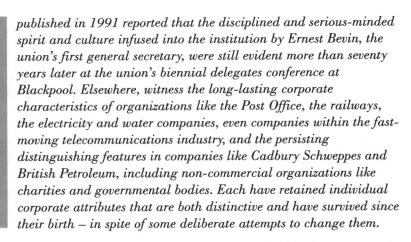

published in 1991 reported that the disciplined and serious-minded spirit and culture infused into the institution by Ernest Bevin, the union's first general secretary, were still evident more than seventy years later at the union's biennial delegates conference at Blackpool. Elsewhere, witness the long-lasting corporate characteristics of organizations like the Post Office, the railways, the electricity and water companies, even companies within the fast-moving telecommunications industry, and the persisting distinguishing features in companies like Cadbury Schweppes and British Petroleum, including non-commercial organizations like charities and governmental bodies. Each have retained individual corporate attributes that are both distinctive and have survived since their birth – in spite of some deliberate attempts to change them.

Most organizations ignore its existence, despite the fact that its nature is ultimately responsible for how almost everything is done. When they do acknowledge it, it is usually in the context of enforced change. When this is deemed advisable, attempts to alter the organizational culture are usually accomplished by wholesale redundancies, the argument being that it is easier to impose a new ethic on a new broom than to transform the old. This happened, for example, when many of the former nationalized industries in the UK were privatized in the 1980s and 1990s, their managements deciding that the former non-commercial culture was no longer relevant to the new corporate paradigm. BA is among the most-quoted of companies that successfully changed its culture this way. One of the problems with this strategy, even if it is successful, is that it also imposes all the consequences of the flexible labour market, with its attendant discontinuity and migratory knowledge. What is often overlooked is the organic – and evolutionary – nature of corporate culture. Above all, it is inherited, the product of cumulative experiences. However they are filtered, all management decisions are made through a set of cultural constructs. To fully understand it – and work with it – an organization needs to be aware of the contributory experiences that shaped its development. And these may go back many, many years.

Corporate culture's accomplice – institutional identity – has a similar importance in the management lexicon. Most human relations experts acknowledge that the stronger the sense of common identity across an organization, the more purposeful the workforce. Like corporate culture, identity is nothing more than the sum of an organization's experiences.

The third argument that gives long-term OM its relevance is a strategic one and concerns how organizations plan their long-term futures, which has to rank among the most important – perhaps *the* most important – of corporate functions. This is the job of the corporate visionary, usually the chairman or president whose office is invariably the gift of proven experience and perceived wisdom, and typically applied alongside the guidance of internal and external industry experts and people like social and political forecasters. So often Western industry has being accused of only been concerned with short-term horizons, a focus that has given 'longer-term' players like the Japanese, whose corporate policies are often designed for periods twenty years hence, a valuable strategic edge, especially in the manufacturing sector; the car, motorcycle and electronics industries are just a few examples.

While the corporate strategists may rightly blame their investors for the short-termism that often issues out of Western boardrooms, I venture another consideration: the dearth of evidence that would otherwise emanate from long-term OM. When it comes to one's own experiences, it is indisputable that a longer-term view is inevitably less rigorous with only short-term perspectives on hand. On this basis, an awareness of one's own longer-term OM can help to provide the additional evidence with which an organization's top strategists can help persuade investors to look longer term.

The US aluminium industry provides a pertinent example of how a company's loss of long-term OM affected its strategic judgement. Going back to the late 1920s, Alcoa – America's premier aluminium producer – had some thirty-two operations underway in countries other than the US. In 1928, a variety of considerations, among them antitrust issues, led management to retrench from its aggressive post-First World War thrust into international activities. Thirty years later all the company remembered was that it was a domestic firm with a domestic orientation. Acknowledging this, a future chairman, Charles W. Parry, recalled[1]: 'Even though opportunities were ripe much earlier, it wasn't until the late 1960s that we again ventured forth, in earnest, into the international arena. World War Two demands for aluminum and the outstanding growth in consumption during the post-war years combined to reinforce what had become Alcoa's strong domestic mindset. It was a mindset that long outlasted the context of its creation.'

In his book *'The Constraints of Corporate Tradition'*[2], Alan Kantrow explains: *'Alcoa was not unusual in the degree to which its communal memory embraced the fact but not the rationale of earlier choices. It was, after all, an emphatically domestic company – and quite a successful one at that and for that reason. Thirty years of industrial experience drove that lesson home, reinforced it, turned it into an article of faith. Thousands of people came to maturity in management swaddled in that lesson's rich cloth of implication and direction. Mentors taught it to their charges, and they in turn spread it among themselves. After a while, though, none of them could remember why it*

was that Arthur Vining Davis [the then chairman] thought it best to retrench in
1928 or that it was Davis who, for a plateful of reasons that must have seemed
good for him at the time, turned an internationally minded organization into
one with strict domestic horizons in its thinking.'

If long-term OM's oversight can be expensive, specific examples of how
its awareness has helped managers influence events is similarly scattered
throughout industry. One instructional example[3] concerns Sir George Blunden,
a former deputy Governor of the Bank of England, whose knowledge of events
in the nineteenth century and the early 1920s led to the rescues in the 1970s
of Slater Walker and Johnson Matthey and helped avert a crisis in both the
London Euromarkets and the gold market. Through his study of the Bank of
England's history, he was mindful of how, in the late 1920s, the Bank helped
to help bring together the armaments and naval shipbuilding businesses of
Vickers and the Newcastle firm of Sir W. G. Armstrong, Whitworth and Co. to
form Vickers-Armstrong. At the time Sir George saw a certain continuity in
the 1920s and 1970s rescues, both of which occurred in significant recessions
during the period in office of non-interventionist governments. *'It (the Bank)*
bears the precedents in mind, learns from experience and each time does a little
bit better than the previous one,' he recounted later.

A similar story[4] is told by the late Sir Alistair Pilkington when, as
chairman of his family the Pilkington Glass Company, he was laying down
a strategy to improve the group's stability. Having studied a commissioned
history of the 155-year-old organization, he became aware of the need not
to repeat the mistakes of several competitors by remaining a one-product
company. *'Our history demonstrated clearly the historical imperative of*
remaining a multi-product manufacturer, sustaining a technological edge
and ensuring that the company was able to compete internationally,' he
recalled. *'It also taught me a lot about changing patterns of management*
through the company's existence. One's own history, really done well,
produces a very penetrating perspective.' To this day the group's historian –
Professor Theo Barker, whom Sir Alistair said knew more about Pilkington
than any man in the world – is consulted by the company.

Both the Bank of England and Pilkington's examples illustrate OM's
role in how organizations can better live with change. It can play another
role in decision making. What ultimately gives managers confidence is
their accumulated knowledge of the way things work for themselves.
Discounting the problems that typically arise from their own short and
selective memories, executives frequently have to consider the experience
of the organization in which their own histories are limited. For this, an
awareness of long-term OM is an invaluable aid to provide both the
hypothesis and the necessary evidence for alternative courses of action.
In short, while the future is never foreseeable, understanding what has

happened before enables managers to make an otherwise more reasoned estimate in the light of past experience. This reduces the uncertainty over decision making.

Finally, there is long-term OM's role in the business of demonstrating worth, which underlies every firm's motivation and activities. Although the calculations of an organization's value are invariably based on *future* potential earnings, the actual numbers – however accurate they might be – always appear as just ethereal figures in a balance sheet or on a Stock Exchange dealing screen. The sums are often astronomical – from £1.37 billion for the relatively small British chemical company Laporte, DM2.7 billion for the smallish German engineering company Thyssen, SKr290 billion for Ericsson, the larger Swedish electronics company and $31 billion for the giant US petroleum company Texaco. Even for the most numerate of number-crunchers, these figures are difficult to comprehend rationally. It is often necessary for a business to demonstrate that worth in a non-digital way, whether to confirm that the numbers are justified or even to reinforce their general perception. How useful might this be when trying to defend oneself in an unwelcome takeover bid or to demonstrate value with the 'For sale' sign outside the factory gates? Evidence of historic events and experiences can do just this – which is where long-term OM comes in again.

When it comes to one's history, organizations usually think in two ways – museums and/or exhibitions and the corporate biography. Few companies utilize either of them in any imaginative way. Of the two, the former is generally thought to be the most appropriate historical agency. While historical interest in specialist subjects like railways and motor cars is widespread, this is characteristically seen as the preoccupation of enthusiasts and largely removed – at least in its applied form – from business affairs. Their application is generally perceived to be a prestigious form of publicity. No accurate information is available as to their numbers in the UK but the British Archives Council (BAC), a body which encourages organizations to preserve and utilize their records, estimates them to be on a par with the number of companies that operate working archives. In fact relatively few British companies preserve their archives in any organized way, the vast majority treating them as dusty and cumbersome piles of paper to be disposed of as soon as the demands for extra space outweighs the mass available. Against the belief that it is a virtue not to 'hoard', the typical attitude is that while archives might have a curiosity value for yet-to-be-born academics, dusty papers occupy space. As such, it is argued, they should be bundled up and hidden from view. Occasionally the company might donate or lodge the records with a university or other repository but, more often, they are simply destroyed after a respectable lapse of time or when the company moves its head office. A BAC directory published in 1992, for example, contains a nationwide listing of just seventy-six established business archives, representing less than half of the BAC's membership.

*Among the companies that have used their archives to create
their own museums are the Bank of England, London Transport,
Bass, the Reckitt & Colman's mustard firm, Blue Circle, British
Telecom, Bulmer, Cable & Wireless, C. & J. Clark, Guinness,
Harveys of Bristol, Irish Distillers, Norwich Union, Pilkington,
Royal Worcester, Sun Life and Wedgwood. Travelling exhibitions
include Harveys' wine glasses and Bryant & May's match-making
archives. Companies which have sponsored single exhibitions at
museums or other venues include Liberty's at the Victoria & Albert
Museum in 1975, Wedgwood at the Science Museum in 1978,
Royal Doulton at the Victoria & Albert Museum in 1979, House
of Fraser at the Museum of London in 1982, Twinings at the
Cutty Sark in London in 1984 and Penguin Books at the Royal
Festival Hall in 1985. Companies with permanent loans to
particular museums include Beatson Clark, which has provided a
special glass gallery at Rotherham Museum in south Yorkshire.*

But in terms of being able to disseminate OM in an efficient and cost-
effective way, it is the other historical medium – the corporate history – that
is probably the most suitable vehicle. Of all the corporate formats – including
company newspapers and corporate videos, even a full-blown film – it is
uniquely able to convey a wealth of corporate information in a highly
communicable way. Done appropriately – the operative word is *appropriately*
– it is an inventory of corporate experiences that can be used to help solve a
whole range of problems that modern business has imposed on itself.

Incredibly, its main employment is typically confined to narrow public
relations once or twice every 100 years. And even then, the way they are
generally produced invariably guarantees that they fall on deaf ears, whether
they are written by scholars or professional writers as academic tomes,
business books or coffee table picture albums.

In the next chapter I explain how an organization's history can be used
for a number of sound corporate applications that go beyond the PR barrier.
In particular, how it can help combat some of the problems created by some
modern business strategies and the flexible labour market.

Take acquisitions and mergers, for example, which in the last three
decades have become the single largest popular short-cut to corporate
growth. In terms of value, they are collectively worth a staggering £62
billion a year in the UK alone. Not many people know this – indeed
companies themselves are often reluctant to admit it, even privately, when
it happens to themselves (defensive reasoning and all that) – but *50 per
cent* of them fail. How can an organization's long-term OM help cut the
rate of attrition?

Then there is the problem of the flexible labour market's effect on job turnover. One solution – oral debriefing – has already been suggested for senior and other key employees, but what about the other workers whose performance is also dependent on a strong sense of institutional identity? Not all can receive an oral debriefing from their predecessor; nor might one be necessary. But if they are going to stay on average just three, four or five years, how can long-term OM shorten their induction period and enhance their real-time contribution?

And finally, how can OM demonstrate the value that an organization's own accountants put on things like their brand names, even the worth that whole companies are given by the market?

References

1. Speech to The Newcomen Society, 12 June 1985. Newcomen Publication No. 1249.
2. A.M. Kantrow, *The Constraints of Corporate Tradition*, Harper & Row, New York. 1984.
3. Conversation with author, 1992.
4. Conversation with author, 1991.

CHAPTER SEVEN

Making acquisitions work by the book, et al.

Western investors, whether they be the banks, institutions or small Stock Exchange punters, are an impatient lot. In contrast to many Pacific Basin countries, their demands generally have short-term horizons. Whereas the investment timetable for a UK or US investor might typically be five years, the equivalent period for their Japanese counterpart would be up to twenty years.

The pressure this puts on Western managers is enormous. In many cases, these demands do not give enough time for companies to develop their activities organically, especially in mature markets, where the opportunities are often limited and margins small. With increased competition ensuring near-saturation participation, expansion for any one company is often dependent on the competition taking its eye off the ball and letting its market share slip. Witness what happens in the cut-throat food retailing, clothing and electrical sectors? The latitude for growth can often be very small indeed.

Hence the disposition for acquisitions and mergers, a corporate stratagem that has been around for most of this century but which has accelerated in recent decades to mammoth proportions. Sharpened to extremely good corporate advantage by acquisition specialists such as Britain's Hanson, America's United Technologies (the Pratt & Whitney aero engine group), ABB and GE Capital, its attraction in a mature market is that, at a stroke, it allows one company to consume someone else's market share and – at least cosmetically – boost sales in either related or unrelated fields of activity. To be successful, the predator then imposes a discipline on the acquired assets that attempts to enhance their prior performance within the enlarged grouping, shared activities usually resulting in 'rationalization'.

While this appraisal of acquisitions and mergers is relatively simplistic – there are other reasons why they take place and scenarios that also lead to job gains – the underlying principle is nevertheless sound. The trick is always to ensure that the purchase price does not exceed the expected benefits – ever a difficult decision before the event. Hence the efforts some companies put into due diligence. With the strategy such an integral part of business life today, and the perception that organic growth is often a more expensive route, it has even become popular in the non-mature sectors of industry, with the result that acquisitions and mergers activity has escalated in real terms over the last two decades.

Acquisitions Monthly, a British journal that monitors M&A activity in Europe, gives an indication of the scale of the industry. In just one year – 1996 – UK acquisitions and mergers within the country totalled a staggering £55.9 billion, up from £27.7 billion in 1990. Cross-border acquisitions – i.e. British acquisitions of companies outside the UK in 1996 – totalled another £6.1 billion. A pointer to the size of the industry elsewhere in the world is the value of cross-border acquisitions by companies of only European Union businesses. In 1996, for example, US companies – the largest buyers and sellers of businesses – spent £15.7 billion on them, Swiss companies £7.63 billion, German companies £6.4 billion, French companies £5.3 billion and Dutch companies £2.5 billion. In the same year European companies spent $67.5 billion on deals in the US, up from $33.3 billion in 1995.

On a worldwide basis, the figures are truly spectacular, even when they just embrace foreign-based purchases. In the first nine months of 1996, the value[1] of international cross-border mergers and acquisition targets totalled $181.7 billion, up from $173.7 billion in 1995. Even the service industry to support this activity – the lawyers, accountants, public relations specialists, etc. – is colossal; it is estimated[2] that the City of London, for example, earned a record £1.1 billion in fees from UK takeovers in 1996.

With their value so high and so many businesses so dependent on their success, it may well come as something of a shock to many acquisitive companies that so few of their acquisitions are successful. The figures, which can be confirmed from a number of different sources, do not reflect well on the managers that carry them out. Statistics from the London Business School show[3] that as many as half of all acquisitions fail, a figure that is confirmed[4] by international accountants Coopers & Lybrand. Elsewhere, the Economist Intelligence Unit's assessment is that fewer than half of all acquisitions and mergers can be considered successful[5] while management consultants McKinsey & Co., whose benchmark of success was a company's ability at least to earn back its cost of capital on the funds invested, puts[6] the failure rate at more than 60 per cent.

In a major Harvard Business School study[7] in 1987 of the records since 1950 of thirty-three large US companies, which diversified through acquisition, the verdict of Professor Michael Porter, who led the research, was that their strategy had largely *'failed'*. Using the divestment rate of earlier acquisitions as the measure of success and failure, he found that even successful diversifiers such as 3M and IBM had *'terrible records when they strayed into unrelated acquisitions'*. By 1980 Cummins Engines, for example, had divested all the unrelated acquisitions it had made since 1950 while companies like Exxon, Gulf & Western and General Mills had each disposed of about 80 per cent of their unrewarding catch.

Research also points to two other significant features – that the failure rate is not substantially different all over the world and the flop ratio has not changed much over at least a twenty-year period. Given the enormity of the sums involved, it is instructive to put the figures into a more understandable context. If the 50 per cent failure rate is applied to just the UK's 1996 figures, the cumulative total of unproductive or loss-making assets is equal to the amount raised by a charge of 27p on the basic rate of national income tax or just short of Denmark's 1993 national budget. The bottom line is that acquisitive companies are wasting shareholders' funds on a truly massive scale.

These figures must be sobering for the scores of companies in the process of going down the acquisition and merger trail. The list is endless. In 1996, for example, Great Universal Stores, the UK's largest mail order group, was looking for £700 million of acquisitions while at GKN, the UK engineering group's war chest was worth £250 million. Among, literally, thousands of other signed deals around the world were the acquisitions by US-based food distribution group JP Foodservice of the food, paper and cleaning products company Rykoff-Sexton for $1.4 billion and the purchase by Dutch-based financial services group ING Group of Equitable of Iowa Companies for $2.6 billion. All eyes are on the $9 billion banking acquisition in 1996 by Travelers of Salomon Brothers, Merrill Lynch's acquisition of Mercury Asset Management and, in the accounting sector, Cooper & Lybrand's merger with Price Waterhouse and KPMG's with Ernst & Young. For the C&L/PW marriage to succeed, Cooper's growth culture will have to be interfused with the smaller Price Waterhouse's less aggressive culture more successfully than Cooper's turbulent acquisition of Deloitte UK in the early 1990s. If the academics and management consultants are right, around half will not earn their keep.

Any constructive assessment of how companies can improve the attrition rate must take account of why so many acquisitions and mergers fail. According to various academic institutions that have investigated the phenomenon over the years – the London Business School, INSEAD and the Harvard Business School included – the most frequent cause of failure among acquisitions is the ethereal culture clash between the parties. More specifically, the LBS research points to an inability to bridge the gap between contrasting values and beliefs, masking what is little more than mutual organizational misunderstanding. This is compounded by little follow-through. While, it seems, companies appear to be happy to spend sizeable amounts to bring themselves together, they puzzlingly allocate very few resources to help keep them together.

However inadequate this might seem in the light of the monies at stake and the numbers of people involved, the LBS research showed that only one buyer in five had any formal operational plan for post-acquisition implementation. More than a tenth of acquirers did not communicate in any way with the seller's staff, presumably hoping, says the research, that the vendor's managers would *pass on the message*. The others communicated with acquired staff through either a personal talk by the chairman and/or through a personal package of information or newsletter. That the efforts to bond with acquired companies are handled badly is confirmed by McKinsey, whose study of the procurement programmes of 116 large US and UK companies to 1972 identified poor post-acquisition integration as one of the predator's three cardinal sins which kept them from generating enough cash flow to offset stock market acquisition premiums.

While bad judgements and the trading environment must also account for some of the attrition, the link between integration failure, cultural differences and mutual misunderstanding is clear, as is the lack of attention to post-acquisition integration.

> *Examples of this can be seen in just a few of the failed acquisitions of recent years. Hill Samuel's purchase of Wood MacKenzie, indeed the TSB's subsequent acquisition of Hill Samuel itself, Mecca of Pleasurama, Midland Bank of Crocker, AT & T and NCR and the Prudential's purchase of a string of estate agents are just a small proportion of the failures arising out of acquisitions in the 1980s that industry observers will readily confirm fell victim to the so-called culture clash. Elsewhere, the marriages between American Express and Shearson Lehman, Pharmacia and Upjohn, Swiss Bank Corporation and S.G. Warburg, Deutsche Bank and Morgan Grenfell, and Merrill Lynch and Smith New Court are all proving to be more painful than envisaged by their instigators, also because of culture clashes.*

So why did these acquisitions fail or falter when, elsewhere in the takeover game, other companies were succeeding at dealing with equally dissimilar cultural mixes? Kingfisher managed to successfully bond with Comet and United Biscuits was successful at linking up with Terry Chocolates. How come, too, Unilever's seizure of Brooke Bond and Grand Metropolitan's procurement of Pillsbury in the US – all of which were hostile acquisitions and at least as culturally different – were integrated successfully?

Out of the LBS research comes another clue. John Hunt, faculty dean and professor of organizational behaviour at LBS, has identified what he calls *'reciprocal organizational understanding'* as one of several key elements to any successful union. Importantly, his research showed that among successful cases, the acquiring managers work hard to deal with conflicting values and beliefs; in the unsuccessful cases, these issues were not tackled.

Hostile acquisitions notwithstanding, the difficulties of 'adaptation' are particularly acute when the takeover is also of a cross-border nature, where new products or new markets are involved and if the digestion process involves getting previous competitors to work together. All experience shows that successful integration can take years, even for the most skilled acquirer. In the case of

Electrolux, for example, rated as one of the foremost takeover specialists, chief executive Gosta Bystedt has admitted that it took five years to digest Electro Helios, a local company. Changing a corporate culture can take even longer. Whether or not a company decides to try to change the acquiree's culture is one of the key decisions of any merger. If it is necessary, how it is done becomes – or should become – the subject of detailed study and professional help. In the meantime, while the longer-term strategy is worked out, it is necessary to get on with life, in particular learn to live and work with each other at all levels on a day-to-day basis.

The evidence is that even the companies most successful at undertaking mergers and acquisitions just adapt the standard processes used for day-to-day induction. What usually happens is that the acquiring company replaces the top layer of the acquiree's management. They might also give a familiarization lecture, show the company video and hand out company pamphlets, hoping that the new group's procedures, values and/or wider culture are transferred quickly and efficiently down the line. Among larger acquisitions, task forces are sometimes created to link the two administrations.

Delta Air Lines, for example, an American company which commands a high degree of corporate loyalty, uses what it calls 'buddy teams', a technique it developed when it acquired Western Airlines in the mid-1980s. When it picked up many of Pan Am's 7,000 employees in 1990, it appointed groups of Delta and Pan Am employees to specifically familiarize former Pan Am staff with the Delta philosophy.

These determined attempts at integration are relatively unusual, however. As the LBS and McKinsey researchers found, most acquirers do relatively little and often generally ignore the all-important process of post-acquisition integration, in spite of the fact that almost all the textbooks emphasize the 'people factor' as a vital element in takeovers. Such examples[8] would include the Imperial Tobacco takeover of Howard Johnsons, Schlumberger of Fairchild Semiconductor, Kennecott of Carborundum, Xerox of Crum and Forster, and Philips of Pye.

What is also clear is that acquisitions are mostly a one-way affair. It is the acquired company that is usually expected to learn to understand the acquirer rather than the other way around. Also, most effort at integrating companies is usually confined to top management; senior, middle management and the shopfloor, where the impact is just as keenly felt, are invariably disregarded, as the 1969 survey[9] by management consultant Charles Handy found. Almost 90 per cent of almost 1,000 middle and senior managers whose organizations had been recently acquired were *'psychologically unprepared'* for the aftermath of the merger. Little appears to have changed since, along with the rate of acquisition failure.

Given the attrition rate, it is clear that the integration factor – the amount of time it takes and the effectiveness with which new arrivals are incorporated into the company – should be of critical concern to all growth companies and their personnel/human resource departments. As such, *all* ways of transferring an awareness of culture and identity – with the intention of encouraging wider understanding and, ultimately, transferring loyalty – should be employed.

If, as the researchers suggest, mutual misunderstanding is much of the problem, what is the best way to deal with factors like conflicting values and beliefs? The answer lies in providing each party with a way of understanding each other through a medium that can successfully transmit 'identity' and 'culture' in an easily communicable way. The logic is that if each party is made familiar with the other, and knows how each other operates, the process of union will be that much quicker and easier. In fact acquisitions and mergers have a lot in common with how people come together at a social level. The first thing that happens is that individuals try to find out something about each other. Only if the information flows will a relationship have any chance of developing and being mutually rewarding. If experience, identity and culture are the lifeblood of a company, then its history – the compilation of its OM – is the artery through which acquired employees can be informed quickly and comprehensively about inherited values, norms, beliefs, systems and the company's individual way of doing business.

Done in a suitable format, the organization's corporate history can be given to acquirees along with other, more statutory, information like new terms of employment, etc. Unlike the company newspaper, pamphlet or corporate video that are the traditional forms of communication for most companies, no other document or medium can impart the type and range of information that a new entrant otherwise takes years to learn, assimilate and apply effectively.

Yet few companies use their corporate history for anything except a celebratory tool for important anniversaries. While some companies do have corporate histories, few of the documents produced are suitable for the purpose of inducting new employees. Even among companies with corporate histories that might suit the task, less than a handful are known to have used the medium for this purpose. This is in spite of the fact that the principle of using history as a component in the induction process is already recognized, at least by some companies. At Burmah Castrol, for example, the company's archivist regularly speaks on an induction course for new entrants while Courage's personnel department has engaged the resources of its archives in making an induction video for new staff. For many years a senior executive at publishers Butterworth, who had a keen interest in the company's history, addressed induction courses for new employees.

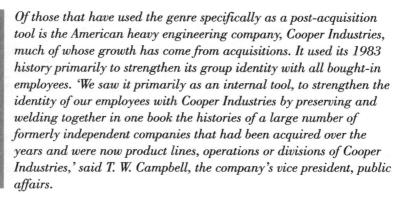

Of those that have used the genre specifically as a post-acquisition tool is the American heavy engineering company, Cooper Industries, much of whose growth has come from acquisitions. It used its 1983 history primarily to strengthen its group identity with all bought-in employees. 'We saw it primarily as an internal tool, to strengthen the identity of our employees with Cooper Industries by preserving and welding together in one book the histories of a large number of formerly independent companies that had been acquired over the years and were now product lines, operations or divisions of Cooper Industries,' said T. W. Campbell, the company's vice president, public affairs.

For conceptual advocacy, LBS's John Hunt confirms history's role as a means of fostering successful bonding. Pointing to religious organizations and the military as examples of institutions with well-planned history-orientated induction processes, Professor Hunt says: *'History can provide the stories, myths and legends for the new or merged culture.'* Alluding directly to the 50 per cent failure rate of acquisitions and mergers, his research says there are compelling financial reasons for assisting in the integration process and transferring the acquired peoples' commitment to the firm's new owners – *'winning the hearts and minds is an immediate necessity. Without their commitment it is difficult to achieve the operational and strategic objectives of the acquisition.'* He points out that employees are at their most receptive at the time they are most inquisitive – immediately after an acquisition.

A well-produced corporate history is not something that can be delivered overnight, so it must be considered as part of the planning process ahead of an acquisition strategy. Once it is produced, however, it can be updated regularly to accommodate recent events. For cross-border acquisitions, a translation would serve the purpose in exactly the same way. In some cases the acquired company might have its own corporate history. In that case – and if it were suitable – it would be prudent to reprint it for distribution to the new owner's relevant employees. If it is important for the acquired to understand the acquirer, it is equally important for the acquirer's employees to understand the acquired.

Done with application, a corporate history can provide a familiarity, knowledge, an understanding of an organization's values, its beliefs and how a company does things. Through it, the acquired company will better understand the acquirer's aims and objectives, as well as its activities, customs and traditions. While, on its own, it cannot save an acquisition from failing it can – done well – go a long way to bridging the gulf of misunderstanding between organizations that suddenly have to learn to live together. Compared with the cost of acquisitions themselves, it is a comparatively inexpensive – and disarmingly simple – way of helping to ensure that miscarriage is not a bride price that companies necessarily have to pay for half their acquisitions and mergers. Along with all the other traditional induction techniques, it is a powerful management tool to help re-employ a huge volume of otherwise unproductive shareholders' funds.

Much the same reasoning can be applied to the needed induction of an organization's appointees that do not come from acquisitions – all those day-to-day appointees who, as a result of the flexible labour market, also have to be inaugurated into the organization. As previous chapters have shown, their tenure will typically only last three to five years, so, if an organization is to extract maximum employment from them, it is important to find ways to shorten their normal period of assimilation and provide a quick means of allowing new entrants to inherit an organization's institutional identity.

> *Confirmation of corporate history's capacity to do this can be seen in the other examples of companies that have specifically used the genre as an induction tool. Procter & Gamble, for example, which has produced two corporate histories over the past four decades, is currently updating its biography expressly as an induction tool for new employees. In Japan, where many companies produce their corporate histories every ten years, NEC, the electronics company, describes its latest history as a 'bible' for new employees; the book, it says, provides a way 'to convey the company's culture of management and tradition to the next generation of employees'.*

Produced in a slightly different way, an organization's history can serve another valuable corporate purpose – to confirm worth. In today's marketplace, where the sales of many companies are greater than the national outputs of some developing countries, millions and billions are, to most people, just figures in a balance sheet separated by a discretionary comma. Their magnitude often dwarfs their reality. Linked to this incomprehension of large measures (what I call digital blindness) is the intangible nature of some financial numbers that are associated with business and accounting – things like goodwill, depreciation and market capitalization. Although they are based on standard forms of computation, how they are calculated – and their perceived worth – are, nevertheless, always subjective until cash actually changes hands. Their contemplative nature will always create a conceptual credibility problem, with the only evidence for their probity lying with the reputations of the auditors that opine on them, the outward signs of corporate 'worth' that emanate from activities like advertising and the actual physical amounts of cash that a willing buyer is prepared to pay.

While it can be argued that the corporate biography's traditional application as a PR document is intended to help bridge this credibility gap, most company histories are only produced with important anniversaries in mind, usually once or twice every 100 years. Moreover, when they are produced, most companies create them in ways that invariably guarantee low readership levels, which immediately confines their PR usage. In the UK, for example, few have print runs that exceed 2,500, ever reach High Street bookshops, appear on reading lists in business schools or even get reviewed by the business press.

While the subject of how organizations can better produce their biographies is dealt with in Chapter Twelve, the fact remains that an organization's OM in its collective configuration – as a corporate narrative – can provide an effective, non-digital means of providing evidence of an organization's value. While corporate histories can do this for companies in their wider context, there is another corporate asset that could benefit from similar treatment. Wholly intangible until someone actually buys them, their perceived value is sometimes greater than many of an organization's other, more traditional assets.

I am referring to brands. It is only little more than a decade since an organization's individual products – through their brand valuations – have been recognized in balance sheets as a major asset in their own right. Even though scores of companies have taken them on board, they still lack broad acceptance in the accountancy and financial communities when their value is computed outside of an actual transaction. The reason is clear: unlike the more tangible assets such as plant and machinery, their value is based on individual judgements or discretion. The subjective nature of their calculation raises the key question of credibility.

To illustrate the problem, the size of which is arguably proportional to the effect they can – and have had – on many organizations' balance sheets, a review of the short history of brand valuations is instructive along with the ways accountants compute brand values.

As a phenomenon, it first surfaced – unheralded – in 1984 when Rupert Murdoch's acquisitive News International included a valuation for publishing titles in its balance sheet. As far as the company was concerned, the effect was dramatic; it offset goodwill write-offs, dramatically reduced gearing and restored the balance sheet. It is arguable that without this simple procedure it is unlikely that the newspaper baron would subsequently have been able to expand his empire as he did.

A year later – also largely unnoticed – the Reckitt & Colman toiletries group capitalized the value of the Airwick brand it had just purchased from Ciba-Geigy. The resultant increase in assets also had a corresponding positive effect on the balance sheet. Next was Grand Metropolitan, which had just acquired Heublein and the Smirnoff brand. In 1988 it put a £588 million value on Smirnoff rather than write off the whole purchase price. The move actually helped the brewing, food and hotel giant conclude the giant Pillsbury deal the following year.

The concept of brand valuation was still largely an unspoken issue – even when they constituted a large element of the two large acquisitions that next hit the marketplace. First came the Swiss food group Nestlé's purchase of the UK chocolate company Rowntree Mackintosh. Rowntree's physical assets – its plant and stock – were worth only a fifth of the £2.55 billion purchase price. The balance was Nestlé's valuation of Rowntree's intangible worth, notably its brands such as KitKat, Smarties, After Eight, Polo Mints and Yorkie. At about the same time Philip Morris, the American food and tobacco giant that owns Marlboro (probably the world's most valuable brand, estimated to be worth at least $31 billion), bought Kraft. The $12.9 billion price tag represented four times the cheese company's tangible assets.

Elsewhere, many more companies were valuing their brands. Rather than just incorporate their worth in the balance sheet, they were also using the valuations for merger and acquisition purposes, brand management strategy, licensing, for fundraising as collateral on loans, as the subject of sale and leaseback arrangements and even to measure the performance of managers. Suddenly, brands had considerable intrinsic worth.

All this was going on without much fuss, even though the consequences of capitalizing brand values were challenging traditional accounting practices. Until, that is, Ranks Hovis McDougall decided to value and capitalize all its brands, acquired or otherwise. The issue hit the headlines in late 1988 when the British bakery product group's balance sheet worth reported a £678 million fillip after incorporating the value of brands such as Hovis, Mr Kipling and Bisto.

The accounting profession found itself unprepared; with companies either using their own in-house resources to put numbers on this intangible of company assets or commissioning the growing band of independent consultancies specializing in the business, there were no acceptable standards by which valuers should do their sums. Concern was raised about the differing methods the different valuers were using, the imprecise nature of the valuations and the dangers of abandoning traditional historical cost accounting practices.

In spite of this, a spate of similar brand valuations were triggered in the balance sheets of companies like Guinness, United Biscuits and Lonrho. Cadbury Schweppes announced it had added £309 million to its balance sheet worth to reflect the value of acquisitions, including Trebor and Bassett. WPP, the marketing services group, also included in its balance sheet the value of the brand names of its well-known subsidiary companies in the advertising and public relations sector.

The reason why companies were turning to brand valuations was clear. Frustrated by the corrosive effect of goodwill write-offs, advocates pointed out that modern business had to concern itself with intangibles such as software and copyright – so why not brands if they had legitimate value? From the corporate point of view, their inclusion in the balance sheet represented a fairer representation of group worth, brand owners arguing that as an asset, well-established brands were often more valuable and longer-lasting than some tangible assets like plant and machinery. With companies like General Cinema of the US building up an uncomfortable stake in Cadbury Schweppes, it was also not lost on them that the inclusion of brand values – or at least the knowledge of perceived worth – would provide useful ammunition to fight off a potential predator and an equally useful indicator of value for a disposal.

The London Stock Exchange ruled that brands should be recognized as part of corporate worth while the Accounting Standards Committee, faced with a *fait accompli*, conceded the difficulties of effective evaluation and immediately set about drawing up new accounting rules, commanding in the meantime that brand worth was part of goodwill and should be amortized. By way of arousing the debate – and providing the renamed Accounting Standards Board with some industry feedback – a group of the top managers of the larger UK companies belonging to the Hundred Group of Finance Directors commissioned Arthur Andersen, the international accountancy company, to produce a set of guidelines for professional valuers. An interim report in April 1992 recommended that if companies included intangible assets in their balance sheets, the accounts should also include detailed information on how the valuations were determined. Brands – or more accurately their valuation – had arrived, with only the techniques for more skilfully calculating their perceived worth to be agreed.

Five years later, there is still no accounting standard for how brands should be valued, with the Accounting Standards Board – in a move to introduce consistency with goodwill – ruling that the only brand valuations that can be included in the balance sheet are those that have been acquired – i.e. those whose values can be demonstrated by an actual purchase, whether individually or part of a larger acquisition. According to a Financial Reporting Standard that is expected to become effective this year, the value of home-grown brands cannot be capitalized. Now, brands that are *not* acquired can only have a perceived value off-balance sheet.

While the ruling has neatly removed the problem of subjective valuations of non-acquired brands appearing in the balance sheet, the move has not stopped companies continuing to value their brands. MCI is an example of a company that has recently valued its brand as a precursor to its projected sale to BT, GTE or WorldCom, while the Nestlé subsidiary Carnation used a recent brand valuation as collateral on a loan. Elsewhere, Procter & Gamble has used valuations for inter-company transfers of royalties and annual fees, and the US chemicals group Du Pont valued some of its brands in order to make decisions on the level of advertising support and whether or not to apportion resources into licensing. Importantly, valuations can still appear in Notes to the Annual Report and Accounts to provide evidence that the company's stated financial worth is understated, which could be useful ammunition in the event of an unwelcome takeover bid or proposed sale.

All these applications notwithstanding, the lack of precise guidelines on how valuations should be calculated has not solved the problem of the reliability – or more accurately the unreliability – of their measure, the imprecise nature of which is illustrated by the dozen or so methods used. Among the various methods are calculations that take into account the estimated future royalty stream, the actual cost of establishing and maintaining the brand, the price difference between the branded product and the identical unbranded product less the cost of brand support, the 'esteem' with which it is held by consumers, assessments of the earnings capacity of the brand with provisions made for the risks the brand faces and a more sophisticated technique based on a multiple of brand earnings, the multiple being determined by so-called 'brand strength'. Yet others include a so-called premium pricing method – the price difference between the branded product and the identical unbranded product less the cost of brand support – and a so-called 'share of mind' method that assesses the awareness of a brand or the esteem with which it is held by consumers, none of which are definitive because of differing criteria for measuring and defining value. The two methods usually seen as the most appropriate, however, are valuations based on assessments of the earnings capacity of the brand with provisions made for the risks the brand faces and a more sophisticated technique based on a multiple of brand earnings, the multiple being determined by perceived brand strength.

Although the concept of brand valuation is fully accepted by tax authorities, the Mergers and Monopolies Commission (MMC) and the High Court in the UK – also in the US – the absence of an agreed standard by which valuers can assess values consistently continues to raise the question of their reliability which – in turn – reinforces their subjective nature. The Accounting Standards Board readily acknowledges its misgivings, one of the members of the team who worked on the Financial Reporting Standard saying: '*The Board remains sceptical about the reliability of valuations when so many different methods are used.*' Equally equivocal are management consultants like Booz Allen & Hamilton, whose chief marketing officer, Sam Hill's opinion[10] is that the question of how brand valuations are arrived at is inseparable from their employment. Referring to the annual league tables of brand values produced by the US journal *Financial World*, which recorded IBM's brand name as having a negative value in 1994 and a massive positive value just two years later, he says: '*Any methodology which tells me my plants were worth zero four years ago and $18 billion now would worry me. A lot of folks would love to measure all the capital employed in their business, but nobody knows how to do that in a replaceable or transferable way.*'

There is even a measure of scepticism from some large brand owners themselves. In 1994 Sir Michael Perry, chairman of Unilever, said: '*The seemingly miraculous conjuring up of intangible asset values, as if from nowhere, only serves to reinforce the view of the consumer sceptics, that brand values are just about high prices and consumer exploitation.'*

For the practitioner, London-based Interbrand, part of the US marketing group Omnicon and a specialist in the field that has valued around 1,600 brands for around 300 companies, explains:

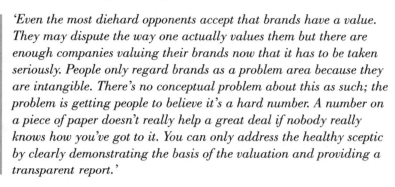

> *'Even the most diehard opponents accept that brands have a value. They may dispute the way one actually values them but there are enough companies valuing their brands now that it has to be taken seriously. People only regard brands as a problem area because they are intangible. There's no conceptual problem about this as such; the problem is getting people to believe it's a hard number. A number on a piece of paper doesn't really help a great deal if nobody really knows how you've got to it. You can only address the healthy sceptic by clearly demonstrating the basis of the valuation and providing a transparent report.'*

It is an issue that valuers can do little about except try to ensure that the methodology they use is plausible, for even an ostensibly plausible valuation technique does not guarantee what an actual sale will yield in a market situation. Examples abound of transactions differing radically from in-house valuations, confirming their subjective nature, their potential to mislead investors and the need to find other, more visible, ways of substantiating value alongside the valuers' bald, final figure.

In addition to helping provide evidence of worth to the wider audience, a serious product history can provide another valuable service – to provide the valuer with an actual document of record with which to arrive at a more accurate value of worth. The rationale for this is explained by the kind of information that an organization typically gives to a valuer to work out the worth of its brands. Whichever technique – or combination – the valuer uses, the fundamental constituent element behind any evaluation is the brand's history. Interbrand puts it this way: *'In essence the brand's stability – which is really all about its longevity, in other words its history – is all part of understanding its value. A brand's history is a vital part of demonstrating worth.'* It is a perspective endorsed by Cooper & Lybrand, which also specializes in brand valuations: *'Value is about consumer loyalty and the demonstrable resources that are committed to brand position and strength. To understand a brand you have to understand its history.'*

Normally the company provides the valuer with an outline of the brand's past, usually no more than a couple of pages in length. Sometimes the material supplied is a glossy brand pamphlet, an updated brand presentation which an executive might have made internally or a schedule of historical figures. The rest is up to the valuer to glean from other sources, both externally (databases, etc.) and inside the company, usually through interviews. In many cases, the flexible labour market's effects means that there are no employees around with a corporate tenure longer than five or six years.

Interbrand describes the problem this way: *'Companies can tell in detail about what has happened in the last quarter but know virtually nothing of the brand twenty years ago, let alone five years ago. Given the long life of many brands and the long memories of many consumers, this is a very short-sighted view of what makes a brand valuable.'* In only a handful of cases – Hovis, Matchbox Toys and some of the car manufacturers in particular – has Interbrand been given anything more, notably a brand or company history. In Cooper & Lybrand's case, only one company, a food manufacturing group, provided the group's corporate history within which the stories of its brands were related. In all the cases, the existence of the brand or business history was coincidental, at least one having been produced for a long-past anniversary and was therefore not up to date. In fact, only few more British companies have ever produced their product histories in anything except pamphlet-style format, in spite of the fact that UK companies are one of the largest brand owners in the world. The nearest books have been geared towards advertising history, such as the 1972 treatment of *The History of Bovril Advertising* and *The Book of Guinness Advertising* in 1985. Add to this product history's potential use as a prestigious marketing tool and as a means for management development/induction for the rolling generations of management and staff, the genre becomes another powerful management tool.

Within the context of a Knowledge Management tool, the issue of brand valuations has also attracted the attention of the Business Archives Council, which has alerted all business archivists that the maintenance or enhancement of brand name value must become more crucial than ever. *'As so many brand names, almost by definition, are historically based, so the work of the archivist, in preserving the evidence and using it to promote the brand, becomes more important than ever,'* it says.

A brand is worth more than a functional equivalent product. Its function is to certify distinction and quality. It often allows the brand owner to charge premium prices and can help secure repeat business. As such, it is a valuable commodity that has been expensive to create, develop, nurture and protect over the years. Its origins, the way the product was launched, the technology it utilizes, how it has changed and developed over the years, its packaging, marketing and advertising, and how it may have contributed to social and industrial change are all clear indicators of value. At one level a product history will give the valuer the necessary full and corroborative raw material on which to base an evaluation. At another it can authenticate the brand's track record and visibly underpin the subsequent valuation. In short, an organization's OM can help turn a soft number into a hard number.

References

1. KPMG Peat Marwick research, November 1996.
2. *Acquisitions Monthly*, Press Release, 20 December 1996.
3. 1991 London Business School research, 'The Human Factor' by Professor John Hunt and Stephen Downing.
4. *Financial Times*, 3 May 1993.
5. *Making Acquisitions Work*, Economist Intelligence Unit study, reported in the Financial Times, 26 January 1996.
6. *Financial Times*, 4 March 1988.
7. *Harvard Business Review*, May/June 1987.
8. McKinsey & Co., quoted in the *Financial Times*, 4 March 1988.
9. How to Face being Taken Over,' *Harvard Business Review* 1969.
10. Management Page, *Financial Times*, 6 December 1996.

CHAPTER EIGHT

OM's wider role

IN 1995, Lord Young, one of British prime minister Margaret Thatcher's architects of her 1979 enterprise revolution, stood up to tell the country's captains of industry the findings of the latest research into industrial attitudes among the country's emerging generation of workers. His report was not inspiring. Two thirds of sixth-form students were more favourably inclined towards public service jobs such as nursing, firefighting and teaching than they were towards positions in industry.

The specially commissioned study[1] by the University of Derby's Centre for Applied Social and Organizational Research, from which he was quoting, also found that students could name only one successful British company and had no idea what the acronyms of the country's representative bodies for industry or the trades unions – the CBI and TUC – stood for. The findings were suspiciously similar to the observations of another rising star forty years earlier. When interviewing graduates for employment at Courtaulds, Sir Arthur Knight, a future chairman of the international textiles company and a key figure behind the creation of the Manchester Business School in the 1960s, became puzzled at the numbers who regarded entry into an industrial job as less appealing than a career in public service.

As the University of Derby's study found, Sir Arthur's perception and underlying attitudes have not changed much over the ensuing period. Neither has much been done to take up his suggestions for changing these non-commercial job aspirations across the community. In fact, Sir Arthur's observations in those post-Second World War days illustrate two of OM's other powerful applications that stretch beyond an organization's internal usage and which go to the heart of how wealth creation and a greater awareness of how business operates can be encouraged in the wider community.

Their nature – also in its collective configuration as corporate narrative – is explained by Sir Arthur's recollections[2] of what happened at the time. One of his responsibilities in Courtaulds's economics department was to interview graduates for employment. Puzzled at the numbers who, though prepared to come to an interview, regarded entry into an industrial job as less appealing than a career in public service, he began to theorize that, possibly, the parents and teachers who had influenced these young people could have no conception of the reality of industrial life. *'In the absence of direct experience, teaching has to be based upon books and there were few books about business, whereas government in all its aspects has been much written about by academics*

and in the memoirs of practicians (politicians and service people in particular),'
he recalls. *'I thought I knew enough of the public service and of industry to
know that the industrial life offered challenges, intellectual and personal, just
as fascinating as those elsewhere.'* Having just read a history of Unilever and
the life story of John Davison Rockefeller, it was clearly possible, he thought,
to write interestingly about business. Why not, he reasoned, encourage the
writing of company histories, which would provide the necessary familiarization
and motivation to influence those who had no conception of the reality of
industrial life? At intervals over the next couple of years, Sir Arthur pressed a
senior colleague to see if a history of Courtaulds could be commissioned.

Some twenty years later, he was asked by the Vice-Chancellor of Oxford
University to discuss the relationship between university and industry. With
management education becoming fashionable and reasoning that Oxford might
be thinking of building its own centre for management studies, Sir Arthur
wrote to recent Oxford graduates who had joined Courtaulds for their views on
Oxford itself, their replies endorsing Oxford's rigorous intellectual discipline
of the tutorial system. Also at around this time Courtaulds had just been the
subject of an adverse report by the Monopolies Commission which Sir Arthur
thought showed *'a complete failure of understanding'*. Disillusioned at the
practical value of economists' *'simplistic'* models, he thought that public policy
could not result in sound prescriptions if based upon unsound notions. What
was needed, he thought, was a multi-discipline approach to understanding.
Could not Oxford be the place where this approach could be nourished?

It was against this background that he advised the Vice-Chancellor of
the need for collaboration between political scientists, economic historians
and economists in the study of the private limited company as a social institution
that was similar to that applied to political affairs generalizing from historical
and contemporary material. He had become convinced that well-written
corporate histories could provide the basis for broader-based business history
which – he believed – should be as important to the education and training of
businessmen as was the study of political history to future statesmen or military
history to future generals.

In the same way many other disciplines operated, he recognized the
educational value of actual business experience, a proposition that would
later influence those who launched the country's flagship business history
institution, the Business History Unit at the London School of Economics,
whose conception mirrored the genre's use as the primary method of teaching
pioneered at Harvard Business School in the US.

More than a quarter of a century later, however, corporate history's spread
in the community is still negligible while business history's employment in
both general education and management education has been indecisive and
correspondingly slow. Take Sir Arthur's suggestion that the writing of company

histories would provide the necessary familiarization and motivation to influence those who had no conception of the reality of industrial life. Forty years on, relatively few businesses still produce their corporate or product histories. When they do, whether they are produced by academics or more popular writer-historians, the majority have only a narrow readership at an important anniversary date and few get seriously reviewed. Unlike equivalent biographies or autobiographies that litter the political, literary, music, art and entertainment worlds, less than a handful of corporate histories ever go on sale in High Street bookshops. And they rarely appear on students' reading lists, including those of business students.

Their widespread scarcity, in fact, attracted the attention of Mrs Thatcher's government in 1988 when Alex Fletcher, a former Secretary of State for corporate and consumer affairs, observed:

> *'There is a great deal of material in our schools and elsewhere about how babies are born but there is a tremendous shortage of publications about how businesses are born. Only a tiny number of people know there really was a Mr Barclay, a Mr Beecham, a Mr Cadbury, a Mr Rolls and a Mr Royce, and the marvellous stories of how they created these now world-famous companies. Generations can only understand these examples if they learn and understand the process, innovation and the leadership that made it possible.'*

Six years later, a similar observation[3] was made in the letters columns of the *Financial Times* by a correspondent complaining that the newspaper's latest review of business books did not contain a biography of a successful leader of a modern business. The writer, one P. V. Zealander, a senior manager in the Post Office, wrote:

> *'A visit to any large bookshop will similarly fail to unearth among the lives of politicians, film stars, novelists and sporting idols any accounts of how the leaders of today's successful companies reached the top and created wealth and worth in getting there. Why is this? There is a great educational value in disseminating the art of business leadership, both to managers in work and to a general readership who are the customers of their enterprise.'*

And what of Sir Arthur's call for the development of broader-based business history and its inclusion into the business curriculum in universities, including business schools? While subjects like political, military, social, music and art history are an integral part of the general educative process, the teaching of business history is still notable for its widespread absence in British universities and business schools, where the history mantle is held almost exclusively by economic historians concerned with macro-fiscal issues that have more to do with how government manages than how business executives manage. In contrast to the US, for example, where both corporate history and business history is a more integral part of teaching in a growing number of universities and business schools, educators in the UK still largely teach the nation's future business executives how to manage without the perspectives of their predecessors or an awareness of their corporate past.

Using Sir Arthur's military analogy, the position in the UK is equivalent to America's West Point and Britain's Sandhurst not referring to the First and Second World Wars, the Korean War, Vietnam, the Falklands or the Gulf. In fact, the genre's neglect is put into perspective by the inconsequential amount of business history research and applied teaching that emanates from a meagre number of specialist academics. By almost every measure, the UK's accomplishments in business history compare dismally with countries like the US and Japan.

Curiously, business history's employment is deliberately shunned by the education system and discouraged by industry, in spite of the fact that the need for the historical perspective is endorsed by patriarch industrialists like former British Rail chairman Sir Peter Parker. At 74, he is the youngest to give the concept any form of recognition as a valid management tool and is on record as saying[4] '... *business history is a missing dimension throughout the educational system. We need to build back into the business school approach the significance of a historical perspective.*'

Educators' dismissive attitude towards the subject is illustrated by Dr Nicholas Tate, chief executive of the School Curriculum and Assessment Authority's comment[5] on the subject. '*Pupils study the industrial revolution in some detail and look at the implications for the economic growth of the nineteenth century. They thus receive an introduction to some important business issues.*' He also notes that the Open University, which is the country's largest business school, uses the Battle of the Somme as one of its case studies for its MBA course. '*It provides an interesting method of helping managers draw upon the lessons of the past.*'

This restrained attitude, which at least acknowledges the principle of experiential learning – albeit from a non-business source – is mirrored in industry, where the view[6] is characterized by Stuart Bishell, chief executive of Understanding Industry, a foundation dedicated to increasing links between business and education: '*I do not believe that historical context is especially useful to students in understanding wealth creation and the position of industry and commerce in the economy and society of the twenty-first century. It is vital that we look forward to the entirely different way in which these processes will work during the working lives of current students and not backwards at how they used to work in the past.*' Coincidentally, Bishell's organization arranged the event at which Lord Young, in 1995, disclosed the high level of pupil ignorance about industry.

It is extraordinary that a country so rich and interested in so many other aspects of its history should be so dismissive about its corporate and business history. It is a concept, for example, that impugns one of the basic tenets of learning that is common in other areas of education – that the younger generation can learn from their predecessor's example.

The existence of a culture is dependent entirely on the level of inherited historical knowledge or tradition, which is usually handed down from one generation to another through the oral, visual and written media. Without it, individuals have to, literally, start from scratch. Business is no different, which may help to explain the University of Derby's findings about discouraging attitudes towards commerce and industry, the constant complaints by captains of industry about widespread employee ignorance of the role of companies, even why the UK's birthrate[7] of new enterprises is relatively low in relation to other OECD countries.

However unrelated these statistics may appear to some, the reality is that corporate enterprise and investment, the foundation of national wealth, is not firmly entrenched in the British national character, an observation described in 1990 by the late Sir Charles Villiers, a former chairman of British Steel, who noted after returning from a business trip to America that enterprise in the US came from the roots up – from home, family, school, college, classmates and a person's home town. In the UK, he reported somewhat gloomily:

> *'British roots go down to mass unemployment, to the disgrace of bankruptcy, to the urge for the safety of the public service, to heavy taxation of the reward for risk – and to the classic story of the teacher emerging with the class from a visit to an engineering works, saying: 'That's what'll happen to you if you don't pass your "O" levels.'*

In the same year Sir Peter Thomson, who as head of the National Freight Corporation led the country's largest employee buyout, admitted that, like many others, he thought the 1980s was the decade when popular capitalism really took root in the UK. The seeds had been planted and all that was required was to sit back and wait for the harvest. In his role as chairman of the Confederation of British Industry's Wider Share Ownership Council at the time, he conceded that the reality was very different. Millions of the new investors had never traded a share, nor did they know how, he said. They owned only one or two shares bought in the generously priced and heavily marketed privatization issues and tended to see share ownership rather as a *'sophisticated gamble than a long-term investment in the wealth creation process'*.

Sir Peter's judgement was that it was unhealthy for the mass of the population not to understand the wealth creation process. *'In any free market economy, ignorance of the wealth creation process is not just regrettable, it is dangerous.'*

His CBI taskforce found that in 1975, individuals accounted for 38 per cent of the value of UK listed equities; this fell to 28 per cent in 1981 and to 20 per cent a decade later. It was not lost on the task force's members that the latest decline occurred during a period when the emphasis on Mrs Thatcher's popular capitalism was at its highest. Barry Riley, the *Financial Times* columnist who served on Sir Peter Thomson's Task Force, followed up the report's conclusions with his own personal lament for the vanishing shareholder. His judgement was that the future of wider share ownership was mostly in industry's own hands.

Two years later – more than a decade after the first efforts to encourage more individual share owners – the Treasury's annual survey of share ownership disclosed that the number of personal shareholders in the UK had fallen from about 11 million in 1990 to 9.8 million in 1991. The survey translated this decline to mean that the proportion of share-owning adults fell from 25 per cent to 22 per cent prompting ProShare, the body that promotes share ownership, to lament: *'Owning shares is not something that a respectable married man does in public.'*

If there is one story that illustrates the nation's relative economic unsophistication, it is what happened in the wake of the privatization of British Gas. Instead of cashing their first dividend cheque, 10,000 investors paid the sum on the cheque back to British Gas, believing that it was a bill.

It is against this background that the British government and British industry – at least during the Conservative government's eighteen years in power – was trying to encourage more constructive attitudes towards industry and commerce. In the education sector their efforts were directed mainly through the inclusion of non-compulsory 'business studies' within the new National Curriculum and the Enterprise in Higher Education initiative.

The experience of Ken Thomas, archivist at Courage, the brewers, demonstrates how little of Britain's business heritage is being inherited. In 1991 he reported to his peers at the British Archives Council that he had had little success in promoting the company's archive as an educational tool, in spite of National Curriculum guidelines.

'In theory, under the National Curriculum schools will be plundering local archives for documents and effectively using archives as source providers for course work and classwork history. I have attended a day school on the National Curriculum and the

role of archives, contacted individual teachers, spoken to County Advisors for history, but all to no avail. Everyone's reticence about developments in education has now rubbed off onto me and I no longer try to promote the use of Courage's archives in this area. My only success in using the archives as an educational tool have been to assist individual pupils in their GCSE course work or on A-level project work. These few successes have not even been in the field of history – rather it has been geographers who have approached the archive. One day I still hope for better results; our company historical archives are rich in records that document great themes in history – the rise of women in employment, the growth of industry in Britain over two centuries, and industry at war in the twentieth century.'

It's not as if the UK does not have any inherent aptitude for enterprise. It is, after all, the world's oldest industrial nation with some extremely successful companies. The point is that, historically, with so few individuals involved in actual wealth creation, it just seems that the required business skills are confined to a small coterie who – as the above evidence would suggest and for other possible reasons that I discuss in Chapter Eleven – have a particular antipathy towards using a tool that would allow others to benefit from their experience. If this is the case, it is also a clear contributory factor that reinforces the country's traditional class system and the cultural divide with workers. It asserts, obliquely but in no less uncertain terms, that the company's operation is not the concern of the mass of people who create the wealth or provide the capital on which the company's success is built.

The new Labour government has gone some way to recognizing the concept of experiential learning by arranging for businessmen like Alan Sugar, the founder of the computer company Amstrad, to speak at a series of seminars for young people interested in business. The view of Chancellor Gordon Brown is that he has *'a wealth of experience and knowledge to offer to our next generation of entrepreneurs – the household names of the future'*. What Mr Sugar will be relating is his own OM.

While all such occasions will no doubt be useful opportunities to pass on his industrial endowment, it takes no imagination to conclude that his addresses to limited audiences is a somewhat inefficient way to achieve what Sir Arthur Knight and Alex Fletcher have already recognized as a valuable classroom and workplace tool. In its composite guise, corporate and business history would allow a wider audience to inherit a business culture without having continually to re-invent the wheel.

To illustrate how organizations and educational institutions – and not only in the UK – are overlooking a valuable resource to motivate a wider constituency, it is instructive to examine the genre's history alongside its usage in various countries. First, corporate history, the bedrock of business history, where the recent rapid dissipation of OM through the flexible labour market both reinforces their need as well as the problem of its production.

References

1. 'Understanding Industry,' research study into attitudes towards industry, University of Derby's Centre for Applied Social and Organisational Research, announced to the Institute of Directors, February 1995.
2. *Business History Newsletter*, Issue No. 8, March 1984.
3. Letters to the Editor, *Financial Times*, 17 March 1994.
4. Correspondence with author, 1992.
5. Correspondence with author, 1994.
6. Correspondence with author, 1994.
7. OECD Annual Report, 1994.

CHAPTER NINE

Literary fiascos and corporate white elephants

While the UK may have a tradition longer than most of producing their corporate histories, relatively few serious or readable accounts, whether academic or otherwise, are ever produced. When they are, they are either designed for – or achieve – minimal audiences, making them one of the most unread of all history books.

Because of their inconspicuous nature, it is difficult to monitor the numbers of corporate histories that are produced. However, some measure can be gleaned from a 1987 bibliography[1]of British business histories, which includes corporate histories of the pamphlet, book and thesis types. In a period spanning about 110 years, about 4,000 titles are listed, equal to less than forty titles a year. Within this, around 340 company histories were published before 1900. The equivalent number for the period to 1940 was around 650. More recently, about sixty corporate histories have been produced since 1970 in the heavyweight, academic style. About 200 theses, articles and books about companies were published in 1990[2].

This compares with Germany, for example, where, in 1987[3] alone, more than 170 businesses commissioned their histories, with another 100 being published without sponsorship. By 1991, the annual production rate was around 500 titles. According to Beate Bruninghaus, manager for the German Society for Business History, at least 25,000 corporate histories have been produced in Germany, '*where companies have become aware that their history is part of their business culture and can therefore be used to develop a corporate identity*'[4].

No firm figures are available for America and Japan but their companies' interest in the genre is also extensive, almost certainly exceeding Germany's.

In Britain, the fate of Courtauld's corporate history, which Sir Arthur Knight wanted produced in the 1950s to familiarize those who had no conception of the reality of industrial life, is illustrative of the small number of books about successful British companies published since the Second World War. Led by Unilever's, the first important post-Second World War corporate history to be produced in the modern manner, Courtauld's history, in fact, created a short-lived mini-boom in the number of academic-style corporate histories in the 1980s that included books on the Rio Tinto Company, Burmah Oil, the National Coal Board, WH Smith, the Inchcape Group, the British Bank of the

Middle East and the Midland Bank. Most were written by a small band of academics who had become interested in the genre. Like most corporate histories elsewhere in the world, they were funded by the subject companies. Courtauld's history was researched and written by Professor Donald Coleman, a professor of economic history at the University of Cambridge, in three editions. The first was published in 1969, almost two decades after it was first proposed, the two subsequent editions appearing over the next eleven years. In spite of Sir Arthur championing the original project, and being chairman of the group in the project's latter stages, there was no widespread circulation to the company's captive audience of employees or shareholders, with only some 300 copies of each volume distributed on a complimentary basis. All three volumes were put on public sale by the publisher, the first two volumes selling just 1,000 copies each and the third about 700.

Of the books' usage, Courtaulds says[5] it is *'not aware of any management application other than it providing a general appreciation of the company's development. We have no views on history as a management tool except in the general sense that we can all learn from our own and our predecessor's experience. By and large we do not spend more time than other companies looking backwards.'* The attitude of Courtaulds towards its OM is not untypical of many other major British organizations that followed the textile company's example of going down either the academic and non-academic route.

Their exposure – represented by the number of copies printed – was grudging. While distribution decisions could also have reflected manuscript quality and perceived interest, the average print run for all the company histories published by the Cambridge University Press during the 1980s, for example, was less than 2,400 copies, with their average outside sale to the general public – at cover prices ranging from nearly three to six times the cost of an average business book – under 750 copies per title. Many observers have estimated that, literally, no more than a handful of people have ever actually read them from cover to cover. As readable books and practical management tools, the vast majority would qualify as literary fiascos and corporate white elephants.

Among them, Bowater's 1981 history had a print run of just 1,000; of this the company's requirement was 300. Phoenix Assurance's order for the 1986 printing of the first volume of its history was even less – 750 copies out of a print run of 1,500. Two volumes of N. V. Philips' history, published in 1986 and 1989 respectively, received company orders of 2,400 copies each out of individual print runs of 3,300. British Rail's order for its 1987 history was 1,000 out of a print run of 1,750. From a print run of 4,400, British Petroleum's requirement for volume one of its 1982 history was 3,500.

Elsewhere, each of the four volumes of the Hongkong & Shanghai Banking Corporation's history, published from 1988 to 1991, received a company order for 1,600 copies out of a print run of 2,300; the majority of the company's requirements are still in store at the company's headquarters cover priced at £65 a volume. In the case of Pilkington's biography, about 50 per cent of the group's order of 6,000 copies of its 1977 edition were still in the company's possession fourteen years later. A limited number of copies were sent to professional and business contacts while employees were offered copies at a discounted price. Elsewhere, the presses printed just 1,900 copies of the Bank of England's most recent history.

Less heavyweight approaches have been given equally parsimonious audiences. When Blue Circle Industries published its corporate history in 1988, 10,000 copies were printed. While books were given to all directors free of charge, an order form was sent out to all shareholders, current and previous employees and pensioners, offering the book at a discount price of £4.95. Only 100 employees and a few shareholders took up the offer. Even fewer copies were sold externally at the published cover price of £14.95. Four years later the company still had a stock of more than 7,000 copies and was unsure how to dispose of them. The book took four years to research and write by a Cambridge history graduate.

The Bradford & Bingley Building Society's distribution experience was equally disappointing. It produced a history in 1989 to mark the retirement of a long-serving chief executive, an event that also coincided with the 25th anniversary of the merger of the two societies making up the society's name. Written by the society's public relations officer, it was edited in-house by the company secretary and other senior executives, who reportedly made numerous changes to the typescript. The society vested copyright in itself and published it itself. The book never went on public sale and was never reviewed. In total 13,000 hardback and softcover copies were printed, almost two thirds of which were still in the company's possession five years later. Apart from its celebratory role, the society – the seventh largest in the country at the time – admitted there was no other particular management application for the book.

In transparently 'PR' books, Empire Stores printed 2,000 copies of its 1981 history, Dawson International 1,000 of its 1986 history, Friends' Provident Life Office 2,000 of its 1982 history, Helix 2,000, Alsford, the timber company, 2,500, Butterley Brick 3,000, Britannia Building Society 2,500, Polands of Lloyds 2,000 and Pillar, the RTZ subsidiary, 500 copies of their corporate histories. Britain's oldest company, the building firm of Richard Durtnell & Sons, printed just 1,000 copies of its 400-year-old history in 1991. Of all the recent corporate histories, just one – Slaughter & May's – is known to have been produced in versions suitable for both academic and wider corporate audiences.

A random comparison of the exposure of similar biographies published by companies elsewhere in the industrialized world is edifying. With distribution decisions presumably also based on manuscript quality and perceived interest, the Japanese car maker Nissan's print run for its 1983 history (*'to ensure that the general public has a correct view of the company and that its employees have an accurate knowledge of their heritage'*) was 100,000 copies. Elsewhere, Toyota's 1987 biography (to present the company to people around the world *'in a way that would allow them to understand Toyota better, both as a Japanese corporation and an international business'*) had a print run of 85,000, the steel-making, engineering and construction company NKK's1992 history (*'to know what the management thought and did to cope with the changes in the environment'*) 38,000 and Fuji-Xerox's 1983 biography (to *'show its appreciation to its customers who had made Fuji-Xerox a fully grown-up company'*) 27,500 copies. Japan's interest in corporate history stems from the reluctance of its companies to be takeover targets, so high priority is given to maintaining their independence. Updated by many companies every ten years, they see company history as being able to reinforce their individual identity; consequently, the company makes a point of distributing copies freely to all employees and, in some cases, shareholders.

In recent years Japanese companies have also found that their histories have a utility outside the country. Most companies with interests in expanding their overseas activities have published foreign-language versions of their corporate histories to enhance their overseas visibility. The rationale is illustrated by Toyota, whose founder, Sakichi Toyoda, who is quoted in Toyota's latest biography, said in 1921: *'The first and most important step in building good relationships with people in other countries is to arouse the interest of entrepreneurs like us.'*

In Germany, BASF's 1990 history (*'so that employees would be able to identify the part they played within the company'*) had a print run of 313,000, Hoechst's 1988 biography (*'to imprint and reinforce an identity and loyalty across a group'*) 170,000 copies plus, Bayer's 1988 history (*'there is a high awareness of history and tradition'*) 185,000 and Deutsche Bank's 1970 history 40,000 copies. In 1994 Deutsche Bank was preparing[3] an updated version *'to take the writing of corporate history to new levels of academic excellence,'* according to the bank's in-house historian, Professor Manfred Pohl. The project, which has been allocated a budget of DM1 million, was initiated by Herr Alfred Herrhausen, the former chief executive of the bank killed by terrorists in 1989.

The German attitude to corporate and business history can be seen in one of the first moves Deutsche Bank made following the unification of the two Germanies in 1991. With new-found access to its pre-1945 archives, which had been held in East Germany, it set up a Historical Association with one of its aims being to make banking history accessible to the general public through publications, lectures, excursions, exhibitions and working groups. It recognized that, with many former East Germans coming into the banking system, a greater degree of historical awareness could contribute to a better understanding of the new banking structures and bring the staff from the old and new federal states closer together. Its history, it believed, could be used to help change disparate attitudes. *'The political and economic unification of Europe as well as the international relations and ties characterizing modern-day banking will no doubt be better understood and become more transparent for the bank's employees if they know the historical background,'* said the company. Speaking at the association's inaugural meeting, Herr Hilmar Kopper, spokesman of the board of managing directors of Deutsche Bank, explained the rationale further:

> *'The political and economic events which have taken place over the past eighteen months have, I believe, demonstrated that a knowledge of history is essential if we are to understand the problems of today. Understanding the present and looking towards the future mean that we need to analyse the past. Only by examining history closely can we establish the necessary distance between ourselves and the world today, and this enables us to see current problems in relative terms and form an independent opinion. I believe that being familiar with and understanding history can contribute substantially towards self-realization and the establishment of identity, not only of an individual but also of an institution, In addition, it educates us in something which is of infinite importance to all of us – a sense of responsibility for the future.'*

He said an awareness of history would enable staff in the new federal states to *'settle down'* easier in their new company. Historical information provided in a clear, straightforward and comprehensive form could, he said, *'establish a bridge on which we could meet, in spite of the differences in mentality which undoubtedly still exists and this could, I feel, act as a unifying force within the bank'.*

In America, the 1983 history of heavy engineering company Cooper Industries (*'to strengthen the group identity with acquired employees'*) had a print run of 75,000, the 1987 biography of Abbott Laboratories 50,000, biomedical company Merck's 1991 history (as *'an employee motivator'*) 37,000, pharmaceutical firm Eli Lilley's 1975 history (*'it's important to us'*) 30,000 copies and the adhesives and speciality chemicals business H. B. Fuller Company's 1987 book 24,000 copies.

The perceived importance of corporate history in the US can be illustrated by the attention given to it in just one sector of American industry – chemicals. A bibliography compiled by The Centre for History of Chemistry (CHOC), a joint endeavour of the American Chemical Society, the American Institute of Chemical Engineers and the University of Pennsylvania, lists twenty-six US chemical companies that have published one or more corporate histories. The total for UK chemical companies is four. CHOC's understanding of the value of history is clear:

> *'One advantage of maturity is the ability to ponder, and to learn from, experience – to profit from history. The choice we face is not between no history and some history, but between good history and bad history. Journalists and critics will always dig around in the past and – if nothing else is saved and nothing else done – the records of court litigation will be the only source from which the story of the chemical industries is constructed. And that history .... runs straight from Silent Spring through Times Beach to Bhopal.'*

The *Silent Spring* reference alludes to the title of a book, which first appeared in 1962, that highlighted the deleterious ecological effects of environmental pollution, specifically DDT. Times Beach is a reference to a notorious case in which dioxine-contaminated sludge was used to spray roads in a small town in Missouri; as a result Times Beach became a virtual ghost town. Bhopal is the name of a town in India which suffered mass deaths and injuries after poisonous gases leaked from a gas plant. CHOC says that the prospect that history's recall will be based on court records *'is not attractive, nor is it good history. Good history requires the preservation and use of a representative range of documents, the existence of archives that will attract imaginative and objective scholars, and the deliberate nourishing of a tradition of research and inquiry. We thus stand at a moment when there is a clear opportunity and great need for modern corporations to sponsor and to create an accurate, authoritative and sophisticated record of the contributions to American life made by chemists, engineers and entrepreneurs.'*

Not all British companies overlook the potential readership opportunities provided by their corporate histories. Marks & Spencer's is the most widely distributed of all British corporate histories. When it published its history to coincide with its centenary in 1984, it printed 60,000 copies for distribution to all staff free of charge, interested public libraries and similar foundations. Elsewhere, Pearl Assurance printed 25,000 copies of its picture-book history to give its staff a feeling of continuity after it was taken over by Australian Mutual Provident Society through its subsidiary AMP (UK) in 1989. Earlier, the 1954 history of Unilever had a print run of 10,000 in English, 3,000 in Dutch and an unknown number in Japanese. Copies were offered to employees and pensioners at a one-third discount to the cover price. By 1968, more than 12,000 were sold. Following this success, the company reprinted a paperback version in 1970 for employees and associates.

In addition to highlighting the low regard most British companies put in their corporate histories' potential utility – their circulation commonly accounting for less than 15 per cent of just their captive audience of employees, customers and suppliers – the typical usage of the genre highlights another characteristic. In spite of the fact, for example, that overseas markets have always been an important source of revenue for UK companies, only one British and one joint British corporate history – Tate & Lyle and Unilever's histories – are known to have been printed in a language other than English. Even then, the reason for printing Tate & Lyle's history in French was that the author was French speaking and the chairman at the time – Sir Neil Shaw – was a French-Canadian. In contrast, the corporate biographies of Japanese and German companies, even many American companies, are often printed in the languages of their main customers. Curiously, few companies put the corporate histories of other companies – even competing companies – on their executive reading list, even when they are done well.

The British attitude is exemplified by the attitude towards its corporate history of one of its largest companies to what is acknowledged to be one of the best and most readable corporate biographies produced over the past forty years. No distribution figures are available for ICI's two-volume history but the author, the late Bill Reader, who is acknowledged as being one of the UK's finest modern corporate historians, once complained to an academic acquaintance that his one professional regret was that companies for which he wrote histories (among them Bowater, Bird's Eye Foods, Metal Box, the Weir Group and the City firm of Foster & Braithwaite) did not utilize his work in any imaginative way. It is interesting to note that when ICI responds to historical enquiries, it often hands out a commercially produced book published by Hutchinson entitled *ICI – The Company That Changed our Lives* rather than its official history.

Given that it is the subject companies that are generally making the distribution decisions, the different company attitudes towards the extent of their exposure does not imply that higher-circulation books automatically reflect better quality content. What is does reflect is the organization's underlying attitude towards OM and the perceived importance of its employment, the application of which provides the opportunity – no more, no less – to use the tried and tested past.

The 'history' of corporate histories is now more than a century old, with many of the early attempts to record the activities of companies confined to relatively benign, albeit colourful chronicles, usually written for the private archives of founding families. With a clear link to industrialization, its development has been confined to four main areas – the US, the UK, Germany and – latterly – Japan. Although, in evolutionary terms, the US is the most advanced, the genre has its origins in the political literature of mid-nineteenth century Germany and associated business history in Britain, Germany and America.

It was Karl Marx whose *Critique of Political Economy* and, later, *Capital* analysed the social dimensions and the consequences of the Industrial Revolution, in particular the effects of manufacturing on the new working classes fresh off the land. Almost immediately his political theology created a multitude of studies on labour relations and the connection between big business and government. This was followed by Max Weber's *The Protestant Ethic* and *Economy and Society*, which proposed a theory of bureaucracy that led to a similar outpouring of works on managers and white collar workers.

In the changing times of the late nineteenth century, emerging business was a political football, as subsequent political developments showed in Eastern Europe. The first literary portrayal of business executives in the modern era – and the companies they created – were highly unflattering. With the example of imported European attitudes to support it, popular journalism and academia in the US started to take an interest in the corrupt practices of businessmen; the perception emerged that they were 'robber barons,' a viewpoint that would be propagated until well into the first half of the twentieth century and, to a lesser extent, even later.

One of the first serious attempts at a corporate history was a remarkable turn-of-the-century narrative of the US refining and transportation conglomerate Standard Oil Company which – under the stewardship of John D. Rockefeller – dominated the American business scene in the last quarter of the nineteenth century. In 1899, Ida Tarbell, a young woman journalist, convinced a senior Standard Oil director, H. H. Rogers, to talk freely and openly about the complex operations of the rapidly developing oil industry in general and the Standard Oil trust in particular. For more than two years Miss Tarbell and a research assistant laboured to assemble the rest of the story from a wide range of sources that included admirers and detractors alike. Her intention was to produce a chronological history of the Standard Oil Company. It was not intended to be controversial, rather *'a straight-forward narrative, as picturesque and dramatic as I can make it of the great monopoly'*, she wrote. In the event she produced a conspicuously influential book.

The story made its first appearance in the November 1902 issue of *McClure's*, one of America's leading periodicals at the time with a circulation of several hundred thousand copies. Over the following twenty-four months of serialization, Tarbell pieced together the genesis of modern American business. Buccaneering entrepreneurs, often working on the fringes of the law, captured the imagination of the American public, which frequently was in two minds whether to cheer or decry some of the tactics of the nascent swashbucklers. Tarbell's series was published in book form in November 1904 under the title *The History of Standard Oil Company*. Contemporaries viewed it then as one of the most remarkable books ever written in America.

Standard Oil, which encountered considerable criticism for some of its competitive practices, was more dissatisfied with the public reaction to the company's image portrayed in the book rather than to the book itself. Later generations of Standard Oil executives would describe it as *'probably more widely purchased and its contents more widely disseminated throughout the general public than any other single work on American economic and business history'*.

Rockefeller and other Standard executives did not realize it at the time, but they had one of the most influential business books ever published in America. The book contained a wealth of management lessons, the most important of which Standard, unfortunately, chose to ignore. Despite the warnings sounded in the book about corporate ethics and public accountability, Standard – along with many of its competitors – continued to operate in an unbridled free-wheeling business fashion. Standard, by this time America's largest corporate enterprise, refined more than three-quarters of all US crude oil and marketed four-fifths of all domestic kerosene. It also maintained its pre-eminence through tough competitive tactics and even developed a particularly efficient network of industrial spies. In conducting business in this fashion, Standard totally misjudged the mood of the times, which was moving against the big conglomerates, or trusts, and in November 1906, the Roosevelt administration charged Standard Oil with violating the Sherman Antitrust Act of 1890 by conspiring to restrain trade.

By ignoring the public response to its corporate activities, Standard's former strengths of size and market dominance quickly became liabilities. The main case against the oil company was proven in court in 1909 and Standard appealed to the US Supreme Court. The entire US business community waited anxiously for the final appeal in May 1911, which went against America's largest corporate enterprise. Standard was given just six months to dissolve itself. The break-up of the company meant the creation of seven new competing parts – the largest of which was the former holding company, Standard Oil of New Jersey (later Exxon). John Archbold, who succeeded Rockefeller in 1897, could only comment to his shell-shocked directors: *'Life's just one damn thing after another.'*

Given the dissolution of the company the book – the only detailed, comprehensive and surviving record of the company during its heyday – has assumed an even greater importance to posterity. It is arguable that it actually triggered the Rockefeller legend.

Eighty-six years after its publication, one of the new generation of business historians, Harvard's Alfred Chandler, was using Standard Oil's competitive example to illustrate how – through a logic he christened *'managerial enterprise'* – Germany became the most powerful industrial nation in Europe before the Second World War, the US became the most productive country of the world for forty years until the 1960s and Japan their most successful competitor since. In 1977 Chandler won a Pulitzer Prize for his 1977 book entitled *The Visible Hand*, the study of managerial capitalism based on the history of US, British and German businesses in modern times.

Since those pioneering days nearly a century ago, the corporate history has developed in fits and starts. Thousands of companies across the industrialized world have put their stories to paper, albeit in their own unique way. The US has been particularly prolific, with the UK, as has been shown, always a hesitant patron. Latterly, the main output comes from Germany and, more recently, from Japan.

In Germany, where business in Europe had seeded its own political genre through the likes of Marx and Weber, relatively few corporate histories were produced before the First World War. One of the earliest full-scale corporate histories was that by an academic for the Siemens company in 1906. It was written by Richard Ehrenberg, Professor of Economics at Rostock University, who is attributed with an influential role in promoting business history at the Harvard Business School.

At about this time, work was starting on another corporate history, that for the giant Krupp steel group, which was published to coincide with its centenary in 1912. By the mid-1920s several hundred corporate histories had been written and published, at which point they began to acquire an academic application.

In 1934 academics such as Walter Dabritz, who was awarded his professorship on the basis of his work on business history, were producing dozens of corporate histories. Dabritz himself wrote histories of the Bochumer Verein steel group, the Disconto-Gesellschaft bank, and the engineering firms of Hanomag and Ludwig Loewe. Another corporate history that was written at about this time was that of the giant AEG electrical group. Scheduled for publication in April 1933, it was suddenly withdrawn from the press. Adolf Hitler had come to power and the portrayal of the exceptional managerial qualities of Emil Rathenau, the company's Jewish founder, was not considered appropriate. The manuscript was eventually published in 1956. While the AEG story had to wait more than twenty years, the account of the Berlin Electricity Supply Company, an early subsidiary of AEG, was published in time for the company's fiftieth anniversary in 1934 since it had been written without mentioning Rathenau too often.

 More recently, literally hundreds of German companies have published their histories, among them Continental Aktiengellschaft in 1971 and, later, BMW, Adam Opel, Daimler-Benz, Goetze,

Europe's largest piston ring manufacturer, Flachglas, whose history as a glassmaker goes back 500 years, the sugar company Suddeutschen Zucker AG and Hamburg traders C. Woermann.

In the UK, one the earliest corporate histories predates the 1902 Standard Oil biography by sixteen years when an author called Charles Hindley wrote the history of the Catnach Press, a hefty illustrated text published under the company's own imprint. In 1889 came histories of the Hawick Co-operative Store Company and Tillicoultry Co-operative Store Coy Ltd followed, in 1891, by a short history of the Hand-in-Hand Fire and Life Assurance Society. The Leeds Industrial Co-operative Society came up with a jubilee history in 1897, the same year the Norwich Union Fire Insurance Society published a short historical narrative of itself. A year later came one Alexander Bruce's account of *The Life of William Denny* of William Denny & Bros, the Dumbarton shipbuilders.

At the turn of the century it was the turn of Charles Cammell & Co., the iron and steel company, and the bankers Messrs Coutts & Co. In 1903 came the histories of bankers Smith, Payne and Smiths, the Halifax Permanent Benefit Building Society and the Amicable and Fraternal Society. Three years later *The Early History of the Old South Wales Iron Works* was published followed, twelve months later, by *The Lloyds of Birmingham: With some Account of the Founding of Lloyds Bank*, written by a member of the founding family, Samuel Lloyd. In 1907 one H. E. Maxwell, who had already acquired some writing experience as a biographer of a prominent politician of the day, produced a fifty-year history of the whisky distillers W. A. Gilbey. Seven years later he turned his hand to the *Annals of the Scottish Widows' Fund Life Assurance Society*. In 1909, another Maxwell, William, did a history of Edinburgh's St Cuthbert's Co-operative Association, one of a number of similar books at the time on other members of the co-operative movement.

Perhaps the earliest history of one of Britain's oldest companies appeared in 1912 when A. M. Broadley penned a 182-page history of Garrard's subtitled *Crown Jewellers and Goldsmiths during Six Reigns and in Three Centuries*. With most companies timing histories to coincide with important anniversaries, Garrard's – curiously – published theirs nine years short of its 300th anniversary. By then, the concept had become reasonably well established, with many being written by businessmen, either the founder himself, members of the surviving family owners or long-serving employees. Rather than being chronological histories in the modern manner, many of them would turn out as diary-type personal recollections. They would be characteristics that would continue down the years.

With a few notable exceptions, they remained mainly short, superficial public relations exercises. Acadamic involvement in UK corporate histories probably started in 1924 when Professor George Unwin and co-author George Taylor published a detailed history of *Samuel Oldknow and the Arkwrights: The Industrial Revolution at Stockport and Marple*. Published by the Manchester University Press, it is thought to be the first British academic corporate history. Then, in 1938, the Bank of England commissioned a two-volume 250-year anniversary history. Written by J. H. (later Sir John) Clapham, professor of economic history at Cambridge, it took six years to produce. It was a transparently celebratory vehicle for a famous British institution.

Between the world wars, the majority of business histories in the UK were house histories, consisting mainly of reminiscences and anecdotes. Only a tiny handful of serious works existed using business records which had found their way into museums, county record offices or the private possession of collectors.

The reason for their existence was usually accidental. The records were often discovered by chance and deemed interesting enough to turn into historical narratives which were funded either by the family descendants of the long-dead businessmen in question or, less frequently, the author in association with a publisher. They had one thing in common – they were generally records of companies that had died or otherwise dropped out of sight.

Up to then, the history of business had generally been sourced through public records. This started to change in 1932 when the British Records Association was formed to champion the cause for saving historical records. Two years later a group of academic historians, led by G. N. (later Sir George) Clark, the newly appointed professor of economic history at Oxford University, and Professor Eileen Power of the London School of Economics, formed a pressure group to lobby against the destruction of business records. Inaugurated in 1934 as the Council for the Preservation of Business Archives with support from eminent bankers, the Master of the Rolls and Sir William Beveridge, then director of the London School of Economics, and a former (and future) prime minister, Stanley Baldwin, it survives today as the Business Archives Council, whose success in encouraging companies to preserve and use their archives constructively remains trifling, in spite of some heroic efforts down the years.

Then came the Second World War. Although there was residual interest in the concept of recording business history on behalf of some businesses, the numbers of companies putting their stories to paper fell away sharply as the country took on a more urgent priority. Even after the war was won, it was some time before some companies resumed an interest in preserving their OM.

As the dust was settling, modern corporate history took its first big conceptual step when, by chance, a hitherto unknown young academic was given the chance of becoming the corporate historian of one of the world's largest manufacturing companies based in the UK. Typically, the opportunity resulted from the personal patronage of a company director who had a casual interest in the value of company history. It was in 1947 that the then chairman of Unilever, Geoffrey Heyworth (later Lord Heyworth), approached G. N. Clark, who had led the national campaign against the destruction of business records, for his advice on writing the history of the Anglo-Dutch manufacturing company. Clark, who had just become a professor of modern history at Oxford, suggested as author a younger colleague, Charles Wilson. The result was a classic, two-volume work that transformed the writing of business history in the UK from a public relations exercise into a reputable branch of scholarship. His authorship of this trail-blazing account of one of Western Europe's most important companies confirmed him as the father of modern corporate histories in the UK.

Corporate history quickly took another leap forward with the arrival on the scene of William (Bill) Reader, who qualifies as perhaps the most celebrated of modern corporate historians in the UK. Combining a recorder's skill with a readable style and a corresponding integrity, his achievements were particularly noteworthy given his non-academic status in a world where the only serious approach to a product was seen as the scholastic one. A history graduate turned advertising/public relations man, Reader was born in 1920, graduated from Jesus College, Cambridge, and after serving in India and Burma during the Second World War, returned to Cambridge to become research assistant to Charles Wilson, who was just embarking on his history for Unilever. After two years he took a job with Unilever's advertising company, Lintas, where he learned the realities of business life. He progressed to writing speeches for Unilever's chairman and started writing company histories on his own account when Unilever asked him to write about the early years of Bird's Eye, its frozen foods business. Thereafter followed a career of writing corporate histories, none of which were ever used imaginatively. He died in 1990 whilst writing a new history of Unilever.

It is against this background that company history has evolved from the private pennings of Victorian industrialists. Although many of the examples mentioned above refer to the more serious attempts at documenting corporate history, the majority of books that continue to be written are still 'PR' projects expressly designed to celebrate important anniversaries. A loosely-based percentage estimate would probably expose a 85:15 bias that would probably be not too dissimilar to equivalent projects in the US and Germany, with the main difference being their utility and the extent of their distribution. Among the most popular formats remain poorly researched glossy coffee table picture books and other 'PR' formats that give little pretence as a repository of OM.

With 'PR' histories representing the vast majority of all corporate histories and many of the more serious examples falling on deaf ears, it is clear that the story of business is not being efficiently passed to successive generations of workers. What is also clear is that the treatments are also restraining the other, wider application of OM – business history, which is the more general historical study of the subject that Sir Arthur Knight, a quarter of a century before, thought was as important to the education and training of businessmen as was the study of political history to future statesmen or military history to future generals. What business history that is produced in the UK generally has to be assembled without the benefit of suitable company histories and company records, circumstances that have led the UK's *Business History* journal having to define business history as the *'more general historical study of the subject which may or may not include the investigation of numbers of company histories and their records'*. Without a sound substructure of business history, this also affects the quality of the more universal-based economic history, which is the main form of history related to business that is utilized in Britain's education system.

References

1. F. Goodall, *A Bibliography of British Business Histories*, Gower, Aldershot. 1997.
2. *Business Archives*, November 1991.
3. Pencorp research study. 1994.
4. *German Yearbook on Business History*. 1988.
5. Correspondence with Author. 1994.

CHAPTER TEN

Education, education, education!
(after the British Labour Party's 1997 election manifesto)

While corporate history is the memoir of individual companies, business history is the more general historical study of the subject that composites the scrutiny of single enterprises into a wider sectoral, industry or other context. Drawing as they do on the evolution of existent business behaviour and policies, they are a highly practical way of demonstrating the exemplar of business in a graphic, informative and substantive manner.

Yet both are notable for their widespread absence in the education systems of many countries, including the UK, where the subjects are also non-existent at most business schools. Instead, 'history'-related business education is largely confined to economic history and the use of so-called 'case studies'. The former is the evolutionary study of fiscal practice as it affects national and international economies, a largely theoretical discipline that is unconnected with the intimate nature of running a real business. The latter are usually summarized snapshot examples that are used to explain the workings of some functional management discipline. Thus, for example, an aspect of a car manufacturing company's sales strategy in the 1970s might be used to illustrate the elements of a modern marketing course. Although more relevant than economic history to how businesses are actually run, they are almost always subject-specific and, as such, disaggregate their inter-relationship with other management factors and influences. In fact, neither economic history nor the use of 'case studies' provide the nation's future business executives with anything other than a conceptual and/or narrow awareness of their corporate past.

Extending Sir Arthur Knight's military analogy, related in Chapter Eight, the position would be the equivalent of not making available within the curriculum subjects like the history of architecture, music history, art history, social history and political history. Universities also offer subjects like the history of decorative arts, the history of photography and the history of film, even, in the UK, the history of popular culture. If these subjects are considered useful in further education and the instruction of other types of professionals, why should corporate history and business history not be equally relevant to the training of business executives?

My observation should not be interpreted as suggesting that economic history or 'case studies' are irrelevant to business training. Or that their employment should be curtailed. Just that corporate and business history, because they are predicated on individual example and provide a wider, more representative context of the craft of business, are – when done well – substantively more relevant to how the nation's future business executives are taught. Also that conventional management training and business history have for too long been disassociated with each other.

The justification for this is that business education, whether in the UK or almost everywhere else, tends to compartmentalize its studies into separate disciplinary boxes. Most management disciplines also deal mainly with the short run and – like techniques such as calculating market share and gearing ratios – are generally taught in theoretical terms. In general, this approach disassembles management functions, restrains the perception of inter-relationships between subjects and means that analysis is often far removed from the real world. Given the present rapid rate of change in day-to-day business, future managers need to be made aware of how long-term changes have affected enterprises and how previous managements have coped with both success and failure. Good business history is multi-disciplinary, is concerned with the dynamics of long-term change and allows more practical contextualization. Because corporate history and business history is driven by actual examples, their study gives aspiring entrepreneurs a more practical orientation to the real world of business than the empirical instruction they otherwise receive. They are, in effect, a simulation exercise for real life.

The use that was made of the biography that Bill Reader wrote for ICI is instructive. Written by one of Britain's most skilled corporate historians, it is an account of one of the UK's most important companies. The book itself is acknowledged as one of the best researched of all the British corporate histories written in the modern manner. In Volume Two, which was published in 1975, a chapter called *Dictatorship in the '30s, Barons Revolt* carries a classic account of insider dealing in the 1930s of how individuals speculated massively against the company. Dr Richard Davenport-Hines, one of the UK's small band of academic business historians and a former editor of the journal *Business History*, comments[1]: *'Nobody's ever cited it as an event ever since. No one knows about it because few have ever read the book. They can't have done because the documentation in the story that Reader got through is stunning.'*

This conspicuous lack of utility – both as a corporate history and its applied use in wider business history – sits uncomfortably with Reader's motive for doing the ICI book in the first place. In his Preface, the author said great corporations were bound to be the subject of public concern and controversy. *'Controversy ought to be founded on fact, and on historical fact not least, for otherwise all manner of mythology, folklore and prejudice will gain currency and respectability.'* Anything that helps to dispel these mental mists or helps to remove the excuse for being misled by them *'must be a contribution worth making to the understanding of industrial society'*, he added.

The fact that ICI's exemplar falls on deaf ears is not untypical of the other relatively few British corporate histories, whether written by academics or other professional historians. With minimal print runs, and few reprints, the majority languish unopened in company libraries and on university bookshelves, and few make it as source material for the wider-based business history that is produced. The result is a genre that is under-developed as a management discipline and under-exploited as an educational tool. By default, it also limits the selection of examples that educators would more conventionally use as case study material to illustrate their abstract instruction.

While the reasons are discussed more fully in Chapter Eleven, the UK's involvement in business history has, over the years, been hesitant, rare and championed by only a small band of academics and an almost invisible number of industrialists and politicians. Although some British business historians have achieved a measure of prominence by the nature of the UK's position as the world's oldest industrial nation, evidence of the genre's lack of utility is obvious.

There are just five professors of business history in the UK within a core community of around forty academics working on the subject. This compares with around 400 in the US and a similar number in Japan, where interest in the genre was triggered as late as the early 1970s when an academic, Professor Yoshitaro Wakimura, persuaded the country's Ministry of Education that every faculty of business and commerce should have its own business historian. By 1981 more than a third of their research and applied teaching was concerned with foreign countries[2]. Japan's Emperor is said to have a keen interest in business history.

In Germany, academic interest in the history of business goes back to the second half of the nineteenth century through the work of Karl Marx, Jurgen Kocka and Max Weber, which was followed up by a historical school of political economy that made business history an integral part of economics. This was helped by a number of monographs of the history of enterprise on which people like J. Riesser developed studies on Germany's banking relationships with big business, H. G. Hetman's study of the steel industry and the work of Otto Jeidels and Robert Leifmann on cartels. Business history, in fact, won an academic reputation in German universities for the first time in the late 1920s when Walter Dabritz became the first professor at a German university to write exclusively on business history. Among his most famous works were studies of Bochumer Verein, Krupp's closest rival in high-grade steel, the bankers Disconto-Gesellschaft and Hanomag, the engineering company. Political and social historians started to incorporate business history into their studies in the late 1960s. Since then, business history in Germany has broadly followed the American exemplar, which has been widely accepted as the academic standard. Where it differs is in a concentration of non-management topics from a wide range of scholars from the social sciences and a long-standing interest in the older literature rooted in other schools of economic thought. In common with the US and the UK, economists have largely kept themselves apart from business historians, approaching business history via regional studies or the history of finance. In general, the genre is still a sub-discipline of social, economic or political history, which continues to determine its research objectives and methodology.

Britain's low number of business history appointees to academic posts has a spin-off in the amount of business history research that emanates from academia. Including the output of the London School of Economic's Business History Unit – England's flagship business history institution – the volume of academic research into business topics is small and education sources report[3] a decline in interest in business history subject matter among higher-degree students.

Its weakness as a subject in the educational system is demonstrated by an examination of an extensive bibliography – twenty-seven pages in length – in a recent major text on modern British economic history. In the second volume of *The Economic History of Britain since 1700* covering the century to the 1970s, there is included just five business histories, two biographies of businessmen, two articles from the British journal *Business History* and four from the American *Business History Review*.

Elsewhere, corporate history and business history on any topic rarely appears on any British business student's reading list – undergraduate or post-graduate. This disinterest in the genre can be gauged by a field study[4] of the nominated corporate and business history literature available for use in academic institutions in the US and the UK. A reading list prepared recently for PhD students taking a minor field in business and economic history at the University of Illinois at Chicago contained around 260 proposed titles[5] compared with around fifteen equivalent texts for business students at Glasgow University, one of just four major British universities that had lists with *any* corporate or business history content for their business students.

Applied teaching of business history is also uncommon, with the subject tending to being taught within economic history and as modules within wider programmes rather than as dedicated programmes at business schools where its employment would – presumably – be more appropriate. Research[6] by the Association of Business Historians (ABH) in 1993 found that just 1,700 students were exposed to the subject in any way. While ABH's figures are not specific, it would not be too speculative to infer that more non-business students than business students in the UK entertained the subject[7]. The example of Manchester Polytechnic, renamed Manchester University, which was the first educational institution in the UK to introduce business history in the 1950s, is a further illustration of the subject's lack of penetration; in a twenty-year period to 1990, no more than 350 of its students[8] were exposed to business history. ABH's study also gave an indicated of the distribution of business history's employment across the nation's 300 universities, among which are more than 100 business schools.

The subject is still absent from the curricula of both London and Manchester Business Schools, whose attitude towards business history has been uncommonly hostile ever since an experiment to introduce it into the LBS through an externally funded research fellowship failed in 1984. Even with an encouraging increase of a third in the number of business history courses introduced since the beginning of the academic year 1990, courses in business history were offered at just twenty British universities and another eleven educational institutions in 1992/3, with student recruitment coming from diverse backgrounds. The ABH reported that while business history courses appeared as an option on a range of economics, social sciences and business studies final degree schemes, the subject was rarely offered in history and MBA degrees. At the undergraduate level a business history course was offered exclusively at only one university; also, just one university offered a business history course in an MBA programme. In a new departure, Cambridge ran two-part business history courses at undergraduate level for fifty students while Oxford ran a part business history course for undergraduates and a business history course for seven graduates on a MSc/MPhil in Economic and Social History. Interestingly, the study found that a high proportion of PhD students in business history were of non-UK origin.

This compares with the US, where more business history is researched, published and taught than anywhere else in the world. Pioneered at the Harvard Business School, where the well-known preoccupation with the practical study of change has focused at least seven generations of its academics on putting business in its historical context, the subject has been one of the most popular electives by business students for a decade at least and is about to become a compulsory component of all first-year teaching. Alongside the work being done by other schools and institutions across the US – such as Ohio State University and The Center for the History of Business, Technology, and Society at the Hagley Museum and Library in

Wilmington, Delaware – the subject is considered important enough to be a separate functional division of America's Academy of Management.

In terms of the genre being developed as a valid educational tool, whole careers – both at Harvard and elsewhere – have been built on researching, writing books, teaching and finding industrial applications for business history research. Among them has been the Harvard economist Alfred Chandler who, in the 1950s, started to use a more systematic and analytical approach which evolved from an intellectual outlook which he labelled 'managerial enterprise', a concept that he explained as moving in two directions – forward from the past to the present and backward from the present to the past. Using the former perspective, he examined why early nineteenth century industry did not employ any managers, a phenomenon which changed decisively and forever in the second half of the nineteenth century. Using the latter perspective, he questioned the 1950s moves by industry towards decentralization of their functionally specialized and multi-departmentalized organizations. His answers – in a landmark book entitled *Strategy and Structure* published in 1962 – took the genre of business history into a new dimension by establishing a fresh framework and rationale for the subject. In particular he introduced the feature of making comparisons within and between industries and over time, and enabled business history to acquire relevance in a wide range of related fields. He revolutionized the business history discipline by refocusing attention away from individual entrepreneurs and seeking patterns in the rise of large-scale modern business.

Chandler, who would become professor of business history at Harvard Business School, won a Pulitzer Prize for his 1977 book entitled *The Visible Hand*, the study of managerial capitalism based on the history of US, British and German businesses in modern times. His other works – including earlier titles such as *The Beginnings of Big Business in American Industry* in 1959 and *Strategy and Structure* in 1962 and the later *The Coming of Managerial Capitalism* with Richard Tedlow – are routinely used in at least thirty higher educational establishments in the US and many more abroad.

While Chandler's work has strongly influenced Japanese, German and other business historians, his efforts have had little impact in the UK. Among the few British business historians to make use of some of Chandler's ideas has been the LSE's Professor Leslie Hannah in a 1976 analysis of merger activity in the twentieth century and described by some of his colleagues as a 'proxy for a proper textbook on twentieth-century British business history'. Elsewhere, Bernard Alford's work in the tobacco industry represented an isolated example of business history's more progressive development. He followed up a 1973 study of W. D. & H. O. Wills in the context of the UK tobacco industry from the eighteenth to the twentieth centuries with a more expansive work in 1977 on *Penny Cigarettes, Oligopoly and Entrepreneurship in the UK tobacco industry in the Late 19th Century*. Taking the concept a stage further he used several company histories in a study of the impact of the First World War on British business. In frustration, and by way of encouraging progress to a higher plane, the British journal *Business History* commissioned six corporate historians to write on a variety of themes to explore Bernard Alford's conclusions through a basket of their own corporate histories. The companies selected were ICI, Courtaulds, Bowater, Pilkington, Colvilles, Harland & Wolff, Kendricks, British Rail, the National Coal Board, W. D. & H. O. Wills, WH Smith and the Midland Bank. The editors of the resulting work, published in a slim volume, lamented that there was still no general introductory text on British business history in the twentieth century. *Business History* said the collection of essays was an attempt to explore major themes in the business history of Britain between 1914 and the 1980s in the hope that the result would assist students looking for general interpretative studies of this era and pave the way towards a fully fledged textbook. It added that much research remained to be done on Britain's business history.

Despite these trailblazing efforts, however. *Business History* was still complaining in 1990 that British business history research projects had few links, not even to the point of using the Chandler model as a standard point of reference. In addition, most projects '*lacked a solid or explicitly stated methodology*'. By way of an explanation, it suggested that the British resistance to Chandlerianism stemmed from an excessive attachment to empirical teaching methods, innate conservatism and '*an insularity of mind which breeds hostility towards innovative ideas originating abroad*'.

Since Chandler's innovative work, business history has further flourished in the US, with the US journal *Business History Review* reporting in 1987 that an explosion of business school enrolments on American campuses had led to a revival of interest in American business history.

Using business history as a teaching tool in the US is even extended to using films. Some educators have used a documentary produced by Forbes Inc., publisher of *Forbes Magazine*, called *Some Call it Greed*, an overview of capitalism in the early twentieth century while the Columbia College in Missouri, a liberal arts college, uses film biographies of Andrew Carnegie, John D. Rockefeller and Henry Ford as well as documentaries on the Sears and Roebuck catalogue and various US railroads produced by the Public Broadcasting Service and the Arts and Entertainment Network: even an independent film called *Roger and Me*, a documentary released in the late 1980s that humorously explores the relationship between General Motors and Flint, Michigan, at a time of corporate downsizing and restructuring. Elsewhere, the Brookings Institution has used several commercial movies, among them the 1940s *The Grapes of Wrath* and *The More the Merrier* as depictions of businessmen as 'robber barons' and the interaction of business and government.

> *One university – Ohio State – is even using the Internet. In 1997 it used a World Wide Web exercise to teach a course that included business history[9]. Of the books assigned in the course, the most popular with students was Harold Livesay's Andrew Carnegie and the Rise of Big Business. The tutor, Austin Kerr, advises that he used the Internet 'to have the students explore aspects of that subject, and of industrialism more generally, on the lives of Americans during 'the gilded age and progressive era'. Although my web exercises are a crude first effort on my part, the students responded favorably. As time and energy allow, I hope to refine these exercises and develop new ones that present some key business history concepts in an interesting and (possibly) interactive way.'*

Further evidence of business history's perceived value is seen in the related science sector in the US, which is one of the more prolific industries at producing individual corporate histories. The broader-based history of science, which has been driven from these individual monographs, was acknowledged as an independent discipline in the 1920s. Since then, the history of science and technology has made significant strides in establishing itself in American academic life. Alongside the enormous number of US-produced books now available on the history of science, there are more than sixty American universities offering dedicated higher degrees in the history of science, technology and medicine. In addition, many colleges offer a concentration in history of science at the undergraduate level. As recently as the 1980s, the subject's importance was endorsed by Secretary of Education William Bennett's declaration that *'all students should study the history of science and technology,'* a sentiment echoed by his successor Lynne Cheney in a report on the role of humanities in American education.

More than seventy years after its importance was first recognized, the chemical industry claims there is a revival in interest in business history and in the history of science and technology that reflects its importance in understanding the subject. The History of Science Society, which promotes US teaching in the field, describes the history of science as a bridging discipline that involves exposing students to more than the technical skills and theories of the natural sciences. Its view is that scientific literacy is a necessity in a culture pervaded by scientific values and crucially dependent on the applications of scientific knowledge – *'one that students, parents, educators, and political leaders in the US all demand'*.

By way of contrast, British industry has been complaining for years that fewer and fewer students are considering science as their vocation or as a career. It is no coincidence – my view at least – that the corporate histories of science-related companies and the history of science, which might otherwise have provided motivational role models for successive generations of new entrants into the profession, is a curricular subject in less than a handful of British schools and universities.

> *A specific example of the effect of its oversight in the UK exists in the aluminium industry, where the sector's own trade body complains that educational institutions and industry are woefully ignorant about its uses, despite the non-ferrous metal having been around since the early 1800s. Little suitable product teaching material is generally available in the educational system. As a result it was felt necessary to embark on a £1 million European-wide programme to rectify what Brian Turner, president of the Aluminium Federation, described in 1993 as 'one of the most appalling educational failures of recent decades'. With the help of twenty-five universities, the industry's objective is to provide 150 hours of teaching material covering technology-transfer aspects of the metal. As it happens the employment of history-related material is conspicuously absent from the package of planned teaching material.*

With the British aluminium industry highlighting just one area of business history's educational neglect, it is instructional to trace the genre's origins which, like corporate history, goes back more than 100 years. Perhaps the earliest example, which was also an extraordinarily influential one at the time, was entitled *A History of Modern Banks of Issue* by Charles Conant, a former member of the Commission on International Exchange at the end of the nineteenth century. First published in 1896, it used the history of banking in countries like Italy, France, Germany, England, Scotland and Ireland to support the argument for America to modernize its monetary system. It was only twelve years earlier that the gold standard had been described as *'a conspiracy against the human race'*. Until then, the US, Russia, Austria-Hungary, Japan and Mexico had joined the gold standard but, as the author argued, if the US wanted to be more competitive it had to establish new principles to govern the issue and distribution of money.

In earlier editions, the author had already identified that financial and economic subjects promised to be one of the paramount issues of American politics for many years to come, in particular the emerging monetary systems that were addressing the increase in world trade. Using *'a summary of the experience of the world in banking,'* he explained how the great banks of the world were powerful factors in the monetary changes that had been accomplished in recent years. His hope was that his historical narrative would contribute *'to the diffusion of those sound views of banking whose adoption into law is essential for the economic progress of our country'*.

By the fifth edition in 1915, the US had finally adopted a comprehensive measure of centralized banking and note issue which, the author, noted, *'if wisely administered, will put her bankers in a position to compete on something like an equal plane with bankers of other countries ...'*. In all, six editions were published over a thirty-year period. The last, in 1927, brought the author's original narrative up to date with the addition of new historical material by another writer, Mr Conant having died a short time before.

His books were clearly ahead of their time, appearing as they did when popular journalism, which was taking an interest in the corrupt practices of politicians and businessmen, was the driving force in how industry was portrayed and perceived. As noted in Chapter Nine, the emphasis in the sensational press was on the immorality of individual business leaders, a portrait encouraged by Gustavuis Myers in his 1909 account of *The History of Great American Fortunes*, Matthew Josephson's *The Robber Barons* in 1934 and Miriam Beard's *A History of the Business Man*. They all presented images of avaricious men with few favourable attributes whose legacy was a vicious and immoral economic system. This only started to change when Joseph Schumpeter's *The Theory of Economic Development*, having been published in German in 1911, was translated into English in 1934. It described the businessman as a force for positive advancement. Schumpeter's view coincided with an awareness that the owner-managed firm was increasingly being replaced by impersonal stockholder ownership of larger-scale managerial enterprises and that new organizations were being created through mergers and acquisitions.

A decade before – in the early 1920s – had come the first involvement of American academics into the field of business history when Edwin Gay, a native American of English stock who had trained as an economic historian in Europe, principally in Germany, replaced William Ashley, a British scholar who had been appointed as the US – and Harvard's – first professor of economic history in 1892. Gay, who was the first dean of the Graduate School of Business Administration at Harvard Business School, had a passionate belief that research in economic history would provide an important foundation for both historical understanding and policy making. For much the same reasons, he believed that companies should not dispose of their archives and in the mid-1920s helped form the Business Historical Society Inc. to *'encourage and aid the study of business in all periods and in all countries'*. The society, which went on to publish *The Bulletin*, the forerunner of America's *Business History Review*, the academic voice of the new academic and literary discipline, found sponsors like Herbert Hoover, the then Secretary of Commerce, Gordon Selfridge, the US-born London department store owner, and Thomas Lamont of merchant bankers J. P. Morgan. Out of Harvard, its sister institution Columbia University and elsewhere came a succession of more appreciative biographies of businessmen and companies by authors such as Norman Gras, Henrietta Larson, Ralph Tidy, Robert Gordon, Adolf Berle and Gardiner Means. Among them, the historian Allan Nivens, who would later establish oral history as a tool for serious scholarship, would re-interpret the same robber barons to be constructive, daring and far-seeing *'industrial statesmen'*. Modelling Joseph Schumpeter's earlier thesis, his argument was that industrialists deserved credit for making the US a predominant economic power whose economy was to generate the highest standard of living in human history and enable the US to defend itself and its allies from the totalitarian assaults on freedom of the twentieth century.

Other historians would subsequently develop the argument whether these huge companies would inevitably create their own inefficiencies and question the economies of managing different kinds of activities under a single managerial structure, the most recent example of which was the multinational company, which came under scrutiny in the third quarter of the twentieth century. In their turn other authors would examine the nature of the business organization and the types of managerial structures.

Since these early days in the 1920s, business history in the US has been inextricably linked with the scholastic world as scholars discovered a new and rich source of material on which to exercise their intellect. Their interest was greeted not without welcome as companies that commissioned their own biographies reasoned, not unreasonably, that academic respectability would help to offset the political propaganda of the previous forty years. By way of observation, the same argument that characterized capitalism as exploiters of the working classes continued unabated in Britain well into the 1970s.

Following the 1920s interest in the subject in the US, a debate about the nature and purpose of business history did start in the UK. Some notable business monographs were also produced by some economic historians, among them works on the English cotton industry, iron and steel, coal, wool and the English copper and brass industries. But, in terms of the genre becoming established as an academic tool in its own right, it would be another thirty years before more practical measures would be taken.

It was in 1958 that an Anglo-American link, forged before the Second World War, burgeoned into the British equivalent of the US *Business History Review*. Called *Business History*, its creation came about through Professor Francis Hyde, who was Professor of Economics at Liverpool University. Twenty-seven years earlier Hyde had won a three-year Commonwealth

Fellowship and had chosen to do research into European investment in the US at the Graduate School of Business Administration at Harvard being run by Edwin Gay. When he arrived, the debate about corporate and business history was at its height. When he returned to England his commitment to the subject was assured. This matured over the next two decades through a series of academic appointments and after co-authoring *Blue Funnel: A History of Alfred Holt & Company*, he launched and edited *Business History*, the editorial offices of which would move from Liverpool to the London School of Economics in 1982.

As *Business History* started spreading the word, it presented *'serious business history'* as appealing to the businessman *'not only as something which can satisfy his curiosity about the past but also as an important public relations activity'*. Significantly, these early aspirations for the genre in the UK have not progressed in the way it has in the US, Germany and Japan.

Although Manchester Polytechnic did introduce an optional business history course to its economic students in 1958, very little else happened for the next fifteen years. Up to then, the country's main interest in the subject was centred in Scotland, where the University of Glasgow's Professor Peter Payne, later to become professor of economic history at the University of Aberdeen, had, since 1960, collected the business archives of defunct companies in the west of Scotland.

The first serious attempt to increase the educational establishment's interest in business history came in 1973 when a symposium was organized at Cranfield's School of Management to get business historians and other management educationalists to talk to each other on the subject. According to some of those who attended, the event was conspicuous for the underlying discomfort and outspoken friction between the two groupings. The business historians were worried that management educators sought historical data to test pet theories, that they did not appreciate their reservations about patterns, predestination and repeatability and the fact that they studied the past to understand it for its own sake rather than providing a blueprint for future action. Endorsing many of these fears, the management educators thought business history painted too broad a brush on too wide a canvas and failed to use relevant analytical tools to explain theories used.

At post-graduate level the conference failed to produce any business history courses in teaching, nor did it encourage any business historians to tailor their output to better suit the needs of the management educators. It *did* spin-off some interest at undergraduate level, however, with the subject of business history – usually widely defined – being introduced as part of history, economic history or economics courses at several polytechnics, notably the Ealing College of Higher Education, which became the second educational establishment to introduce a history element to its business course in 1966. This was followed in 1979 by Bristol Polytechnic, which introduced business history to its social science students.

Later that year came the creation of the Business History Unit at the London School of Economics. Until then, the country's few business historians, styling themselves as economic historians, had been located within broader departments in some British universities, colleges and polytechnics. The BHU was the first dedicated department with the objective of shifting the emphasis away from narrow-focus company history towards broader comparative studies. It was time, it said, to move on from company history to *'wider conceptual studies'*.

Ironically, its creation was the result of at least two unconnected events involving two of Britain's best-known corporate figures at the time. The first was Sir Arthur Knight's advice that the Courtauld's chairman had given to the vice-chancellor of Oxford University urging the need for a more multi-disciplinary approach to business education. The second event concerned Pilkington Brothers, where Professor Theo Barker, one of the doyens of British business history, was working on a commissioned book for the St Helens-based glassmaker on the company's revolutionary float glass process. When it was completed, the company's lawyers became extremely distressed about its possible implications *vis-à-vis* American antitrust laws. There were a number of important court cases pending where the company needed to defend its position worldwide on know-how issues. Pilkington's lawyers decided that the company could not have something like a book put in the public domain where every word and every date would be examined by other lawyers.

Somewhat embarrassed, Sir Alistair Pilkington, who personally invented the float glass process, went back to Professor Barker and offered to finance a solicitor to help him fight a case against the company. Barker refused and suggested that the book remain on ice until a more opportune time. As a *quid pro quo*, Sir Alistair asked Professor Barker what else the company might do. He replied that business history had generally been ignored in the UK. Would Pilkington help get the concept established on a formal academic footing? As a result Pilkington donated £15,000 and launched an appeal to other businessmen to set up the BHU at the London School of Economics, Sir Arthur Knight's support for the concept of its wider utilization being instrumental in its eventual creation. The sponsors hoped that the unit would eventually be subsumed into the university.

On the back of just £250,000 raised, the BHU was – coincidentally – formed just as Mrs Thatcher's government was elected to office with a vision of popular capitalism. As the interest in business history grew among some academics and a few of the larger companies, there were strong hopes[10] from Downing Street that it might make some contribution towards improving the quality of British management; even that it might, by example, further seed the efforts to cultivate the enterprise economy. At a more specific level perhaps, it was hoped it would make some inroads into conventional attitudes towards business, notably that a career in industry might make a more attractive option than the civil service – exactly the argument used by Sir Arthur Knight nearly thirty years before.

Later that year the newly formed BHU attempted to encourage the teaching of business history at a one-day conference on the subject. Like the earlier effort at Cranfield's School of Management, this, too, was largely a failure, with the delegates consisting mainly of the country's few fledgling business historians. Attendees remember the conference mostly preaching to the converted. With interest at post-graduate level almost non-existent, the next initiative was a top-level investigation into economic and business history teaching in the UK and the US. In 1980, the newly-appointed director of the BHU, Leslie Hannah, was despatched to the US by the SSRC's Economic and Social History Committee. His report, which highlighted a number of key differences between the UK and the US, suggested that if business history was to be adopted in UK business schools, the research undertaken would need to be modern, policy-orientated and theoretically based. To draw business historians into business schools, he recommended that the SSRC fund several post-doctoral fellowships to provide a model teaching post. The argument was that once the appointments proved themselves, the universities could take over the funding themselves – in exactly the same way as, it was hoped, the LSE would assume financial responsibility for the BHU. In 1982 the SSRC agreed to fund two such posts at Bath University of Technology and the London Business School, where appointments were eventually made in 1983 and 1984 respectively. Like the other initiatives to introduce more business history into management education, the outcome of the SSRC's – now renamed ESRC – fellowships was a failure. Neither post was made permanent and both incumbents left their posts.

Also, at the LSE's BHU, its pioneering efforts have had to contend with the government's financial strictures on all academic institutions, which has led to the withdrawal of promises of permanent funding. When the Unit ran short of funds in the late 1980s, Sir Alistair Pilkington, its original champion, personally injected a further £90,000 to keep it running. With its survival constantly in doubt, its output continues – both as a research and teaching body – to fall short of the vision of its industrial founders.

While the creation, in 1987, of the first permanently funded research centre within the University of Glasgow's Economic History Department under the directorship of Professor Tony Slaven livened up the prospects for the genre, business history's most extensive offering by the end of the decade was at Bristol Polytechnic where students reading for an MA in Historical

Studies could specialize in business history following a common course in historical theory and practice. Elsewhere, the University of Reading planned a new MA in International Business History that included a history-related course in 'entrepreneurism'.

Since then, business history's progress has depended almost entirely on the efforts of smaller academic institutions creating BHU-style clones. This has increased the amount of business history employed at institutions like the former polytechnics at Coventry, Bristol and Manchester and universities at Glasgow, Edinburgh, Reading, London's Royal Holloway, Brunel, Aston, Lancaster, East Anglia and the Cardiff Business School but, as the 1993 research study by the ABH showed, the subject's exposure across the student population is still very small.

Several business historians have at last produced some general textbooks on British business[11] while, for the first time, business history has been identified as a core management subject in the 1996 Research Assessment Exercise (RAE) with Reading University's top ranking of its submission by its revamped Centre for International Business History. *'This RAE development is important because if business schools see that business history research can deliver a high RAE ranking in management, they will begin to take it seriously'*, says Reading's Professor Geoffrey Jones. That British business history has, at last, registered with the academic establishment is encouraging. That it has taken so long confirms how unreceptive almost everyone has been to it for so long. Leaving it to the end of the last decade of the twentieth century has clearly wasted a lot of time when, as the next chapter shows, its exponents have been prescribing its employment for a goodly long time.

References

1. Interview with author, 1991.
2. *Business History* journal. 1981.
3. *BAC Newsletter,* June 1992.
4. Pencorp research, 1997.
5. H-Business posting on Internet, August 1997.
6. 1993 research study into business history teaching in the UK, Association of Business Historians.
7. Based on Department of Education statistics, which reveals that numbers of business students on the UK mainland totalled 28,853 in 1993.
8. University's own estimate given to author, 1994.
9. See http://www.history.ohio-state.edu/courses/hist563/default.htm
10. *Business History Newsletter.* 1986.
11. J. Wilson, *British Business History 1720-1994*, Manchester University Press, 1995, M. Kirby and M. Rose (eds), *Business Enterprise in Modern Britain*, Routledge, London, 1994 and G. Jones, *The Evolution of International Business*, Routledge, London. 1996.

CHAPTER ELEVEN

History provides experience cheaply

History as an instructional medium has been referred to almost as many times as there are philosophers, academics and writers. Philosophers have been particularly prolific on the subject. Cicero recognized its relevance back in 46 BC when he wrote that *'To be ignorant of what occurred before you were born is to remain always a child. For what is the worth of human life unless it is woven into the life of our ancestors by the records of history?'* At around the same time one Dionysius of Halicar-Nassus, who died at the then princely age of 32, said: *'History is philosophy drawn from examples.'*

For the seventeenth-century English philosopher, Francis Bacon, *'Histories makes men wise'* while the German Romanticist, Friedrich von Schlegel, wrote nearly two hundred years later that *'the historian is a prophet in reverse'*. In the same period the American politician Adlai Stevenson believed that mankind could chart its future clearly and wisely only when it knew the path that had led to the present. Abraham Lincoln's judgement[1] was that *'We cannot escape history'*, Winston Churchill's *'The further backward you can look, the further forward you can see'* and Mikhail Gorbachev's *'History decides the future.'* Even the youthful William Hague, the new leader of Britain's Conservative Party[2] has a view: *'In looking to the future, we have to be informed by the past.'* While their commentaries could arguably be described as a representative selection of views on experience's efficacy in the non-business world, it is instructive that few management educationalists and industrialists have equivalent sentiments about their own activities.

Except, perhaps, one of the most famous of all businessmen. In any discussion of the validity of history at a business level, the most quoted men on the subject is Henry Ford, the legendary American tycoon with history's own verdict of being the father of popular motoring. His much-publicized statement[3] that 'History is more or less bunk' is a convenient conversational rejection for the subject as a whole.

Ford's affirmation of experience's lack of authority, the defence of which took eight days of cross-examination in a successful court case for libel against the *Chicago Tribune* (which had described him as an *'anarchist'* and *'ignorant idealist'*) survives as one of the most often quoted aphorisms alongside the declaration that past models don't apply because circumstances/tools change. Between them, they are responsible for stopping dead in its tracks the application of more Organizational Memory than possibly anything else, despite the fact that the principle of history's utility is demonstrably evident in other areas of human endeavour. Although it is not practised much, it is accepted, for example, that the lessons of history in *other* disciplines can be applied to the business world, even the experiential examples of other businesses. But not – it seems – an organization's *own* hindsight. Then, the notion founders on the back of the widespread predisposition towards non-reflectivity.

As already attested, the principle of using the past as a learning tool is well established in a whole range of disciplines including, music, art, religion, architecture and politics, among others. In the armed forces, military history is an important element of education, the effectiveness of which can be clearly demonstrated in the 1991 Gulf War against Iraq. When General Norman Schwarzkopf, Commander-in-Chief, Allied Coalition Forces, was training as a soldier, one of the major components of his curriculum was military history. One of the wars he studied was the 218 BC battle waged by the Carthaginian military genius Hannibal, whose tactics defeated the Romans and set up his assault on the most powerful empire of the age. *'The first thing I ever learned in the study of military art was about the great captains – and the great captains start with people like Hannibal,'* he recalled[4] later. *'We went back and looked at manoeuvres used by the ancients to win battles and more importantly the fundamental principles of war that caused them to prevail. Those same principles that applied to the days of Hannibal apply today. I learned many things from the study of the battle of Cannae that I applied in Desert Storm,'* an admission that also rebuts the other anti-history argument that past models don't apply because circumstances or tools change; Hannibal's bows and arrows cannot be more dissimilar to the modern tools of war. Debriefings after campaigns – even after training exercises – are also standard procedure in the armed forces, as is the whole role of the military historian, whose job it is to document carefully the experiences of war.

> *In the Second World War, for example, US military strategists recognized that they and future generations of naval planners would have plenty to learn from their ensuing experiences. As a result, the American Navy recruited Harvard University's Samuel Elion Morison, a reserve naval officer and respected scholar of American maritime history, to document the war in the Pacific as it happened.*

The proposition is also evident in how the modern Labour Party in Britain formulated its policy on the Internet. The decision to invite private companies to set up a 'National Grid for Learning', providing high-quality services on the superhighway for schools and universities, was modelled on the way radio manufacturers clubbed together seventy-five years ago to create the organization that eventually became the BBC. It is now not unusual for government to learn from the experiences of other countries; among a string of examples, the British criminal justice system is experimenting with so-called 'Restorative Justice' schemes tried in Canada and New Zealand where young offenders meet their victims while traffic planners in London are cooperating with their Tokyo counterparts to share experiences and practices.

In the US, the Institute for Humanities in Management at Hartwick College has developed cases for classroom use from 100 great works of history and literature from Homer's *Iliad* to Winston Churchill's *The Gathering Storm*. More than 150 academic and corporate institutions currently use cases developed by the college. One of these, American Cyanamid, uses the material to reinforce the interpersonal skills of middle managers. The company says: *'History and literature broaden the perspective of managers and underscore the leadership issues that are important to them both today and as they progress to high-level positions in the future.'*

Elsewhere, James Utterbach of MIT's Sloan School of Management draws on extended industry studies to demonstrate technological innovation, many beginning in the nineteenth century. He says: *'The advantage of viewing change over broad sweeps of time is that you can gain understandings that are simply not available when you focus on contemporary developments. Viewing industries and the course of innovation over very long periods makes it possible to identify patterns of change that would otherwise be missed by standing too close to the subject.'* Among the lessons he draws[5] are how, with disturbing regularity, leading companies *'follow their core technologies into obsolence and obscurity'*, for example the near-lethal resistance of Goodyear and Firestone to Michelin's radial type technology in the 1970s.

When it comes to illustrating how other lessons are being applied from one industry to another, the newfound popularity of business history among high-tech executives in California is a good example. In 1992 the Corporation for National Research Initiatives (CNRI), a think-tank founded in 1986 by one of the new generation of IT whizkids to study how earlier technological revolutions might give pointers to how the Internet could develop, commissioned a historian to write three books about the origins of electricity, railroads and telephones. CNRI's creator, Robert Kahn, who co-invented TCP/IP, the Internet's basic communications protocol, then sent the books to many of the new technology's main innovators. *Fortune* magazine has reported[6] that they have become a cult hit among the lords of cybercapitalism, among them Netscape's Marc Andreessen, Microsoft's Nathan Myhrvoid and Sun Microsystems' Robert Bressler, who also encourages his colleagues to read the books.

'As the Internet begins to hook us all together, you look for precedents to help figure out what will happen next,' says Myhrvoid. *'The analogies with telephones or electricity are fairly strong'*, while Brian Arthur, an economist at the Sante Fe Institute in New Mexico, affirms that the rise of the railroads *'can tell us much about the net.'*

A rare example of a company wanting to learn from its own experiences is the American Telegraph and Telephone Company, which specifically commissioned a history of itself for management training and as a point of reference for other studies. The breakup of the Bell system in 1984 was an event which affected almost every consumer in the US. A major development in American economic policy, it even had an effect internationally. The breakup meant that, after a century, the Bell system, which provided local telephone service for most of the country, was divested from its AT&T parent. In effect the company, the backbone of the American telephone service, would no longer exist. As a result of a settlement of the government's antitrust suit against AT&T, no single company would be able to exercise the responsibility that AT&T had long held for most telecommunications in the US. The Fall of the Bell System *was written by Peter Temin, a professor of economics at the Massachusetts Institute of Technology. In common with most projects of this nature, the decision to record this historic event was the vision of one man, in this case the chairman of AT&T, Charles L. Brown. With a keen sense of history he thought that the best time to record the story was while the participants themselves could recall it.*

While these examples testify to the principle of history's learning potential, it remains true that business executives are still largely resistant to its attractions. In conversations[7] with two of Britain's most prominent academic business historians – Dr Terry Gourvitch of the London School of Economic's Business History Unit and Professor Geoffrey Jones of the University of Reading – not one senior or influential British business executives under the age of 65 could be named who would fall into the category of a sympathetic industrialist who understood the potential of business and corporate history as a live management tool. Young industrial exponents of the utility of history are non-existent, or at least invisible.

Alongside the likes of Sir Arthur Knight and Sir Peter Parker, whose views have been referred to in previous chapters, the genre's only industrial allies have been a small band of patriarchal businessmen like Sir Alistair Pilkington, the original sponsor of the LSE's BHU, who said[8] shortly before his death: *'To me it is profoundly important to look back and learn from the past. There's really no point in making the same mistakes over and over again.'* In not ruling out the possible connection between the disinterest in corporate history and lack of enterprise in the UK, he added: *'Lack of awareness must put us at a disadvantage.'* Elsewhere, Sir George Blunden, a former deputy Governor of the Bank of England, says[9]:

> *'I think it is very silly to run any business without having some knowledge of the lessons that can be learned from people having similar experiences in the past because events do repeat themselves, albeit in different forms. It's obviously wise not to make the same mistakes again. How stupid it is if you make the same mistakes when you haven't bothered to learn about those mistakes. Why reinvent the wheel? If you're looking long term you're very foolish not to look back.'*

Thereafter, the only champions are a marginally larger group of business academics whose long-standing and stalwart efforts to promote the genre through their work and media like *Business History* and The British Archives Council's publications have made little headway. Rarely is the subject discussed in educational or industry circles, the BHU's funding difficulties over its twenty-year life span illustrating the level of disinterest in the medium. This is in contrast to the US, Germany and Japan, where the subject thrives to a much greater extent both inside and outside the classroom, albeit at levels that local business historians would still like to see widened.

For the past sixty years at least, business history's leader has been the Harvard Business School, out of which a succession of innovators have influenced whole generations of academics at home and abroad. Their best-known modern business historian is Pulitzer Prize winner Professor Alfred Chandler, who said back in 1962 that *'any meaningful analysis of an organization today must be based on an accurate understanding of its history'*. His view[10] is that the value of teaching business histories in universities is to make MBA students and those in more advanced management courses aware of recent, as well as long-term, changes in functional activities such as production, marketing, research and development, finance, labour relations and the like; also in monitoring and co-ordinating the activities of the current operations of an enterprise as well as in locating resources for future production and distribution. *'Not only can the students learn something about the nature of the functions, but also the complexities of carrying out change,'* he says.

At his university – Harvard – where the concept comes into its own through the business school's preoccupation with the study of change, the attention given to history as a management tool can be illustrated by the comments of a group of academics and businessmen recorded in a 1986 issue of *Harvard Business Review*. Under the headline *'Why History Matters to*

Managers', the journal observed that if the quality of executives' judgement is to improve and if executives are to be able to draw with confidence and intelligence on the experience of others, they must first know how to read the lessons embedded in that experience.

Using the mechanism of a round-table discussion, Alonzo McDonald, a former president and vice-chairman of Bendix Corporation, a former managing director of McKinsey & Co. and, at the time, chairman of Avenir Group and counsel to the Dean at the Harvard Business School, disclosed that one of the first things he did when looking at a major problem was to try to define the context or environment in which to place the problem.

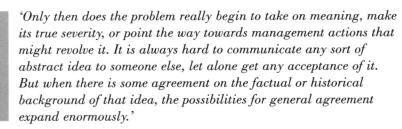

> *'Only then does the problem really begin to take on meaning, make its true severity, or point the way towards management actions that might revolve it. It is always hard to communicate any sort of abstract idea to someone else, let alone get any acceptance of it. But when there is some agreement on the factual or historical background of that idea, the possibilities for general agreement expand enormously.'*

Enlarging on his role as a management consultant, he said an underlying concept or vision was fundamental to all the major decisions that were made at the top of a corporation. *'One of the most important things a chief executive officer can say is: 'This is our philosophy, this is the general direction in which we are going, this is the perspective from which we need to view the issues before us at the moment. Having a historical concept supplies a solid reference point.'* He recalled a saying at McKinsey that they could export ways of thinking about a problem but they could not export solutions. In each case they had to go back to the thought process itself in order to come up with the appropriate solutions because each case took place in a different historical and cultural context and in a different environment.

> *'Now if you don't have this kind of idea or historical perspective, there is an enormous temptation to make a managerial mistake that could be financially traumatic – and to make it simply by using aspiration instead of reality in the decision framework. You just don't want to be in the position of going to your board and saying the situation you face is unique, has never confronted human beings before, and demand a course of action no one has ever tried. True, no two sets of circumstances are ever entirely identical, but often there is a general pattern which does repeat from setting to setting. …. in addition to the changes that are precipitated by external actions that come as a complete shock, there are plenty of changes that people with foresight can plan for and can accommodate. They are predictable.'*

McDonald drew the example of changes that come when an operation moved from a start-up phase into a growth posture and then into a mature business.

> *'We know within general limits what is required to manage at each of these stages, to run things appropriately within these levels. When you don't know any history, however, you are always surprised at what is demanded of you at each of these stages. Managers often do absolutely stupid things that they do not have to do and would not have done if they only understood more about the whole historical sequence.'*

In the same conversation Thomas McCraw, another Pulitzer Prize winner for his 1984 *Prophets of Regulation*, described history as a way of thinking – *'a way of searching for patterns and trying to see if such patterns recur from one situation to another'*. A professor of general management at Harvard Business School, he said: *'It helps us think about the parameters of what's possible, what the boundaries of likely action or possible success are. It is a search for pattern. History offers another way of thinking that helps teach people to accept ambiguity, to be comfortable with, and to reject formulas.'*

To Richard Tedlow, assistant professor in marketing at Harvard Business School and editor of the *Business History Review*, history is a way of getting *'things, events, and facts'* into shared memory. He believed that one of the most valuable things that could be learned from history *'was what you cannot learn from history. It's good to be reminded that there are no keys, no formulas. Just look at the number of people who drew perfectly reasonable conclusions from what had happened in the past but were terribly wrong.'*

From Germany, where corporate and business history is seen as a powerful way to communicate a corporate culture, comes advocates like Dr Dieter Lindenlaub, chief archivist at the Federal Bank Archives in Frankfurt, who believes[11] that history imparts a knowledge of how to act that can help target identification and the allocation of resources in a company. In a paper entitled *'What can the Businessman Learn from History, especially Business History'*[12], he wrote:

> *'We need theories to help us learn from the study of experience. Only then will we be in a position to say that if certain conditions prevail certain events (perhaps events that are desired) will occur. We can only learn from history if we can test theories against historical experience and then develop them further.'*

Lindenlaub, who has published widely on the history of engine building in the first half of the twentieth century and on German social history in the nineteenth century, acknowledged the arguments of some sceptics that each past event is unique and a complete break with the past, or that conditions change so fast that past experience can no longer be drawn upon. To them, he says that such doubters are probably limiting themselves to a comparison of the immediate past.

'History shows us how to absorb experience from periods before the immediate past .... who is so bold as to say that the greater uncertainty in the economy, which replaced the relatively stable growth phase of the post-war years, did not have a parallel in the 1920s, the 1870s or even certain phases of the sixteenth century.'

In the area of formulating business policy, Lindenlaub believes history is of two-fold importance. It first opened the way to general hypothesis on conditions for business success and to alternative courses of action with which companies may not be familiar; second, it lent greater psychological weight to the hypotheses. By giving concrete examples in support of hypotheses it strengthened confidence in their validity. He believes that if history is to help formulate business policy, companies have to be prepared to learn from more than the history of their own activities. *'History is largely a process of learning from others and for companies this means not blinding themselves to the activities of others.'*

Dieter Schneider, professor for controlling and business taxes at the Ruhruniversität Bochum, who has published widely on investment and finance and, particularly, on the *Theory of Uncertainty*, reinforces[12] this view, albeit with a nationalist perspective. In a paper entitled *'Management Mistakes'* [13], he said that many businessmen and too many academics believed that because management techniques had to be up to date, the best way was to translate the latest or most fashionable British or American literature on management methods. Their argument was that the older tradition that had been handed down through history would not stand up to competition; it was antiquated and should be forgotten. This attitude, he said, denies the value of history. Using the example of what is now known as the 'break-even' point – the quantity of output at which sales will for the first time cover total costs – Schneider maintained that a mining official in Dortmund made this precise calculation in 1822 – eighty years before the American engineer Henry Hess published his famous break-even charts which probably gave rise to the term.

In another example of what is now known as the method of critical values or sensitivity analysis, Schneider said that the concept had only become generally known through research over the previous twenty years. Through the study of history, however, a clear and precise account of the method could have been found in the writings of Johann von Thunen, a prominent German landowner in the nineteenth century. *'...why did we have to wait for it to be translated from English management literature?'* Schneider added:

'With rather more concern for the historical background basic business economics, planning, planning cost accounting and investment accounting could have been taught half a century earlier. If the current techniques of business management really mean anything in practice it is at least conceivable that some companies might have mastered the crisis in the early 1930s better had modern planning techniques and control instruments been available.'

Turning away from history did not help to make the science of management more up to date; it simply meant that many ideas of practical use were perceived centuries too late.

'Fashions are mistaken for new knowledge, although often this is only old wine in new bottles. Without a knowledge of history we do not recognize this. What business history can offer is examples from the great range of its experience and knowledge that will confirm or refute individual theories of business economics. In doing so it serves both the science of business economics and the practice of management.'

If history's precedent is accepted in others areas of endeavour – and by these industrialists and business academics – why is it so resisted as an experiential learning tool within companies and at business schools?

I have already outlined the reality and extent of corporate amnesia and industry's consequential poor capacity to learn effectively from its own experiences. That the phenomenon is not new can be related by the observations of Harvard's Robert Hayes, who thought[15] he had discovered something new when he noticed that business pundits seemed to be forever rediscovering the truths known to those who lived two generations earlier. He considered calling this his *'Hayes Law of Circular Progress'* until he discovered a similar proposition in an 1843 edition of *The Edinburgh Review*, which said: *'In the pure and physical sciences, each generation inherits the conquests made by its predecessors. But in the moral sciences, particularly the arts of administration, the ground never seems to be incontestably won.'* For the reasons, the answers revert to the management of OM, covering the attitude of companies towards their past, the attitude towards experiential learning of educationists, and management educators in particular, and the special nature of the medium in its main recorded format.

Companies have a curious relationship with their history, mostly paying lip service to its portent and treating it as something in which to be indulged only at important anniversaries, when it is often simply recorded as a sort of maraschino cherry to be popped on decoratively and sometimes rather smugly.

Most modern managers consider it to be an inert function of time's difficult passage, akin to their schoolroom learning of the dates of British kings and queens. They most often equate it with tradition and the belief that its reminder discourages the ability to change. This is reinforced by the perception that the current rate of change is always more rapid than any other period of history, the speed of which makes tracking unmanageable. Typically, the attitude is: *'History is about the past. We don't want to be reminded about what has already happened. We need to think about the future.'*

The view that past models are irrelevant is predicated on the belief that one man's success cannot be repeated in the context of others' circumstances. The operative word is always *'repeated'*, evidence of a belief – which is seemingly intractable – that history's example is immutable to the observer rather than being inherently organic. Coupled with this is an almost obsessive concern with short-term objectives, at least in the West. With mature markets giving internal expansion too slow a growth track, there is a consequent focus on acquisitions. Both as a predator or as a victim, the company's concentration is rarely on the longer view and definitely not on perceived 'finished business'.

In the UK this is underscored by another immutable characteristic that equates failure with disgrace and prosperity with embarrassment, an idiosyncrasy that has the effect of heightening sensitivities to everyday business occurrences like setbacks, downturns, mistakes and success. In effect, the reality of history's recall – whatever its nature – becomes discomforting. With an amplified self-consciousness, managers also think history's recall will undermine their belief in the necessity to reinforce the notion of executive infallibility. As a consequence the majority display a proprietary defensiveness about themselves and their colleagues with a deafening silence.

Spread across industry, this makes business curiously detached from its origins and evolution. Writing in *Business History* in 1985, Christopher Cook of the Central College of Design, observed: *'Business is notoriously unaware of the historical context in which it operates and certainly businessmen, unlike their political and diplomatic cousins, are remarkably unconcerned about keeping an eye on how the future may judge their past and present actions.'*

Any in-built resistance is not helped by the transformed nature of education and the attitudes of educationists, particularly management educators, towards experiential learning. They are reasons that an observer might readily recognize in other Western countries, albeit less aggressively deployed than in the UK.

Changed educational backgrounds, for example, have made modern managers much less history orientated. Terry Gourvitch, the director of the Business History Unit at the London School of Economics, explains[16]: *'Contemporary thinking has been that society's problems are best solved through technology, psychology-orientated procedures and the application of macro subjects like economics. The result has been a proliferation of the social sciences in higher education.'* The effect of this has been that there are fewer arts/history graduates among senior business leaders than there were forty years ago, with the not too unsurprising result that learning through historical precedent and association has been largely replaced with hi-tech approaches to management solutions.

Management education, too, has largely avoided the historical approach, preferring the more empirical methodologies dominated by macro-economics and quantitive analysis. John Armstrong, a former editor of the British Archive Council's journal *Business Archives* spells it out[17]:

> *'Current management education in the UK tends to compartmentalize its studies into separate disciplinary boxes. This inhibits the perception of interrelationships between subjects. On the other hand, business history is multi-disciplinary. Although it disaggregates to examine particular aspects of the business, it then puts these pieces back together to make an overall judgement. Top-level managers need to take the same approach.*
>
> *'Current management disciplines often deal with an idealized, sanitized world in which basic assumptions are made to facilitate the analysis. This means that some of the analysis is far removed from the real world. In contrast, business history deals only with what actually happened and so can show what assumptions are valid.*
>
> *'Many management disciplines deal mainly with the short run. Theories explaining long-term changes are fewer and less well developed. Business history is essentially interested in the dynamics of long-term change. It deals with how and why the firm has responded to long-run external trends and how its performance has carried over decades, not days. Given the present rapid rate of change, managers need to be made aware of how long-term changes have affected enterprises, how previous managements have coped and the penalties for failing to adapt.*
>
> *'Many management techniques are apparently clean, neat and objective, giving a numerical result to be acted upon – a gearing ratio, a market share, but in fact interpretation of such ratios requires careful contextualizing. They need to be put into the overall pattern of such results and the particular environment must be considered for any freak effects. Contextualization is another strength of business history. It explains how particular political, natural or economic circumstances which the individual firm cannot affect, impact upon it and the type of response that it*

provoked. There is the danger if too much stress is laid upon techniques and pure theory that the manager will not adopt these to the context of the real world. Business history will help to show the wider reality of business.'

Corporate and business history's neglect can also be explained by the traditional rivalry between economic and business historians, on the one hand, and the underlying antipathy between business historians and management educators on the other. With a much longer tenure to their discipline, economic historians have always felt threatened by business historians' incursions into what they see as their traditional territory. Life has not been made any easier by the fact that business historians have to exist within already-established economic departments with their own financial strictures over the past two to three decades. Alongside this, business historians have generally insisted on studying the past to understand it for its own sake rather than provide a blueprint for future action; management educators, for their part, believe business historians paint too broad a brush on too wide a canvas and that, for them at least, this approach does not provide corporate or business history with any utility.

This difference also masks an unresolved debate among business historians that goes back to the early 1930s when Edwin Gay, founder of the Business History Society at Harvard, started editing *The Bulletin* with one of his students, N. S. B. Gras, who became the first Strauss professor of business history at Harvard. Gay and other economic historians believed[18] that business should contribute to the view of economic history they were seeking to construct – that it was precisely because businesses were subjected to the discipline of the market that their records could provide insight into larger economic processes. Gras, on the other hand, believed that business behaviour should be studied for its own sake and that new generalizations would emerge from the case studies amassed by scholars doing highly focused research on the internal operations of particular enterprises. This difference of opinion ended their editorial co-operation and sparked a debate that has gone on ever since, in the US and elsewhere.

At a wider level the dismissal of business history as a teaching tool can also be explained by the British attitude to management education which can best be described as an 'ivory tower' approach. Corporate and business history is predicated on the production of individual monographs, which necessitates a close relationship with individual companies at the time of production. In contrast with the US, Germany and Japan, there has never been a real intellectual partnership between the academic world and the people who run industry, with many British universities, including business schools, uneasy about aligning academic and vocational aspirations.

This tension was observed by the Franks Report in the 1960s ahead of the setting up of the London and Manchester Business Schools. Thirty years later business is still not a respectable subject for academics and academia still has only an arm's-length relationship with industry. This independence is often jealously protected, a characteristic demonstrated in 1992 when the Manchester Business School's academics dissolved the governing council after disagreeing with the council's lay/industry appointees over a plan to model the school after management centres like Harvard or Stamford. The academics preferred that the school reinforce its traditional links with other departments rather than choose a more independent future where highly paid staff would be recruited from around the world to train Britain's next generation of managers and industrialists. One of those who resigned from the ruling council, Bill Jordan, president of the Amalgamated Engineers' and Electricians' Union, described the academics as *'short-sighted 'Teflon' dons. They sit cocooned from reality in their safe jobs paid for by the very industry they refuse to cooperate with.'*

Academic business historians, as well as their non-scholarly counterparts, must also take some of the blame. As the main progenitors of the medium, they have been singularly ineffectual at demonstrating the genre's endowment to their educational and industrial colleagues, particularly in the UK. Many British business historians have also not been particularly successful at maturing the genre in any purposeful way beyond its original conception – unlike their US, German and Japanese counterparts. As distinct from other areas of historical activity, there is also a strong academic elitism that manifests itself dismissively of the non-scholarly author, the common attitude being that if corporate history is not done in a donnish fashion, it must lack integrity or rigour. The evidence for this antiquarian pedantry is that few – if any – non-academic corporate histories are ever used as source material in the construction of wider-based business history, at least in the UK. A comparison of corporate and business history's appraisement by senior British academic business historians over a 25-year-period shows what little progress has been made.

At the first serious attempt to promote business history as an educational medium – at the symposium at Cranfield back in 1973 – Oxford University's Professor Peter Mathias, a president of the British Archives Council, berated business historians for approaching their job in a loose, empirical manner. Author of a broad-based 1967 history of multiple retailing in the food industry through a study of the Allied Suppliers Group and, later, works on the margarine and brewing industries, he said:

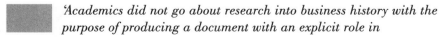 *'Academics did not go about research into business history with the purpose of producing a document with an explicit role in*

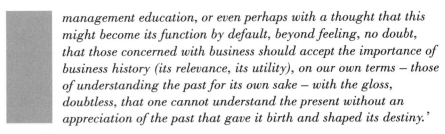

management education, or even perhaps with a thought that this might become its function by default, beyond feeling, no doubt, that those concerned with business should accept the importance of business history (its relevance, its utility), on our own terms – those of understanding the past for its own sake – with the gloss, doubtless, that one cannot understand the present without an appreciation of the past that gave it birth and shaped its destiny.'

His view was that if history did turn out sometimes to have an empirical usefulness, academics preferred to think that it came *'as a sort of bonus, an unearthed increment, from the proper motivation and the hard work of trying to understand the past for its own sake'*. The *'focus'* of the business historian and the management studies specialist looking for data were very different, he added. He suggested that the approach most likely to suit the purposes of management education was *'traditional business history turned inside out'*.

'The business corporation has proved the most influential institution of the twentieth century for shaping the destiny of western countries in times of peace. Most productive assets in western economies remain with business in the private sector: the instrumental decisions which shape economic change in these countries – decisions to invest and to adopt technological change – remain for the most part in the hands of business firms. Clearly the more historians can learn about the evolution of the business firm and business systems the better. And present problems cannot be understood without some historical dimension being applied to them.'

Fourteen years later – in 1987 – Professor Leslie Hannah, the then director of the LSE's Business History Unit, which had been specifically established to liberate the whole subject, bleakly described progress in systematic integrative work, going beyond company history towards comparative business history dealing with wider themes, as *'halting'*. Signs of progress in allying theory and applied research in the genre were not encouraging, he told fellow business historians, a verdict confirmed by Professor Donald Coleman, who said that while some work had served to widen the scope and treatment of the subject and some contributions had been very good and genuinely comparative, the range had been limited and the standards had varied considerably. *'I have seen little sign of really substantial comparative studies, taking specific business situations or problems and analysing the way they have been confronted or tackled over time in different sorts of companies.'* His censure[19] of academic-style corporate histories was equally blunt and uncompromising.

'*They are very largely unread by anyone except other business historians. Apart from the originating inspirer of a history, who will read it, members of the commissioning company will merely dip into it out of curiosity about past leaders of the firm; those to whom complimentary copies have been distributed will glance at the illustrations. In those very rare cases of histories dealing with very recent times former members of the firm who have left in less than harmonious circumstances will look to see if there are any possible grounds for a libel action.*

'*Few businessmen from companies other than the commissioning company will be in the least interested. Few professional economists, inside or outside of the university world, will pay any heed to them because the history of individual firms is not seen as helping the theory of the firm. Business schools will very largely ignore them in the teaching of the nation's future management.*'

Most orthodox political historians, he says, will not only deem such histories irrelevant but will doubt if such remunerated historical writing is quite proper as a form of scholarship. Referring to a description by a distinguished academic historian of business history as '*applied history*', he added: '*This view from the heights of orthodoxy is not made any the less jaundiced by the fact that business history has had to seek academic status against a prior background in which the writing of company histories was seen as a form of inferior journalistic hack-work. It was something done to supplement income otherwise got from more reputable literary activities.*'

While admitting[20] that he gave little thought to its potential educational value when he wrote the three-volume history of Courtaulds, his more recent judgement[21] is that there has only been some small progress in comparative business history in Britain, largely taking the form of collections of specially commissioned essays or articles, some of them appearing in the limited-circulation *Business History* and being subsequently reprinted in equally limited-circulation books. '*It remains true that Britain has not made much progress towards Leslie Hannah of the Business History Unit's call in 1983 for a systematic integrative work going beyond company history towards comparative business history dealing with wider themes.*'

As the above remarks show, the problem of corporate and business history's lack of impact are not entirely lost on some business historians. Aware that their efforts have, over the past thirty years, consistently fallen short of their potential, some have even been prepared publicly to venture the reasons. Among the most forthcoming is Reading University's Professor Geoffrey Jones, who believes companies don't understand how to use their history.

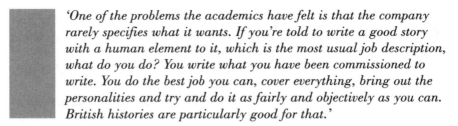

'One of the problems the academics have felt is that the company rarely specifies what it wants. If you're told to write a good story with a human element to it, which is the most usual job description, what do you do? You write what you have been commissioned to write. You do the best job you can, cover everything, bring out the personalities and try and do it as fairly and objectively as you can. British histories are particularly good for that.'

Author and editor of around a dozen corporate and business histories, a co-editor of the academic journal *Business History*, a trustee of the Business History Conference of the United States and one of the five full-time professors of business history in the UK, his general view of British corporate and business history is stingingly censorial[22].

'... there is no evidence that this torrent of scholarship is making any impact on anybody. Few, if any, company histories ever appear on economic history reading lists, and in any case, economic history is almost extinct in schools and is an endangered species in higher education. The companies which spend hundreds of thousands of pounds commissioning corporate history projects never utilize them for in-house management training. British business schools show no interest in business history ..... The overwhelming majority of people considering employment in business, and people already employed in business, are unlikely to have ever heard the term "business history" let alone had their behaviour changed by it.'

Referring specifically to why business history as a discipline has failed to make an impact, he admits that the *'nature of our product'* must take much of the blame.

'At the most basic level, many company histories are over-long and appallingly dull. Has anyone but a reviewer ever read a major company history from cover to cover? Business is as intellectually challenging and frustrating as other spheres of life, but business historians seem less able to convey this reality than, say, political historians. Economic historians – the main authors of academic business histories – seem to have lost the art of writing lucid and precise prose. Anthony's Sampson's books on the oil industry, banks and airlines are essentially business history; it is an indictment of academic business historians that while nobody reads their products, hundreds of thousands buy Sampson's books.'

Referring to the wider failure in business history, Professor Jones adds: *'Bookshelves sag under the weight of gargantuan business histories .... but no one uses this material to write the general interpretations which non-specialists might read. The LSE's Business History Unit was established to help liberate the subject from its narrow preoccupation with company case studies. Some thematic studies are now emerging from this source, but there is no sign of the general textbooks or popular works which might reach a wider audience.'*

He suggests that the impact of Professor Chandler's work in the US – and the fact that he is the only business historian regularly quoted in British books on management – shows what can be achieved.

'We still need more in-depth company histories and case studies, but it is time that business historians began to use the plentiful material that they have accumulated. I believe that British business can learn from the past, and that one – but not the only – function of business history is to help educate British management to perform more effectively than their predecessors. There is evidence, too, that economists and management theorists want and need the kind of empirical evidence generated by business historians. If business history is made accessible, readable and as intellectually challenging as the subject it describes, there will be no problem finding markets for its wares.'

Professor Coleman's earlier references to remunerated historical writing being seen as a *'not quite proper'* form of scholarship raises the other reason why the genre is so overlooked as a corporate repository of OM and as an educational tool. It concerns the way they are produced. Constructed from external sources alone – i.e. newspaper cuttings, public records, the recollections of retired employees and hearsay – it tells only half the story. For it to be roundly accurate, it needs the full input of the company's own archives and employees, access to which always requires the subject company's permission. Companies have a proprietorial attitude towards their own documentation and employees which invariably invokes an insistence that any interpretation of their history is subject to company veto, a position which immediately introduces the prospect of any construction being perceived as less than faithful.

This impediment to objectivity is further complicated by how they are typically funded. Because of the perceived small audience of most corporate histories, few independent institutions or publishers consider it cost-effective to invest on their own account the necessary resources to produce them. As a result, those corporate histories which see the light of day are invariably done at the behest of the subject company and – significantly – with their funding.

The effect of client subsidy is that most corporate histories – even those that are produced seriously and objectively by academics and other professional historians – are usually dismissed outright as being less than credible, a perception not helped by the first-hand association between historian and subject company, and the typically pretentious contractual relationship between the two.

The traditional direct relationship between historian and subject raises a raft of problems. It always holds, for example, the unspoken prospect for the author that the project will lead to future research contracts, consultancy and even directorships. It also puts overt pressure on authors to make changes that may subtly manifest itself in the author deciding to omit potentially controversial bits from their drafts submitted to the company. The contractual arrangements between the two parties are also usually no more than legal window dressing, their unique shape springing from traditional over-sensitivity, concerns that the disclosure of some information might be either price-sensitive or useful to a competitor, the insecurity of not knowing how the final product will turn out and the unspoken dread that the author will unearth some unwelcome skeletons. Given that we're funding it, they argue, is it not unreasonable that we should exercise some sort of control over the final product?

Their production is perverse in other respects, too. Examples of exotic author choices, for example, abound. The history of a top international trader was written by a former war correspondent and BBC commentator. The history of one of the oldest stockbrokers was written by an former MP who was also the golf correspondent of a major newspaper. The history of a well-known stockbroker was written by an academic whose speciality was railways. The author choice of the updated version of Professor Francis Hyde's Blue Funnel corporate history, which was published in 1986, was curiously contradictory; the company's explanation was that the chosen author was *'a historian with a strong feeling for the Far East and its mercantile history'*, yet in the text the author admits to not being a maritime historian and knowing scarcely more than the company's existence when he was commissioned.

In many cases the subject companies edit the final manuscript, insist on vesting copyright in themselves, even publish it themselves. By so doing they publicly attest that the documents – however well they might actually be done – are partisan, company productions. While there are fine examples of corporate histories that survive this gauntlet, this view is entirely justified in many cases and covers histories produced by both academic and other professional historians.

The list of company histories that have been affected in this way are long. In the recent history of a major financial services company, for example, the company insisted that the name of a director who

had been responsible for serious illegal acts – for which he was
prosecuted – be expunged from the manuscript. The author – a
well-known academic – eventually agreed after some difficult
discussions. As a result the text refers to the individual only as 'a
director'. By way of a private protest at the guileless attempt to
disguise the individual concerned, the author used the Index to
disclose the individual's name. Another example concerns the
history of one of the UK's biggest employers. At one stage in the
early 1970s the company's chief executive resigned after only a
short period in the job. The author – also a well-known academic –
devoted a page in the book listing the different reasons why he
might have resigned, all of which were disingenuous. The actual
reason, which was not mentioned, was that the individual had been
accused of a criminal act. Many other examples exist of authors
being pressured to make amendments because senior executives were
not mentioned sufficiently often or subsidiary companies were
portrayed in a less than efficient light. One of Britain's senior
academic business historians[23] who was familiar with many of the
projects undertaken in the 1980s asserts he knows of 'censorship in
every sort of book of this kind'.

Corporate history's lack of esteem is further reinforced by the attitudes of many of the publishers who are approached to print the books and place them alongside their listings of commercial titles. Usually they are pre-financed through a guaranteed print run paid for by the subject company, so the publishers do not generally have to take any commercial risks. In some cases companies try to recoup some of their investment on editorial expenses by selling copies, either directly or through their publisher. Often, the arrangements that are made allow the publisher to sell the book on their own account. Invariably, the publishers seem comfortable to print whatever their clients want them to without imposing the same professional editorial standards they would insist on for other, more commercial, titles.

Their decisions on cover price are a further inhibiting factor to wider readability, often deeming them not to be price sensitive. Typically, corporate histories published by the presses of academic institutions, for example, are cover-priced at upwards of £30, in several cases around £70 each, in spite of client funding. At this level few people can afford to read them – even if they were interested. In general, publishers find these arrangements lucrative enough not to have to devote the marketing resources that are given to more commercial books. The inevitable result is a minimal audience, an outcome illustrated by the average outside sale for all the company histories published by the Cambridge University Press during the 1980s[24] – just 700 copies per title.

All these arguments combine to produce the unavoidable conclusion that, thanks to the attitudes of industry and the academic establishment, the authors that write them and the publishers that print them, the typical treatment of corporate history largely serves to bury the messages of industry – to industry's substantial disadvantage.

While corporate history appears to be particularly predisposed to a cynical reception, it is instructive that the same response does not readily occur in other areas of client sponsorship in academia, architecture, art and entertainment, the BBC being – perhaps – the best example. In terms of its production, the genre is also little different from the product and services of external accountants/auditors and lawyers, who are also funded by the company and whose professional standing and perceived independence is miles ahead of the corporate historian.

Given that, done well, corporate history is still the most efficient repository of OM and, along with business history one of the most powerful educational tools than can both familiarize new entrants to the economy with the realities of business life and train the future generations of entrepreneurs, can the genre ever gain the authority it needs to become a legitimate corporate and educational tool? If it is professionalized, yes!

References

1. Annual Message to Congress, 1 December 1862, in R. P. Basler (ed.) *Collected Works*, (1953) Vol. 5, p. 537, 1953.
2. Closing speech, Tory Party conference, Blackpool, October 1997.
3. Interview with Charles Wheeler, *Chicago Tribune*, 25 May 1916.
4. BBC2 Timewatch programme, 'Hannibal and Desert Storm', 10 September 1996.
5. *Mastering the Dynamics of Innovation*, Harvard Business School Press, Cambridge, MA, 1994.
6. *Fortune* magazine, 3 March 1997.
7. Separate interviews with author, in 1992 and 1993.
8. Interview with author, 1992.
9. Interview with author, 1992.
10. Correspondence with author, 1982.
11. *German Yearbook on Business History*, 1984.
12. Ibid.
13. *German Yearbook on Business History*, 1985.
14. *German Yearbook on Business History*, 1996.
15. 'The Timeless Secrets of Industrial Success', classroom discussion paper, Professor Robert Hayes, Harvard Business School, 1984.
16. 1992 interview with author.
17. 'Business History and Management Education', *BAC's Journal*, Business Archives, 1988.
18. N.R. Lamoreaux, D. Raff, and P. Temin, 'New Economic Approaches to the Study of Business History', *Business and Economic History*, Vol. 26. No 1. 1997.
19. *Business History*, 1987.
20. Interview with author, 1991.
21. Interview with author, 1994.
22. *Business History Newsletter*, October 1986.
23. Interview with author, 1992, with individual who requested anonymity.
24. Pencorp research study, 1992.

CHAPTER TWELVE

Mending the Emperor's new clothes

If it is as powerful as its champions claim, how can corporate and business history become as important to the education and training of business executives as is the study of political history to future statesmen or military history to future generals? How might it, too, provide the necessary familiarization and motivation to influence those who have no conception of the reality of industrial life – and also profitably address many of the tenure- and experience-related problems that workplace discontinuity has imposed on Western industry in recent years?

What is needed is a fundamental reappraisal of the genre's utility as an educational and management development tool by industry, education and, because it controls the latter's policy and purse strings, government. Underlying this has to be a broader philosophical re-examination of the nature of history and its relationship with learning. Should it be taught as a sequence of dates of important milestones – the traditional approach – or as, as this book proposes, a vehicle to apply the knowledge of tried and tested experience?

If the proposition survives, a better accommodation must then be found between educationists, particularly business educationists, and business historians, as well as business historians and economic historians, with a view to improving constructively the quality, methodology and application of the genre in the classroom. American business historians, for example, are currently calling for a completely new relationship – what they call an *'interdisciplinary dialogue'* – with their counterparts in the economic history world[1]. In the journal *Business and Economic History*, three senior business historians suggest that despite their very different interests, the two groups have much to gain from the exchange of ideas.

'We are not calling for a hierarchical conception of scholarship that Gay attempted to impose on Gras during the 1930s – we do not see business historians as research assistants for economists who engage in a higher level of thinking. Although we hope that a by-product of this dialogue will be better modelling by economists, our main concern is that the work of individual business historians redound to the credit of the field of business history as a whole. The real benefit of recent theoretical developments in economics is that they enable business historians to recognize the essential unity that underlies a

great number of the problems with which they are concerned. As a result, studies on one topic can resonate with studies on others, strengthening them all and, in turn, the field as a whole.'

Thereafter, more and better research is needed into relevant business history topics with the prospect that its scholarship will also transfer into academia and the active business world. To ensure this, its teaching needs to be formalized – and actively promoted – in schools and universities, and especially business schools. In this, government and representative bodies within industry and education themselves have to be key players in helping to guide, direct and influence curricular policy.

But it is at industry level that most pace can probably be achieved. Simply, if commerce and industry demanded it and helped it on its way, academia and government should – theoretically at least – respond. For this to happen, companies have to rethink their attitudes towards being constructively reflective which, at root, involves ranking the management of Organizational Memory alongside the other corporate assets such as labour, capital and land. If it was important before, it is now doubly significant because of the flexible labour market whose main advantage – the ability to be discontinuous at will – is also its biggest handicap. This involves understanding that – in the words of Procter & Gamble's former Vice President J. G. Pleasants – no company can afford the luxury of having to rediscover its own experiences. Like it or not, the past affects all the decisions a company ever makes. Whatever happened cannot be changed. But it can – instead of being ignored – be used as a powerful learning tool in a variety of ways to help managers and other workers perform more effectively than their predecessors. Rather than being the change inhibitor it is traditionally perceived to be, it can – when skilfully managed – be transformed into a potent change *agent*.

Having accepted the principle of experiential learning and taken on board the precepts of Knowledge Management and the Learning Organization, the single other most effective move would be to support the professionalization of the most efficient and portable repository of OM – the corporate history, whose typical treatment to date has turned it into one of the most devalued of corporate tools. Rather than treating it as ornamental public relations to glorify the past, it needs to be transformed into a comprehensive, objective and communicable inventory of corporate experiences that can be used for other corporate applications. Using the domino theory, its metamorphosis into 'proper' history would then enable increased and more legitimate spin-off into wider-based business history, where it would find a more effective role in education. In so doing, it will be necessary to nurture a whole new culture and tradition of recording – and a new generation of skilled corporate and business historians to match.

In previous chapters I have related why the automatic reflex is to discredit most company attempts to capture their OM. In an attempt to consider how this might be overcome, it is instructive to examine how many modern corporate histories are produced.

Among a variety of types of history-related 'corporate books', there are first the books written by independent authors who are funded by publishers completely independently of the subject company. Sometimes the company cooperates with the author and often not – depending on the sensitivities of individuals within the corporation. In this category would fit books on the Rothschild banking family company, Ford, Jaguar and foundations like Lloyd's of London. The excellent *The Rothschilds – A Family of Fortune* was written in 1973 by the popular historian and journalist Virginia Cowles. Equally impressive was the 1986 novel-like account of Henry Ford and his Michigan empire, which was written by the journalist Robert Lacey.

When the books do not have the cooperation of the subject company, they are sometimes called 'investigative' works. These are often quick-off-the-presses books on subjects like the Guinness and BCCI scandals in the late 1980s and early 1990s but they also include attempts at full-blown corporate 'histories'. One example was Lonrho's, the multinational trading company run by Roland 'Tiny' Rowland who ran foul of prime minister Edward Heath in the 1970s. Before starting to research, the authors approached members of the board with requests for information. They record that 'it was impossible to arrange a meeting on terms acceptable to Lonrho'. On completion of the manuscript the authors presented the company with a draft for comment. It was this stage that some information was provided. When Lonrho. A Portrait of a Multinational was published in 1976, the publisher described it as 'a sustained piece of investigative journalism'.

This type of book is also called an 'unauthorized' biography, a recent example being the 1992 'history' of Ireland's most famous businessman, Tony O'Reilly, president of the Pittsburg-based H. J. Heinz food company. In this case the author relied almost exclusively on public archives, newspaper cuttings, various editors and journalists and the hear-say evidence of unidentified people in Europe, the US, Africa, Australia, New Zealand and Ireland. In *Oh really O'Reilly*, legal proceedings were instituted to try to prevent publication – without success. The author, whose acquaintance with the subject was limited to a mutual interest in sport, used his own resources to publish the book. Any pretentions towards publishing professionalism was discharged by a loose insert to the book which regretted any grammatical and typographical errors, and adding: '.... *we trust you will understand these shortcomings in the light of the legal efforts made to prevent the printing, publishing and distribution of this work.'*

Few in number, the choice and interpretation of OM in these types of book is exclusively the mandate of the author and publisher. In many cases, the emphasis is on the sensational at the expense of more useful OM. Equally few in number is the type of independently produced book where the subject company cooperates with the author. In this case it is sometimes called an authorized biography. But even then, things do not always go smoothly. Like *Oh really O'Reilly*, Nomura, the giant Japanese securities house's experience with its corporate history ended up in the courts, costing both the author and the company an estimated £1 million in costs. When *House of Nomura* was published in 1990, the company immediately started legal proceedings against the author, Al Allethauser, an American stockbroker, and his British publisher, for libel. Solicitors Linklaters & Paines claimed that the book suggested the Japanese securities house had had dealings with gangsters. The author, who researched the book in his spare time while working as a stock salesman in Tokyo, maintained that he obtained permission from the Nomura family for access to archives and the interview of 100 company executives. The author also claimed that the Nomura family read the proofs before publication. In its action Nomura claimed there were *'many false stories in the book'* and wanted a retraction, payment of damages and a promise that alleged libels would not be repeated. Preparations for a trial were still underway in July 1991 when the company's chairman and vice chairman resigned after taking responsibility for a series of scandals. The chairman, Setsuya Tabuchi, said his resignation would show that the company genuinely regretted its improper behaviour, which also included compensating favoured clients for trading losses and lending to a gangster group. Nomura dropped its libel action in July 1992 under a so-called 'drop hands settlement' under which both sides covered their own costs.

More often, though, if an independent author is known to be doing a book about a company, the company will become defensive at the outset. In Morgan Grenfell's case, legal moves were also taken to try to stop publication of an independent book on the company by a former employee. While the action occurred shortly after the company was involved in one of the biggest scandals to hit the City of London, it also coincided with postponed plans to publish the company's own corporate history. Controversy is often a factor that postpones a corporate history indefinitely, the company reasoning that it does not want to resurrect public attention to contentious events unnecessarily. However, the decision by Morgan Grenfell to publish its official corporate history before the dust had settled is enlightening.

Research for the book began in the mid-1980s, when the company commissioned an academic, Dr Kathleen Burk, to write its corporate history to coincide with its 150th anniversary in 1988. Alongside J. P. Morgan, its sister bank in the US, Morgan Grenfell had a prestigious history financing the overseas purchases of the allies during the First World War and, later, helping to reconstruct Europe. A pioneer of corporate finance, an important issuer of fixed interest securities, the organizer of the first privatization in 1953 of the steel industry and the operator of a successful asset management business, the history would – supposedly – crown an unusual and important success story. As 1986 went by – it was the year it was floated on the London Stock Exchange after a five-times over-subscription – the timing for publication looked perfect. Over the previous five years it had doubled in size and profits had quadrupled. But then scandal struck. By the end of that same year senior heads started to roll ahead of one of the most celebrated insider dealings trials in the Old Bailey. Within two years, just as the company was celebrating its important anniversary, the company's securities division was closed down in disgrace. With the company's corporate history by now written up to date, the scandal was hardly a positive note on which to end a book about an illustrious bank. The decision whether or not to publish was complicated by the attempt by the former employee – a relatively junior one at that – to publish his own account of the bank's history, including the events surrounding the scandal.

Morgan Grenfell had been asked by Dominic Hobson, who had worked for the company for almost five years, to cooperate in the production of his book. Despite his undertakings not to publish confidential material that had come to his attention during the period of his employment, the company had grave misgivings and instituted legal proceedings to prevent publication. However that would turn out, it still left a question mark over what to do about the company's own history. Kill it off? Given that it was public knowledge that the book was being written, this course of action ran the risk of being seen to be too defensive.

At first the company decided to postpone publication. At the time the company's chairman, Sir Peter Carey, argued that another City scandal – the Guinness affair – was still too much of a live issue and anyway, many of the protagonists, including a former member of his own corporate finance department, could still face trial. Internally, the company had decided that it didn't want any publicity – good, bad or indifferent – after the Guinness affair. Privately, the company assured the author that it intended to publish eventually, possibly in 1990 or 1991.

In the event, it was the author who swung the argument against further postponement. She pointed out that since Morgan Grenfell could not prevent publication of the Hobson book, they *'should get mine out if only to claim the ground, as it were'*. Once this strategy was agreed, it was decided to drop the final chapter and include, instead, an epilogue abridging the recent events. After two attempts at writing the summary, it went to the Oxford University Press for speedy publication. The Burk book finally came out several months

ahead of the independent Hobson book, which was published early in 1990. To
Morgan Grenfell, publication was a pro-active defensive action. To Hobson, the
move was a spoiling tactic.

While Hobson's book traced the history through to the events of the late
1980s, Morgan Grenfell's account of its history effectively stopped at 1981. The
rest of the 1980s expansion, the purchase of a US-based stockbroker, a UK
jobber and gilt-edged broker, the introduction of a new shareholder – Deutsche
Bank – its public listing, the move into equities and government securities, the
scandal and the subsequent rationalization and top management shake-up were
dealt with cursorily in a three-page Epilogue at the end of the narrative.

Among the most recent successful 'authorized' corporate histories produced
independently of the company is one produced on International Telephone and
Telegraph Corporation (ITT). In the late 1970s, Robert Sobel, professor of
business history at New College of Hofstra and a financial columnist for *Newsday*,
was approached by the company's public relations department to write the
group's history. The company, with interests ranging from seeds and hotels to
creating the electronics-based technologies of the future, was coming up to its
fiftieth anniversary and the directors had decided to make a record of the past.
Told that ITT was prepared to sponsor a full-scale work, Sobel replied that he
believed subsidized histories were of limited and questionable worth since the
payment of funds established a dubious nexus between the writer and the subject.

Intrigued by the opportunity to do a major work, he bravely offered to find
an independent publisher and enter into a contract that did not require or
involve any direct or indirect ITT subsidy. In return, he suggested, ITT would
have to ensure him complete access to records, files and individuals except for
matters in litigation. ITT would have the right to see the finished manuscript
and to comment on questions of style or content but could not demand changes
or alterations of any kind. The company agreed.

Four years later, in 1982, Truman Talley Books/Times Books published
I.T.T. The Management of Opportunity, a warts-and-all look at the world's largest
conglomerate. Notable for its candour, it laid to rest long-held accusations that
founder Sosthenes Behn aided the Axis powers in the Second World War; it also
revealed unpublicized aspects of ITT's damning behaviour in Chile during the
Nixon era. Above all, it gave a valuable insight into the workings of a major
American institution. In spite of the controversial aspects of some of its top
personalities, and the fact that there was no editorial control over the manuscript
by the company, ITT executives were delighted with the result. Significantly,
the group's UK subsidiary, Standard Telephones and Cables, was taking a different
route in commissioning its centenary history, which was published a year later.
It chose a former company employee as author and preferred to vest copyright
in the book in itself. The book, perhaps predictably, had less of an impact than
its US counterpart.

At around the same time, another notable corporate history was in the making. Like Sobel's book, it concerned an American company, would be independently written, unsubsidized and have the full cooperation of the subject company. Not at first, though. The book had its genesis when a young sociologist took an interest in the secretive activities of Wall Street law firms. One that caught Nancy Lisagor's eye was Sullivan & Cromwell, which had not written its own history. Its client list was unmatched in Wall Street, among them a large percentage of Wall Street banks, a number of oil giants and top Japanese companies. With a secretary of state, director of the Central Intelligence Agency, Supreme Court justice and test-ban negotiator among its distinguished alumni, the firm ranked high among unexplored subjects in the law.

She started her research at Princeton University, which houses the archives of John Foster Dulles and his brother Allen Welsh Dulles. The former had been senior partner in Sullivan & Cromwell for twenty years before becoming Secretary of State while the latter also spent twenty years at the company prior to his move to the CIA. Supplementing her researches with National Archives material she eventually decided to approach the firm to see whether they would allow her to talk to employees and pensioners. After trying to arrange a meeting with a pensioner whose great uncle might have introduced Sullivan and Cromwell, the two founders, she discovered that the firm disapproved of the book. Even though lawyers were by now allowed to 'advertise' and take a more public profile, it seemed the main reason was their tradition of secrecy and that they distrusted an outside company assessment over which they would have no control; no doubt there was also an element of embarrassment over revelations unearthed by Lisagor in the public archives that the company co-operated with Adolph Hitler until the US entered the Second World War.

It was at this stage that Lisagor brought on board her husband, Frank Lipsius, a journalist with the *Financial Times* and *The Economist*. Together they tried once again to elicit the help of the company, emphasizing that the firm's input would, if nothing else, make the book more accurate. Insisting that it was a firm tradition to avoid the modern practice of soliciting press coverage, the company again refused to co-operate, although they did advise all former employees who telephoned in to enquire about company policy towards the project that they could talk to Lisagor and Lipsius if they were so inclined. Once again research stalled.

A year later things suddenly changed when the firm changed its chairman. The switch coincided with four embarrassing incidents in which the firm's lawyers, three of them important partners, had become the object of headline-making law suits, prosecutions or investigations. More interested in the need to present the firm's side of the case rather than retain its constricting traditions, the new chairman agreed to cooperate with no conditions attached to the interviews.

In 1988, four years after starting the research, *A Law Unto Itself* was published. It was the first social history of an American law firm, showing how the firm's partners had a crucial impact on American business, government and international relations for more than a century. While it recorded the firm's assistance to the Nazi government, it registered the fact that this co-operation occurred pre-war; it also chronicled the firm's influence on the building of the Panama Canal, the Great Depression, the post-Second World War Two recovery (especially in Japan) and the mergers and acquisition boom of the 1980s which reorganized much of America's business.

In their preface, authors Lisagor and Lipsius wrote:

> *'Afterward we speculated on how the book might have turned out had we had the firm's co-operation at the beginning of the project nearly five years before. We realized the result would have been quite different, relying much more on the firm's persuasive opinion of its own accomplishments and less on the public record. We thank the partners for their interviews and assure them that the process of writing the book has enhanced our respect for their intelligence and devotion to their clients and work. If we raise the wider issues of those loyalties, we do so in part because of the very effectiveness of their professional achievements.'*

While the numbers in these categories of corporate book are extremely small, there is another class of history-related corporate books that sometimes get external funding. These are the autobiographies of business executives, some recent examples being Margery Hurst's 1967 *No Glass Slipper*, an account of how she formed the Brook Street Bureau chain of employment agencies, the 1968 account by Percy Hunting entitled *The Group and I*, of the story of the transportation group bearing his name, the 1970 *Memoirs* of Marks & Spencer's Israel Moses Seiff and, in 1991, Anita Roddick's *Body and Soul*, the story of how she created The Body Shop. In many cases these types of books are ghosted by professional writers. Lee Iacocca, for example, the plain-speaking boss of Chrysler, used the services of novelist William Novak to write the best-seller *Iacocca*. Victor Kiam's *Going for It!* was written by Richard Lally, a former sports journalist who had previously written an autobiography of a famous baseball player. In the UK Sir Ian MacGregor's *The Enemy Within*, the story of the British miners' strike of 1984, was written by an investigative reporter while, in his *Off The Rails*, British Rail's Sir Richard Marsh collaborated with the biographer and historian who also provided professional assistance to Lord Forte in his *Forte*. But the most popular approach to recording a company's OM remains the authorized books written by employees or external authors and funded by the subject companies. It is in this category of OM books that the genre frequently falls apart as a legitimate management tool.

Among examples of the former are the 1926 and 1972 books on Barclays Bank. The earlier book was compiled by an employee who became chief inspector of the Bankers' Clearing House and edited by a branch director, Anthony Tuke. It was clearly intended for a narrow in-house audience only, with many of the chapters chronicles of the admission and death of successive partners. Forty-six years later Tuke, who in the meantime had risen to become the group's chairman, co-authored the sequel with a former company secretary, R. J. H. Gillman. The result, this time, was sub-titled *Some Recollections*, containing a large element of personal comments and reflections of the interim period and personalities of the day.

More commonly, though, companies choose external authors to write their histories, either academics or professional writers. In this category, the experience of several other companies gives an indication of the completely different approaches taken in their production.

Unusually, bankers Coutts, which decided on a serious approach to its biography, had a largely problem-free experience with their corporate history, although it did miss its original publication deadline by a year and the company's distribution policy was affected by a remarkably high printing cost imposed by the publisher. It was notable for the amount of pre-project planning, in particular their efforts to give the author clear editorial guidelines.

The commission to write the history was started in 1984 for planned publication in 1991, a year ahead of the 1992 tercentenary. In the event the manuscript was completed in June 1991 and publication took place in February 1992. Its brief was that the book was not intended to be a definitive, complete history. *'While an accurate and sound historical basis is required it should be impressionistic rather than precisely photographic,'* the brief said. *'It should be more a history of people and their influence on the bank and of the bank's influence on people and events than a financial business history. The business history must not, however, be totally neglected. The relationships between partners may well lead to the influence of certain families or personalities giving a theme to the book but the part played by staff will hopefully come in.'* No doubt referring to the Royal Family in particular, the 'thoughts' added: *'The trap should not be fallen into of writing about interesting customers apart from their influence on the development of the bank or the bank's influence on their careers.'*

The company's brief to the author also covered more general editorial aspirations. *'It should be a book that would (and hopefully will) sell as well as being given away. If it can give rise later to television productions so much the better, provided it is not, as a book, too episodic. It should be almost an historical novel or saga rather than a history – a biography of the bank rather than a history of it.'* As author, the company used both a well-known 'name' and an Oxford English graduate to write the 300-year history. Edna Healey, wife of the Labour politician Denis Healey, was selected because of her association with the bank through another book, *Lady Unknown*, a biography of the philanthropist Angela Burdett-Coutts, the grand-daughter of one of the family members who gave the bank its name. However, although the company employed the resources of an outside writer with a high profile, it chose not to assign copyright to the author. When the manuscript was handed in, there were two 'editing' processes – a team of in-house editors undertook what the company describes as 'fairly intensive' factual corrections and elaborations while more stylistic editing was done by the publisher.

While it commissioned and managed the author directly, it used the resources of the author's literary agent to select an outside publisher and negotiate a printing fee. In deciding how many copies it needed, the bank first considered its possible applications. Among these were to use it as a corporate marketing device and *'inculcating the culture'* with new younger staff and mature recruits. At first Coutts thought it might be given to the bank's entire customer base of 50,000 on the basis that selective distribution would cause rancour. However, on the 'advice' of the author's literary agent that the retail cover price of the intended hard-back edition should be in the region of about £20 and that the company could anticipate a discount of up to 50 per cent on bulk purchase, the projected cost – at £50,0000 – was considered exhorbitant. In the event the company decided on a more limited print run of almost 14,000, with the publisher printing an additional 2,500 for outside sales at a cover price of £25. Distribution was restricted to long-standing customers amounting to 10 per cent of the customer base. In addition, copies were given to all staff and pensioners, so-called 'influencers' or 'introducers' of business, journalists and 'dignitaries', including Royal Households.

Glaxo's experience was less smooth. The pharmaceuticals giant decided to produce its history in 1982 and approached the recently-formed Business History Unit at the LSE to do the job. In the event, the Unit appointed as author one of its part-time staff, Dr Richard Davenport-Hines, who had just written *Dudley Docker: The Life and Times of a Trade Warrior*, which would win the Wolfson Literary Prize in 1985 and the Wadsworth Prize for Business History in 1986. Docker was a highly influential, right-wing Midlands industrialist and international financier who founded, in 1916, the Federation of British Industries, the forerunner of the Confederation of British Industry.

The university had another reason for appointing Davenport-Hines – it wanted to employ him on a more permanent basis. Using an arm's-length arrangement Glaxo employed the university as project manager; the university, in turn, commissioned Davenport-Hines through a separate contract which gave the university copyright of the manuscript and Glaxo copyright of all the quoted material in the manuscript. Davenport-Hines spent four years working on the commission – with Glaxo's full co-operation. When it was handed in in 1986, it was rejected. The author admits the manuscript was unsatisfactory. He explains the circumstances:

'I was originally hired to write the company's history to 1963. I was later asked to bring the book up to date to the 1980s, which I started to do. That decision was referred to the board that became upset at the idea. That instruction was then withdrawn.

'When the manuscript was handed in, it was shown to a former chairman who, I was told, strongly disliked it. He apparently thought the historical method entirely inappropriate because the book was initially conceived as a management textbook on marketing, the company being particularly proud of its marketing of products like Zantac and their global strategy plan based on Italy. The former chairman was apparently against the project on grounds of principle. Over the research period the nature and purpose of the project changed three times. As a result I had to chop and change the manuscript. There were clear errors in liaison between the university and the company. It was dogged by misfortunes and was badly handled – both by myself and the university.'

Davenport-Hines attaches no blame to the way Glaxo handled the project. *'We were under no obligation to accept the company's suggestions for changing the goalposts. We were incautious. With hindsight we should have said "no" but we were awed, anxious to please a benefactor and agreed to the idea unreflectingly.'*

Davenport-Hines also admits that, as author, he was a bad choice. *'I think I was ill-suited to write the book on temperamental grounds. Also, my writing style is quite unsuitable for that type of book. In the meantime I had had various disagreements with people at the university, which had been building up for some time. In addition I had no faith in what was being proposed to resuscitate the project.'*

In the event, the only way to revive the project was to bring in another author. In 1987 Judy Slinn, who had just completed the histories of May & Baker and Freshfields, was commissioned to recast the manuscript. The book was eventually published under the joint authorship of Davenport-Hines and Slinn in 1992 – ten years after it was first conceived by Glaxo. Like most other company biographies in the UK, it was given no explicit corporate application in spite of the fact that the timing of publication provided a propitious opportunity to use it as an induction tool for the soon-to-be Wellcome merger.

While the Coutts and Glaxo projects represent corporate history at the 'serious' end of the genre, most company biographies, which are assembled in quite short periods, are still produced virtually exclusively as inexpensive 'PR'. The 'histories' of Staveley Industries, Britannia Building Society and Fyffes represent fairly typical examples.

While the relationship between Davenport-Hines and Glaxo survived, albeit with some trials, the example of Staveley's corporate history is one where the relationship between the author and client broke down. Staveley, one of Britain's oldest publicly quoted companies, decided to do its corporate history after arranging an exhibition at one of its annual general meetings. When interesting material started to come in the chairman, Brian Kent, decided to produce a full corporate history. Having decided against using a professional project manager and publisher, the company commissioned an author directly, choosing a freelance writer, Patrick Beaver, who had previously written around ten 'PR'-style histories of companies like the Initial Group, Empire Stores and Bryant & May. Beaver, whose subsequent experience is not uncommon, recollects the one-year project with not a little anger and frustration. *'They employed an outside journalist to reduce the text from 70,000 words to about 25,000 without any consultation with me. Consequently I refused to allow my name to appear anywhere in the history.'* Staveley admits to having changed the text *'rather a lot'*. The final document was published anonymously in booklet form by the company in 1988. In a Foreword to *Survival Against the Odds*, the chairman wrote: *'We have tried to give only a "flavour" of Staveley's somewhat tortuous progress through this century of industrial revolution and change. In doing so, we may be guilty of some omissions.'*

The 1985 history of the 128-year-old Britannia Building Society was produced to coincide with the retirement of its chairman, Sir Hubert Newton, after 51 years of service. The building society had previously published softcover narratives to celebrate anniversaries after 50 years and, in 1958, its centenary. On the first page its author, who came by way of recommendation, illustrates Sir Hubert's *'kindliness and good humour'* by recalling that the 80-year-old took him to see a match by *'his beloved Stoke City FC on the dreadful day in the 1984-85 season that they first plunged to bottom place in the First Division'*. In recording that Sir Hubert was appointed president of Stoke City Football Club in 1982, the narrative, which was edited in-house, does not make clear the relationship between the Britannia's business activities and the chairman's interest in football.

In the 1976 history of Fyffes, produced to celebrate the shipping and banana importer's 75th anniversary, the company admitted that, in terms of objectivity, the document *'looked on the bright side'*. Entitled *Yes? We Have Some*, any pretentions towards seriousness was discharged by reference to *'sleeping'* as one of the author's spare-time occupations.

Illustrating a lost opportunity for even a PR approach was the corporate history of Addis, the brush and housewares company, which published a 55-page biography to celebrate its bicentenary in 1980. The company decided to do its history because of the Addis family's early involvement in toothbrush manufacture. It said it also hoped to gain some unusual publicity from the book. Through a brief

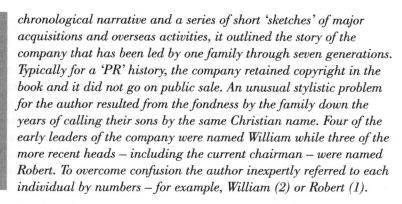

chronological narrative and a series of short 'sketches' of major acquisitions and overseas activities, it outlined the story of the company that has been led by one family through seven generations. Typically for a 'PR' history, the company retained copyright in the book and it did not go on public sale. An unusual stylistic problem for the author resulted from the fondness by the family down the years of calling their sons by the same Christian name. Four of the early leaders of the company were named William while three of the more recent heads – including the current chairman – were named Robert. To overcome confusion the author inexpertly referred to each individual by numbers – for example, William (2) or Robert (1).

In other examples, which indicate the extent of their OM, 160 years of the 1991 history of Scotch whisky distillers, George Ballantine, part of the Allied Distillers Group, were covered in 61 heavily illustrated pages. The history of the group's Teacher's Whisky subsidiary, whose origins go back to 1830, was even shorter, with the author tactlessly concluding the 47-page illustrated narrative with the words 'The End'.

One of the most guileless 'PR' histories in recent years was Lonrho's, which used a 1988 book about itself as a lobby tool against the interest of the Egyptian al-Fayed brothers. At the time the company was enmeshed in its long-running tussle with the brothers who, in 1985, had acquired House of Fraser and its flagship Harrods. Department of Trade and Industry investigators were investigating the takeover. As part of its campaign, Lonrho published its own account of the saga to put pressure on the government to publish the DTI Inspectors' report. Differing radically from the investigative history written twelve years before, the 185-page product, entitled *A Hero from Zero*, was written anonymously in flowery prose and contained chapters entitled Pharaonic Fantasies, Eastern Folly and Hapless Harrods. A group subsidiary printing company printed, it is thought, about 15,000 copies for distribution to merchant bankers, lawyers, MPs and the media.

There is also a significant number of books that do not see the light of day. The history of the Institute of Chartered Secretaries & Administrators, one of Britain's oldest professional associations which was planned to coincide with an important anniversary in 1991, was shelved[2] because of what the association's own chief executive admitted was *'less than constructive cooperation by the committee set up to manage the project'*. The author, an award-winning business writer, eventually gave up in despair having spent eighteen months trying to accommodate hundreds of comments, many of them contradictory, from individual committee members. Elsewhere, the Association of British Chemical Manufacturers, the Federation of British Industries, Guinness, Kleinwort Benson, Carr's Milling Industries, William Heaton & Sons and J. & J. Colman, the foods company, have all kept accounts of their OM firmly under wraps.

To help ensure editorial objectivity, some companies form special committees to oversee the project. Others use academics as supervisers. In BP's case, the company's chairman formed a special editorial advisory board to help choose the author and assist in consultation during the compilation. The committee, formed to safeguard the independence of the history, the integrity of the historian and the company, consisted of himself, a former chairman, three outside academics, a past president of the British Academy and two successive company secretaries. The decision to authorize the writing was taken without any strings attached. For their history Ernst & Whinney formed a History Committee to *'correct misconceptions'* and provide other assistance. An outside academic historian was brought in to supervise the author, who was given full access to all surviving documents. In the case of Butterworth's *History of a Publishing House*, the company hired an outsider to act as final editor, his *'skilled diplomatic help'* helping to ameliorate defects in structure and sequence.

And what of the cost of these efforts to document companies' OM? In the world of corporate history there is a curious mixture of famine and feast in terms of allocated budgets, with author budgets almost always being the poor relation of printing costs, at least in the UK. I have heard of cases of companies apportioning total budgets equal to little more than the annual cost of a single secretary to one example where the author was offered a project fee of £200,000, even if the manuscript was never published. For my part, the answers, while interesting in their own right, need to be judged against their utilization, which is always the ultimate demonstration of their perceived added value. In this light British corporate histories, because of their minimal exposures, generally give extremely poor value for money.

> *Among a string of examples is the first volume of Phoenix Assurance's history, which received a company order of just 750 copies. Taking eight years to produce, it cost[3] more than £350,000. Elsewhere, Royal Insurance's 1995 history cost[4] £360,000; the 287-page book, which did not go on public sale, attracted a two-inch review from the* Financial Times, *which said: 'Unfortunately its attempts to pep up the history of insurance by linking developments to contemporary events leave a bit to be desired.'*

As the record shows, many repositories of OM are poorly researched, less than incisive and, at the behest of their sponsor, unmistakably self-serving, often so much so that any application they might have – even as PR – is completely lost. With few exceptions, they largely fall on deaf ears. In many cases the companies that fund them are completely unaware of their transparency and lack of subtlety; shades of the parable of the Emperor's New Clothes.

What the record also shows is that corporate history is one of the most difficult of corporate documents to produce – for the company as well as the individual author. The internal author, usually flattered by the invitation from his or her peers, invariably finds the job more onerous than it was ever believed at the outset. Archibald Richards, a former chairman of the board of partners at chartered accountants Touche Ross & Co., recalled: *'When the board asked me to write a history of the firm, I readily agreed – believing in my innocence that I already knew a great deal about the firm. Had I known then the enormity of the task and the great amount of research it would entail I am sure I would have respectfully declined.'* About his efforts to write his autobiography, which was done with the help of a professional writer, Lord Forte, chairman of Trusthouse Forte, said: *'.... writing a book is a damned sight harder than cutting sandwiches'* while S. T. Roberts, the employee author of *The History of Pitney Bowes*, admitted that the task was *'formidable'*. For an external author, the difficulties are no less forbidding. Academic David Kynaston, who wrote the 1990 *The Financial Times: A Centenary History*, said of his two-and-a-half-year project:

> *'Researching and writing a company history is rather like playing a game of Chinese whispers. Rumours which turned into anecdotes pass down from one generation to another and become accepted facts, and reasonably well-adjusted personalities achieve legendary status for one or two exaggerated traits. The living have highly contradictory accounts of past events and the dead of course can only bear witness through fading documents and board minutes.'*

Alongside the practical difficulties are the imposed structural pitfalls that include the disposition towards inappropriate author choices, the direct association between author and subject company, the commonplace decision to sequester copyright from the author and, when not printed in-house, the use of publishers that often neglect to impose professional editorial standards on client-funded books.

While the quoted examples in this and previous chapters will give companies some clues how (and how not to) produce them, it follows that companies have to reassess fundamentally the way they construct this most corporate of documents. A useful corporate history is unlike conventional corporate documentation such as pamphlets, brochures, company newspapers and corporate videos. As such, it needs to be produced differently.

For the subject company, it is essential to confront the choice between making a faithful record and presenting a good PR profile. Even though companies may believe these treatments to be contradictory, they are, in fact, complementary. Good history is actually a prerequisite to good PR. Above all, a faithful treatment demonstrates a corporate maturity that extends beyond the defensive posture of the insecure. Thereafter, corporate histories need to be professionally produced as 'real' books, with an authoritative author, careful structuring around a predetermined application, rigorous research, stylish writing and editing, and professional publishing, including committed marketing where they are suitable for an outside audience.

The decision to use an in-house author is usually made because companies believe they will receive a more 'sympathetic' treatment and/or that an outsider will know less about the organization than someone not steeped in its culture and tradition. Although internal authorship does not invalidate any account as a historical document, company employees are invariably better at making money than trying to explain how they did it, generally lacking the necessary perspective and writing skills. As an alternative, many companies choose to give their histories the 'scholastic' treatment in the belief that the mortar board will disguise any perceived lack of credibility. As the record shows, this treatment is invariably at the expense of an audience. The other option, using professional writers, is also less than ideal when communicability is offset by a lack of perceptivity. The broad rule of thumb is that the author should be an individual whose business knowledge and insight is at least matched by an ability to research and write. However obvious this might seem, real life dictates that the message is invariably lost without the ability to convey it.

Whichever choice the company makes, there is still the credibility problem surrounding the issue of client patronage. Up to now companies have depended almost entirely on institutional and individual writer integrity to overcome the wide misgivings over perceived objectivity. As the record shows, the typical arrangements between author and client to guarantee the manuscript's integrity are rarely convincing. While this can be helped by operationally constructing projects so that management, production, copyright and publication are at arm's length from the subject organization, nowhere in the world have corporate historians developed an agreed Code of Conduct for the authors that write them, the companies that fund them and the publishers that print them.

An ethics code would help to ensure that all corporate histories are not tarred with the same brush. It would also demonstrate the determination of corporate historians to have their work taken seriously, marginalize the PR product and enhance the received worth of the genre in industry and academia. In addition to the UK, a number of academics and corporate historians in the US, Germany and Japan, where client patronage similarly undermines the genre, have indicated to me they would welcome a formal Code of Conduct to combat the genre's automatic lack of perceived credibility. As models, several have mentioned the existence of formal codes that exist to oversee the behaviour of academics in research projects funded by commercial organizations. The proposition, in fact, stimulated a round-table discussion[5] in 1997 between senior US business academics at Ohio State University, the University of Houston, the University of Maryland and the Winthrop Group, the main US private sector producer of corporate histories, with a view to professionalizing the business history profession and expanding economic and business historians' influence in the academic and corporate worlds. It was noted by them that sociologists, archaeologists and anthropologists had had some success in professionalizing themselves, with the latter being hired as corporate consultants to suggest, for example, whether or not proposed mergers would work. *'Surely business historians have something to offer here?'* The organizations that could jointly formulate such a code might be the UK's Association of Business Historians, the newly-formed European Business History Association, the Business History Conference in the US and/or the Economic and Business Historical Society, the Business History Society of Japan and the German Society for Business History.

Given the importance of Organizational Memory, the professionalization of its main portable repository is long overdue. If the product had the necessary credibility, they could have profitable employment beyond restrained PR and go some way to achieving the aspirations of people like Sir Arthur Knight, Sir Peter Parker and Professor Geoffrey Jones. The trick, which government, educators and industry seem to have overlooked up to now, is to enfranchize the corporate past. Businesses are the single biggest contributors to the standard of living in the twentieth century. Their experiences deserve more shelf space and a less dusty fate.

References

1. N.R. Lamoreaux, D.M.G. Raff and P. Temin, 'New Economic Approaches to the Study of Business History', *Business and Economic History*, Vol. 26, No 1. Fall 1997.
2. Pencorp research study, 1994.
3. Phoenix Assurance assessment given to author on book's launch.
4. Pencorp research study, 1995.
5. *Essays in Economic & Business History*, Vol. XV, 1997 (the journal of the Economic and Business Historical Society).

EPILOGUE

'.... when experience is not retained, infancy is perpetual'

It's a funny thing, experience! The encyclopaedia of life, its conveyance is dependent entirely on two media – memory and the instruments of the written word and/or the printed picture. Depending only on the former is not very reliable. Its recall, at least in any accurate form, has the tendency to deteriorate into legend and myth. When that happens, whatever transpired has a way of disappearing from view. Witness some of the great Middle Eastern, African or South American civilizations. Of those that did not have a tradition of recording their experiences, how many survived? Can the ability to be accurately reflective have something to do with it?

Authorship of this chapter's related title[1] belongs to the US philosopher and poet George Santayana, whose more famous quote on the subject – *'Those who cannot remember the past are condemned to repeat it'* – was used by historian William L. Shirer as an epigraph in his 1959 book on *The Rise and Fall of the Third Reich*. However elegantly simplistic his words may appear to some, the relationship between Santayana's commentary and progress is not obscure. Except for those who choose to forget, or remember selectively, it is no coincidence that those civilizations that endured developed a recording tradition that – however unconsciously – provided a reference point from which individuals at one level and nations at another acquire the ability to learn experientially and incrementally. As all the great established religions have shown, the practice is moreover an extremely powerful way of embedding and reinforcing a tradition and a culture. It is, at root, the most efficient medium of inheritance that many agencies already use to their considerable advantage. The Chinese proverb *'The palest ink is better than the best memory'* is apposite.

If one extrapolates this theme into the business world, it is of no little concern, then, that the education systems of so may countries provide so little *historical* awareness of their companies in particular or business in general; without any inheritance, the learning curve for new entrants to the economy is steeper and longer than it might otherwise be. Neither do many organizations make any effort to pass on their experiences from one generation to another; for the individual company, whose staff can today be displaced every five years, corporate 'memory' is increasingly other employers' experiences, which is not necessarily always relevant.

In this book I have sketched out the effects on institutions of 'unlearning', 'forgetting' or 'losing' one's own experiences, what I have described as corporate amnesia, and its effect on how effectively organizations learn their own lessons. The answer – as this book also relates – is not very well, whether in the UK or elsewhere.

Taking just the UK example in this last decade of the twentieth century, the concluding evidence I can proffer traces how much progress has been made in improving the nation's industrial productivity. In 1993 – at the tail end of the country's deepest recession for more than half a century – the *Financial Times*[2] quoted the results of a Cranfield Business School study that showed that only 2 per cent – yes 2 per cent – of British companies were world class. The survey, which also found that British managers thought they were the best in Europe, caught the attention of deputy prime minister Michael Heseltine, also Britain's Trade and Industry Secretary and a successful businessman in his own right, who rebuked the nation's managers for over-confidence. In front of businessmen at the annual dinner of the Institute of Directors, he asked his audience for a clear recognition that there was a gap between the UK's industrial performance and the best in the world. In spite of increases in productivity, he said, the UK was still 25 per cent behind its main European competitors and even further behind the US.

Four years later – in a boom period that was generating profits and employment which were the envy of many of its European competitors, a Royal Society of Arts (RSA) study[3], which was part sponsored by the deputy prime minister's Competitiveness Unit in the Cabinet Office, rediscovered the unflattering position in Britain's comparative performance with its main competitors. '*We seem as a nation unable to close the gap between our industrial performance and that of other major manufacturing nations*', it concluded. Just months later, after the Conservative government's disastrous defeat at the polls, Margaret Becket, Mr Heseltine's successor, was echoing[4] the same message. A government benchmarking exercise had found, she said, that the task faced by UK business in catching up with the best in the world was '*bigger than we thought*'. The performance of companies throughout the supply chain, even at the top, '*isn't as good as the performance of companies overseas*'.

This, and the fact that UK productivity has lagged behind almost all of its First World competitors for most of the post-Second World War period, confirms that not much learning from experience is taking place. Or that others are better at experiential learning than we are.

To try to find an explanation, the *Financial Times* published an article[5] under the headline '*Why Michael Heseltine is absolutely right*.' Referring to Britain's managers as '*myopic*', it quoted Mark Smalley, who headed PA Consulting's strategy unit and directs its Midlands office, as saying the reason was British managers' self-delusion, arrogance, insularity and unwillingness to learn, in particular a reluctance – or inability – to learn from the discomforting experience of others. In this book it has been my contention that PA Consulting's observation extends to companies' widespread inability to learn from their own experiences.

For further support of this conviction, I venture another set of statistics. More veteran companies failed in the last recession than in any other previous economic slump[6] this century. A massive 10 per cent of firms that had survived two world wars, the bleak 1930s depression and the succession of cyclical downturns crashed between 1989 and 1993, which also happened to coincide with the height of the downsizing boom. Why were they able to survive previous recessions? Because, I contend, there was less discontinuity – and an organizational memory that provided them with the benefit of how they manoeuvred their way out of previous crises.

Whether in the UK or elsewhere, experiential learning depends on an unambiguous awareness of one's own experiences, which is the prime constituent of that emigrating resource, Organizational Memory. Organizations have already paid for their OM once. If it is not to pass beyond reach, it needs to be managed professionally – just like any other corporate asset.

References

1. 'Progress, far from consisting in change, depends on retentiveness. When change is absolute there remains no being to improve and no direction is set for possible improvement: and when experience is not retained, as among savages, infancy is perpetual'. From *The Life of Reason*, Chapter 12, by George Santayana.
2. *Financial Times*, 24 November 1993.
3. 'Reassessing the Context of Manufacturing Success', Royal Society of Arts, January 1997 study.
4. CBI Conference, Birmingham, reported in the *Financial Times*, 11 November 1997.
5. *Financial Times*, 26 November 1993.
6. 1994 National Westminster Bank Review of Small Business Trends.

Bibliography

Abernathy W. and Corcoran J., 'Relearning from the Old Masters', *Journal of Operations Management*, August 1983.

Anderlohr G., 'Determining the Cost of Production Breaks,' *Management Review*, Vol. 58, No. 12, 1969.

Argyris C., 'Double Loop Learning in Organisations', *Harvard Business Review*, September/October 1997.

Argyris C. and Schon D.A., *Organizational Learning*, Addison-Wesley, Reading, MA, 1978.

Bailey C.D. and McIntyre E.V.V., 'Some Evidence on the Nature of Relearning Curves', *Accounting Review*, April 1992.

Bateson G., *Steps to an Ecology of Mind*, Paladin, London, 1973.

Bateson G., *Mind and Nature, A necessary unity*, Bantam Books, New York, 1979.

Boone Pickens T. Jr, *Boone*, New English Library, London, 1987.

Boulding K.E., *The Image: Knowledge in Life and Society*, University of Michigan, Ann Arbor, 1956.

Bowen H.K., Clark K., Holloway C. and Wheelwright S., *The Perpetual Enterprise Machine*, Oxford University Press, Oxford, 1994.

Bower T., *Maxwell*, Mandarin, London, 1992.

Bowker G.C., 'Lest we Remember: Organizational Forgetting and the Production of Knowledge', *Accounting, Management & Information Technology*, Vol. 7, No. 3, 1997.

Brown M., *Richard Branson: The Inside Story*, Headline, London, 1988.

Carlson J.G. and Rowe R.J., 'How Much Does Forgetting Cost?' *Industrial Engineering*, Vol. 8, No. 9, 1976.

Cassell M., *The Readymixers*, Pencorp, London, 1986.

Cassell M., *Dig It, Burn It, Sell It*, Pencorp, London, 1990.

Cassell M., *Long Lease, Pencorp*, London, 1991.

Chandler A.D., *Strategy and Structure*, MIT Press, Cambridge, MA, 1962.

Clemens J.K, *The Classic Touch, Lessons in Leadership from Homer to Hemingway*, Dow-Jones-Irwin, Holmwood, IL, 1987.

Cusumano M. and Selby R., *Microsoft Secrets*, The Free Press, New York, 1995/ HarperCollins, London, 1996.

de Bono E., *The Use of Lateral Thinking*, Jonathan Cape, 1967.

de Bono E., *Lateral Thinking: A textbook of creativity*, Ward Lock Educational, 1970.

de Geus A., *The Living Company*, Harvard Business School Press, Cambridge, MA, 1997.

Deutsch K.W., *The Nerves of Government*, The Free Press, New York, 1964.

Drosrin, M., *Citizen Hughes*, Bantam Books, New York, 1985.

Drucker P.F., *The New Realities*, Harper & Row, New York, 1989.

Drucker P.F., *Post-Capitalist Society*, Butterworth-Heinemann, Oxford, 1992.

Easton D., *A Framework for Political Analysis*, Prentice Hall, Englewood Cliffs, NJ, 1965.

Fallon I., and Stodes J., *Delorean: The Rise and Fall of a Dream Maker*, Hamish Hamilton, London, 1993.

Friedman, A., *Agnelli and the Network of Italian Power*, Harrap, London, 1988.

Frisch M., *Shared Authority, essays on the craft and meaning of oral and public history*, British Archives Council, London, 1990.

Garratt B., *The Learning Organization*, Fontana, London, 1989.

Garratt B., *Learning to Lead*, Fontana, London, 1990.

Garratt B., (ed.) *Developing Strategic Thought*, McGraw-Hill, London, 1995.

Garratt B., *The Fish Rots from the Head*, HarperCollins, New York, 1996.

Goldstein N., *Trading Up*, Sidgwick & Jackson, London, 1988.

Grele R.J., *Envelopes of Sound: the art of oral history*, British Archives Council, London, 1991.

Hamel G. and Prahalad C.K., *Competing for the Future*, Harvard Business School Press, 1994.

Hannah L., *New Horizons for Business History*, Social Science Research Council, London, 1981.

Harvey-Jones, J, *Making it Happen*, HarperCollins, London, 1988.

Herriot P. and Pemberton C., *Competitive Advantage through Diversity*, Sage, London, 1993.

Hindle T. , *The Sultan of Berkeley Square: Asil Nadir and the Thatcher Years*, Macmillan, London, 1991.

Hoffman R.J.S., *Great Britain and the German Trade Rivalry*, University of Pennsylvania Press, 1933.

Honey P., 'The Learning Organization Simplified', *Training & Development*, July 1991.

Hurst D.K., *Crisis & Renewal: Meeting the Challenge of Organisation Change*, Harvard Business School Press, Cambridge, MA, 1996.

Hurt H., *Lost Tycoon: The Many Lives of Donald Trump*, Weidenfeld, London, 1993.

Jobs, S., *The Journey is the Reward*, Glenview, 1988.

Jones G., 'Business History: Theory and Concepts', discussion paper in *Economics*, Series A, Vol. VII, University of Reading Department of Economics, 1994/5.

Kantrow A.M., *The Constraints of Corporate Tradition*, Harper & Row, New York, 1987.

Kimberley J.R. and R.H. Miles and Associates, *The Organizational Life Cycle*, Jossey-Bass, San Francisco, CA, 1980.

Kletz, T., *Lessons from Disaster: How Organizations Have no Memory and Accidents Recur*, Institution of Chemical Engineers, 1993.

Kofman F. and Senge P.M., 'The Heart of Learning Organizations', *Organization Dynamics*, Vol. 22, No. 2, 1993.

Kolb D., *Experiential Learning*, Prentice-Hall, Eglewood Cliffs, NJ, 1984.

Landes D., 'Watchmaking: A Case Study of Enterprise and Change', *Business History Review*, Spring, 1979.

Leucke R.A., *Scuttle Your Ships before Advancing: and other lessons from history on leadership and change for today's managers*, Oxford University Press, New York, 1994.

Maidique M.A. and Zirger B.J., 'The New Product Learning Cycle', *Research Policy*, Vol. 14, No. 6, 1985

Maira A. and Scott-Morgan P., *The Accelerating Organization*, McGraw-Hill, New York, 1997.

Mbaye S., *Oral Archives*, ICA, London, 1988.

McCall M., *High Flyers: Developing the Next Generation of Leaders*, Harvard Business School Press, Cambridge, MA, 1997.

McCall M., Lombardo M. and Morrison A., *The Lessons of Experience*, Lexington Books, Lexington, MA, 1988.

McClelland C.A., 'Systems History in International Relations', *General Systems Yearbook*, Louisville, 1958.

Moss W. and Mazikana P.C., 'Archives, Oral History and Oral Tradition', *RAMP*, 1986.

Mumford A., 'Four Approaches to Learning from Experience', *The Learning Organization*, Vol. 1, No. 1, 1994.

Mumford A., Honey P. and Robinson G., D*irectors' Development Guidebook: making experience count*, Training Agency/Institute of Directors, London, 1989.

Neustadt R. and May E., *Thinking in Time: The Uses of History for Decision-Makers*, Collier Macmillan, 1986.

Noer D., *Healing the Wounds: Overcoming the Trauma of Layoffs and Revitalizing Downsized Organizations*, Jossey-Bass, San Francisco, MA, 1993.

Nonaka I. and Takeuchi H., *The Knowledge Creating Company*, Oxford University Press, New York, 1995.

O'Toole J. M. (ed.), *The Records of American Business*, Society of American Archivists, Chicago, 1997.

Parsons T. and Shils E.A., *Towards a General Theory of Action*, Harper & Row/Torchbooks, New York, 1962.

Pedler M., Burgoyne J. and Boydell T., *The Learning Company, A strategy for sustainable growth*, McGraw-Hill, Maidenhead, 1991.

Peters T.J. and Waterman R.H., *In Search of Excellence*, Harper & Row, London, 1994.

Pfeffer J., *Management as Symbolic Action in Research in Organizational Behaviour*, JAI Press, Greenwich, CT, 1981.

Polanyi M., *The Tacit Dimension*, Routledge & Kegan Paul, London, 1966.

Quinn J.B., *Intelligent Enterprise: A Knowledge and Service Based Paradigm for Industry*, The Free Press, New York, 1992.

Raw C., *Slater Walker: An Investigation of a Financial Phenomenon*, André Deutsch, London, 1977.

Reid M., *Abbey National: Conversion to PLC*, Pencorp, London, 1991.

Roddick A., *Body and Soul*, Ebury Press, London, 1991.

Saunders J., *Nightmare*, Hutchinson, London, 1989.

Schein E.H., *Organizational Culture and Leadership*, Jossey-Bass, San Francisco, CA, 1985.

Schon D.A., *The Reflective Practitioner*, Basic Books, New York, 1993.

Scully J., *Odyssey: Pepsi to Apple*, HarperCollins, New York, 1987.

Senge P.M., *The Fifth Discipline:The Age and Practice of the Learning Organization*, Century Business, London, 1990.

Senge P.M., *The Fifth Discipline Fieldbook*, Currency, 1994.

Smith G.D. and Stedman L.E., 'The Present Value of Corporate History', *Harvard Business Review*, November/December 1981.

Stewart T.A., *Intellectual Capital, the New Wealth of Organisations*, Nicholas Brealey, London, 1997.

Swieringa J. and Wierdsma A., *Becoming a Learning Organization: Beyond the Learning Curve*, Addison-Wesley, Reading, MA, 1992.

Terkel S., *Envelopes of Sound: The art of oral history*, Precedent Publications, Chicago, 1985.

Terkel S., *Hard Times: An oral history of the Great Depression*, Random House, London, 1988.

Terkel S., *American Dream Lost and Found*, Hodder & Stoughton, London, 1981.

Terkel S., *Good War Oral History WW2*, Ballantine, New York, 1995.

Terkel S., *Coming of Age: The story of our century by those who've lived it*, Penguin, London, 1995.

Thomas D., *Alan Sugar: The Amstrad Story*, Century, London, 1990.

Thompson P., *The Voice of the Past: Oral History*, Oxford University Press, Oxford, 1978.

Tichy N.M., with Cohen E., *The Leadership Engine*, HarperBusiness, New York, 1997.

Toffler A., *Future Shock*, Bantam Books, New York, 1970.

Toffler A., *Powershift Knowledge, Wealth and Violence at the Edge of the 21st Century*, Bantam Books, New York, 1990.

Tosches N., *Power on Earth: Michael Sindona's Explosive Story*, Arbor House, Ann Arbor, MI, 1986.

Townsend P.L. and Gebhardt J.E., *Five-Star Leadership*, John Wiley, New York, 1997.

Underwood J., *The Will to Win: John Egan and Jaguar*, W.H. Allen, London, 1989.

Wallace J. and Erickson J., *Hard Drive: Bill Gates and the Making of the Microsoft Empire*, John Wiley, New York, 1992.

Trump D.J. with Leerhsen C., *Trump: Surviving at the Top*, Century, New York, 1990.

Utterbach J., *Mastering the Dynamics of Innovation*, Harvard Business School Press, Cambridge, MA, 1994.

Vanderbilt A., *Fortune's Children: The Fall of the House of Vanderbilt*, Sphere, London, 1986.

von Bartalanffy L., *General Systems Theory*, General Systems, New York, 1956.

Walsh J.P. and Ungson G.R., *Organizational Memory: Structure, Functions and Application*, Amos Tuck School of Business Administration, 1990.

Walsh J.P., 'Managerial and Organizational Cognition; Notes from a Trip Down Memory Lane', *Organization Science*, Vol. 6, No. 3, 1995.

'What Production Breaks Cost', *Industrial Engineering*, September 1969.

INDEX